forever in my Heart

ALSO BY CHARLENE CARR

A New Start Series
When Comes The Joy
Where There Is Life
By What We Love
Whispers of Hope

Behind Our Lives Trilogy
Behind Our Lives
What We See
The Stories We Tell

Standalone
Beneath the Silence
Before I Knew You

Forever In My Heart

A New Start, Book 4

Charlene Carr

Published by Coastal Lines, 2019.

Copyright © 2019 Charlene Carr

Published in Canada by Coastal Lines
www.coastallines.ca

All rights reserved. No portion of this book may be reproduced, stored in a retrieval system, or transmitted in any form or by any means—electronic, mechanical, photocopy, recording, scanning, etc.—except for quotations in reviews or articles, without the prior permission of the author. For information regarding permission contact the author at
contact@charlenecarr.com

Library and Archives Canada

Forever In My Heart
Book Four of the A New Start Series
ISBN: 978-1-988232-18-8

This novel is a work of fiction. Names, characters, places, and incidents either are the product of the author's imagination or are used fictitiously. Any resemblance to actual events, locales, organizations, or persons living or dead is entirely coincidental and beyond the intent of the author.

Typography by Coastal Lines
Cover Design by Coastal Lines

Second Edition, November 2019

This work is also available in electronic format:
Forever In My Heart
ISBN: 978-0-9939238-9-0

To Peter,

who loves me through all my imperfections.

CHAPTER ONE

Elation. That's what I expected at this moment. A moment that should have been filled with joy. Instead, I feel paralyzed.

"Miss, do you need any help?"

Learn to take it slow. Learn to be happy with myself first. Don't rely on finding happiness with a man. That was my mantra.

"We have a lot of options."

It still is my mantra.

"Miss?"

And it's brought me Adrian. Adrian, who makes me laugh. Adrian, who I've been wary with, who, amazingly, has stayed despite the way I tried to push him away, despite my fear of getting attached to someone again. I smile. Who, when I get close enough, always seems to smell faintly of cinnamon.

"Miss. Are you al—"

"Sorry?" I snap to attention. A woman stands beside me. She could be my mother. Her dark hair curls around her head. Her blouse, which has probably been pressed, fits impeccably. Her smile is both matronly and authoritative. This is a woman who appreciates and cultivates perfection. I take a step back.

"Would you like some help? It's a nervous time, isn't it? But exciting." She smiles.

I glance at the shelf in front of me—the myriad of

options—then back at the woman. "Yes. Thank you." I struggle to keep my voice even, polite.

The woman wears a question on her face. Perhaps she expected elation too, when she saw me in this aisle, in front of these shelves. A glance at my hand and her smile starts to fade, then softens into sweetness. "You'll figure it out. No matter what, it'll be okay." She places one hand on my shoulder and reaches to the shelf with the other. "Use this one. It's cheapest and really they're all pretty much the same."

"Thank you." I offer a smile. My normal smile. My seemingly natural smile. Inside, I crumble into a scary mess.

En route to the cash, I almost trip over a little girl in a pink tutu style dress who walks right into me. An armload of toiletries and makeup fall to the floor. Lipstick and eyeliner, conditioner and nail polish roll between us. The girl freezes. Her lip trembles. "It's okay." I smile and crouch to gather the items. A quick grin coats her face as she squats to help me. In under a minute everything is safely back in her arms. She gives a little laugh, disaster averted. A young woman—her mother?—turns up the aisle and calls her away, her voice harsh and grating. I can only wonder why she's angry—perhaps a mother who wasn't ready to be one?

At the cash I pay, wrap the box in a bag, and stuff it to the bottom of my purse. The weight of it feels too much to carry. The pharmacy door squeaks closed and I step onto the busy foot traffic of Spring Garden Road.

Outside, I squint in the sunlight. "Tracey!" Through a halo of light, Eloise strides toward me.

I meet her smile with my own. "Hey, lovely." Always the one to initiate contact, I hug her, though today I'd rather run in the other direction. Eloise is one of my closest friends. I should be happy to see her. Just like I should be happy this box is in my purse—it could hold the realization of one of my earliest dreams, what I've always wanted. But not like this. I didn't want this. The box sits in my mind like a rock. The thought of holding it there, while I pretend to chat happily with my friends, feels like an anchor ready to pull me under.

"I'm glad I caught you." Eloise links her arm in mine. "I wanted to chat about some new ideas for Aspire. The girls are so excited for the district-wide conference and…"

My thoughts bounce and scatter like ping-pong balls: Eloise's words lost among them.

She puts her hand on my arm. "You feel good about that?"

"Yeah, I mean…what?" My cheeks warm.

"Are you all right?"

"I'm sorry. I lost focus. I'm listening now."

"I suggested we let the core girls take over the conference presentation. It would be a great way for them to put into practice the skills they've built these past few months."

"Yes, absolutely." My voice is high with enthusiasm. Too high. "That's a perfect idea."

Eloise pulls me to a stop as we approach the café doors. Her head tilts as her gaze narrows. "You sure you're okay? You seem…not yourself…and pale."

"Oh." I wave my arm as if I'm waving away her words. "Not enough sleep last night. You know how I need my sleep."

"Sure." Eloise releases my arm as we turn into the café. Everyone but Allison, who is chronically late, is gathered around our usual booth. It's been over a year since we've all been here. Today Autumn's cousin Jennifer joins us as well. I smile and gush and comment on how fabulous Autumn looks, how London and her new man, Jakob, must be treating her well. The ping-ponging persists but I ignore it as best I can. The balls of thought settle as Autumn's arms wrap around me. She hugs me as if my presence alone brings her joy.

"It's good to have you home," I whisper.

"It's good to be home." She pulls out of our embrace and joy sparkles in her eyes. She doesn't just look good, she looks happy, which calms me. If she can be happy, it means goodness can come out of tragedy. Not that this would be a tragedy. Not at all. Autumn losing her husband the day after their marriage was a tragedy. This is…well, it's not that.

"And my news…" Jennifer grins once the initial round of greetings and questions have died down. She pulls her flouncy shirt flat against her stomach, revealing an undeniable baby bump.

Excitement and questions explode around us, and I join right in. The only one who doesn't act enthused is Sheila, who is generally uncomfortable around all things decidedly feminine.

"That's so wonderful," reitcrates Eloise as we sit down. "Autumn mentioned you and Rajeev eloped a while back."

"We sure did." Jennifer grins. She rests a hand on her belly. Her diamond ring sparkles. "Everyone assumed we had a shotgun wedding. Their suspicions seemed verified when I announced this little one, but she or he's a honeymoon baby." She shrugs. "A little too excited to remember my birth control. So, not planned," she rubs the bump, "but very much wanted." She takes a sip of her smoothie. "It's kind of ridiculous, my first thought when I found out was—I'll get fat. I can't get fat. I was terrified!" She shakes her head. "I wasn't even thinking about the baby, just about seeing that scale creep up."

"Well," says Autumn, "you weren't planning a baby, and you worked so hard—"

My mind drifts again. What was my first thought when I realized it'd been almost two-and-a-half months since my last period? Fear. I have a plan, a specific plan, and for the first time in almost ten years I'm with a man who could be part of that plan. A baby right now wouldn't necessarily ruin the plan, but it could. Adrian and I haven't been together long. He could bolt, leaving me a single mother. I would still have a child, that true family I've always dreamed of…but not in the way I dreamed, not with a man I know loves me, a man who won't leave.

I look to Jenn as she talks on, not hearing the words, but seeing her laugh, seeing how at ease she seems. This wasn't part of her plan. From what she said, she and Rajeev wanted to wait at least two years. But they're happy now. Elated. Exactly what I want to be.

"My ladies!" Our heads turn as Allison breezes into the café. Her red hair glistens. "Sorry I'm late." She winks. "I was with this dreamboat of a man who wanted a few more sets."

Autumn stands and Allison wraps her in what's more of a tackle than an embrace.

"Well, how could you resist that?" says Eloise.

"I couldn't. It's been so long…" Allison slides into the booth. "You should know." She elbows Eloise. "We've both had a horrendous dry spell. Look at that." She laughs. "Three and three. So, Tracey, Autumn, Jennifer, while you catch me up on anything I've missed, be sure to drop some love hints to help out us single ladies."

"I'm fine." Eloise holds up her hands. "It'll happen when it happens."

"Oh, sure." Allison groans. "You say that, but you've had what, a measly year and a half since anything serious? Back me up here, Sheila. You and I must be pretty neck and neck. It's been almost three for me. What are you at?"

"Four." Sheila's lips form a tight, thin line. "Since anything serious, anyway."

"Yeah, we need help." Allison leans forward, her elbows on the table. "Who's first? Autumn, I'm pretty up to date on you and your British love." She turns her head toward me. "Tracey, all I know is that you're seeing a fella. A journalist?"

"Umm, yeah," I shift in my seat. "Eloise and Autumn already know all the details. I don't want to bore them with a rehash." My stomach twists. I had been excited to tell my friends all about Adrian, my first relationship to extend past three months in a decade. But what's the point in getting them excited if whatever's happening inside of me scares him away?

"Rehash away." Allison offers a wink. "They can soak it in again."

I take a breath and try to slip back into that feeling of happiness, of feeling secure in a man, to not suspect he's cheating, or sly, or trying to pass the time. "It was at an Aspire fundraiser. He was covering it." I smile. "So, of course he wanted to interview the founder."

Eloise grins at me, then interrupts. "All the girls were whispering about him, how dashing he was. His broad shoulders, his burnt sienna skin."

"Burnt sienna?" asks Allison.

Eloise laughs. "That's what Jayden, one of the girls, referred to it as."

"Okay, okay," says Allison. "Go on."

"He came over to interview me." I look away as I remember his stride, slow but purposeful, strong and confident. His green eyes, so clear and focused. His smile, the way it grew as he got closer, as his gaze connected to mine. "Instantly I felt a little something."

I'm in the moment again: He reached out his hand. Our skin touched. My stomach fluttered. Actually fluttered. I had always thought that was something people just said, not something that really happened.

"Just a little something?" Allison leans in farther, clearly eager to hear the story in full.

"Maybe a little more than a little." For the second time today my cheeks warm. My whole face is probably flushed. I can't hold back all of the excitement of those first moments. "He was so handsome, and he looked at me like I was the only woman in the room. I loved how he seemed entirely comfortable in his own skin." I sigh inwardly as my friends' interest piques. This is not what I wanted, them excited, not if he leaves. I shrug. "Nothing much else happened that night. He did the interview, his questions were direct, thoughtful, challenging at times. He wanted to know why the school board wouldn't have fulfilled this need years ago if it was as much of a need as I stated." I pause. "He stayed for the event, talked to a few of the students, then left."

"Not playing it too forward." Jenn grins. "A risky ploy. And then?"

"And then he called me the next day, said he needed to do some fact checking. They were ridiculous things to check. The answers were on the school board's website. I called him out on it." A grin erupts. "And he asked me out."

"Nice, nice." Allison laughs.

"And it kind of stemmed from there. Nothing too fabulous."

"But is he fabulous?" asks Jenn.

I can't deny it. "Yeah." I smile at her, but that twist of fear grips me again. "He is. The other girls know I haven't had the greatest history in the love department."

"That's an understatement." Allison rolls her eyes. "After her first big love it's been nothing but cheaters, commitment-phobes, and guys who can't seem to keep a job."

"Allison." Sheila shakes her head.

"No, it's okay." I push out a laugh. "She's right. And with all of those guys I knew from the start something was off. This gut feeling, you know? But I'd stick with the guy, hoping I was wrong, hoping things would work out because I wanted it to work out so badly with someone."

I look to the table a moment. The memories pass through me. When Adrian called, it had been almost a year since I'd been on a date. Men asked, but I said no, too afraid of finding someone like the last guy—Thomas, the schoolteacher who turned me into the other woman. Still, I wanted love.

At first I said no to Adrian too, but he'd been persuasive, said we didn't have to call it a date. He'd edged and pushed. He made me laugh. Despite what he'd said, from the moment he picked me up it was a date. And I liked it.

He got to know me, let me know him. He was curious. Open. I tried to resist his attentions, scared it couldn't be real, scared he'd disappoint me like so many others. He didn't let me. Three dates in he invited me to a BBQ at his brother's house. I belonged. Seeing him laugh with them, the ease, it hooked me. He hooked me. I look up at my friends. "With Adrian I never got the feeling something was wrong. It felt right."

"And it still does?" asks Eloise.

"Yeah. Absolutely." I hesitate. "It still does."

Allison breaks into an eager smile. "So, does this mean we'll be meeting him soon? And is his brother single?"

I laugh, because I know that's what's expected, that's what I'd usually do, but will they meet him? It all depends on the little box in my purse, what it has to tell, and how he reacts to it. "We'll see. And no, I'm sorry. The brother has a lovely wife and two rambunctious kids."

"Drat." Allison glances around the table. "So, other news?"

Autumn mentions Jennifer's pregnancy.

"My condolences," says Allison. "Oh, I mean congratulations." She winks. "No, really, that's awesome. Super happy for you and Rajeev. Just say goodbye to sleep, sex, clean clothes, and showers for a few years." Allison laughs. "At least that's what my sister says. Her kid's three, and my sis says she's just starting to get her life back."

"Not all kids are as rough as your sister's was," says Eloise. "Lori had some rough patches with Trisa, but it hasn't been that bad."

Allison tilts her head back and forth. "Well, your sister and her fella also have you living there to help, and then nearby your Dad and Evelyn, his parents, Junior."

"And Jennifer and Rajeev will have a lot of support too," says Autumn.

How much support would I have? Mom and Dad for sure. They'd be disappointed that another one of their children would be an unwed mother, but they'd embrace this child as their own, just as they embraced me. Of course, they live two hours away.

And Adrian's family? They joke about how he needs to settle down again, nudge that I'm exactly what he needs and I shouldn't let him forget it. He's been married before and he left that relationship. Would a baby feel like pressure toward something he doesn't want? Or worse, scare him away?

The talking stops. I've zoned out again. Each face at the table stares at me.

"What?" I let out a little laugh.

"Autumn asked if you can come to a BBQ at her parents' place this weekend," Sheila raps her fingers on the table, "and if you'd bring Adrian."

"Oh, I. Yes. I can. When?"

"Saturday at three," says Autumn.

"Fine for me." I notice my foot tapping and stop it. "I'll have to check with Adrian."

"Great."

The conversation shifts to Autumn's business ventures in London. I attempt to listen with a focused intensity, though I've heard much of this already. She started off slow—one on one and small group training in people's homes and, when the weather allows, public parks—and has enough of a following that she's thinking of renting a small studio space several times a week.

Next the group transitions to a case Shelia is trying: a young pregnant woman filing charges of incest and statutory rape against her uncle. It's easy to see why Sheila tends to be so reserved and distant. If she kept herself open, I have no idea how she'd deal with the world she sees on a daily basis.

The story makes my fear and stress seem unwarranted. At least I'm not that girl.

Allison talks about her fitness studio, and Eloise brings everyone up to speed on the Aspire group. For this part of the conversation, I need to do more than listen. I push the constant stream of 'what if's' out of my head and join Eloise in excitement and wonderment over how in a little over two years this youth empowerment program has gone from the group of ten students I'd bring into my classroom once a week for skills training and lectures from successful business women, to a program that now has Eloise as a full-time employee, two part-time workers, and involves three high schools and fifty-five young women learning the skills to either start their own business or excel in their field of choice.

When everyone is caught up, Sheila stands. "Time to head back to the office."

Allison pops up beside her. "The gym calls me."

"And I need a nap." Jenn stretches. "This baby is stealing all my energy."

Her words snap me back to the fears I'd put aside to talk about the Aspire program. In just a few hours, my life could change forever.

"I have nowhere I have to be." Autumn turns to me.

"Neither do I." Eloise reaches for her purse. "I got a ton of work done this morning. What about you, Trace? Should we put off the prep for a few hours, get some quality Autumn time in?"

Her question is interrupted by a round of hugs before Sheila, Allison, and Jenn all head away from the café.

"Umm…the summer program starts in a week. Do you think we have time to—"

"I'd love to catch up more." Autumn rests her hand on my shoulder. "And…" she hesitates, "I'm worried about you."

"You're not yourself today." Eloise pauses, a look of

concern in her eyes. "Don't try to hide it."

I avoid their faces, scared of what they'll think and scared saying the words will somehow make my fears real. But my mind is about to burst. I have to tell someone.

Autumn gives my arm a squeeze. "It's okay."

I take a deep breath then let the words ease out. "I think I'm pregnant."

CHAPTER TWO

Eloise motions us toward Victoria Park. "Are you sure you're pregnant?"

"No." I hesitate. "The test is in my purse."

Eloise and Autumn sit across from me at a picnic table by the fountain. Autumn smiles. "So, you may not be pregnant."

"I'm over a month and a half late."

"Wow." Eloise breathes. "And you're just testing now?"

"Life's been so crazy—the Aspire group blowing up, meeting Adrian, and then I just got through with all the end-of-year marking."

"It's totally understandable." Autumn glances at Eloise then back to me. "But isn't this a good thing? I mean, isn't this what you've always wanted? Children. A family."

"Yeah." I speak evenly, refusing the whimper that tries to enter my voice. Are they judging me? Are they thinking how stupid I am for getting knocked up? This is what Eloise's sixteen-year-old sister did. I'm thirty. I should know better. I did know better. We always used a condom. "But not like this. I wanted a husband. I wanted—"

"This isn't nineteen-twenty." Eloise leans forward. "You don't have to do things in a certain order. Lot's of women—"

"But that's the way she wanted to do it." Autumn reaches across the table for my hand. "It'll be okay."

"Will it?"

"If there's one thing I've learned," says Eloise, "life has a way of working out, sometimes in ways we'd never expect it to."

"Absolutely." Autumn nods.

I stare at them, not knowing what to say. They've both lived that lesson.

"How do you think Adrian will take it?" asks Eloise.

"I have no idea." I lay my hands on the table. "We've been together a while now. Over five months. But we rarely see each other more than two or three times a week. We've never made plans more than a week or two in advance."

Autumn purses her lips. "Has he talked about wanting children?"

"No."

"Has he talked about not wanting children?" asks Eloise.

"No. I've gotten the impression, though, that his divorce had something to do with children."

"Really?" Autumn shifts.

"He made a comment when we were watching a movie. I tried to dig deeper, but he changed the subject. It was the first time he's ever given me what seemed like a brush off."

Eloise waves a hand. "Well, there's no point hypothesizing. That could mean anything. Heck, it could have been like my situation, he's the one who wanted kids and I'm the one who didn't."

"Absolutely," says Autumn.

I sink my head into my hands and stare at the table. "I feel so stupid."

"Don't say that," says Autumn. "It could happen to anyone. We all make mistakes."

"I didn't though, not really."

"Hmm?"

"Well, I mean, I probably should have been on birth control or gotten an IUD or something. Extra protection, you know? But I went off of birth control after things ended with Thomas. I felt so much better off it. The chemicals must have been messing with me. So we were just using condoms and—"

Eloise leans forward. "Did one break?"

"Not to my knowledge."

"Oh," she leans back again, "well, you're probably not pregnant. Those things are ninety-nine point ninety-five percent effective or something. Maybe you're having some hormonal issues. That happens."

"Has it happened to you?"

Autumn and Eloise shake their heads.

"I was somewhat irregular as a teenager, but I was on birth control from what…first year University? I decided to get off of it last year."

Autumn nods. "Why don't you do the test? All this wondering, it could be for nothing."

"I'm scared." If it's positive my whole life, my whole vision of my life, won't be what I imagined.

"We'll go with you," says Eloise. "Even look at the stick for you if you like."

I laugh. "I don't think that's necessary."

"We can be with you, though," says Autumn.

"I don't know." I shake my head. "I think if it's…I think I'd want to be alone."

They're both silent. "You should do it sooner than later." Autumn slaps her hands on the table. "Stop stressing about it. Get it over with."

Eloise nods.

I lift my purse and shake it. "I guess I should." I stand and Autumn and Eloise follow my lead.

"We'll see you at the BBQ Saturday, right? Come no matter what. Even if…even if Adrian's busy or something. You come." Autumn reaches for a hug.

"Yeah, I'll come." If I am pregnant, if my life is about to change, the last thing I want to do is push these friends away. Eloise and Autumn, more than anyone else, more than my family, are the two people I'm almost never afraid will leave me.

"And call, okay? Or at least feel free to call. Do you want us to—"

I shake my head.

Eloise grasps my hand, squeezes it. I lift my arm in a wave and walk down the lawn to the sidewalk. When I glance back, the two of them still stand in the park, arms around each other's waists, watching me.

THE WALK TO MY apartment seems long, but Autumn and Eloise are right. There could be another explanation. Women have false alarms all the time, at least according to movies and TV shows. From what I can remember, though, the women in those false alarms are a week or two late. Maybe just days. I'm a month and a half.

A husband, a family, a white picket fence…not literally, but what that fence represents, is what I've always wanted. A real family. A family whose blood I share. But if Adrian leaves me, decides he wants nothing to do with me or the baby I carry…

It wouldn't be the worst thing; I'd still have a child. My own child. I stop to lean against the brick wall of a building just a few lots down from mine and place my hand over my abdomen, like Jenn had. I can almost feel a child growing there. Blood of my blood and flesh of my flesh. Of our flesh. Would the baby have Adrian's fervent curiosity? His boisterous laugh? His confidence? A smile creeps across my face. No, being pregnant wouldn't be the worst thing. Whether Adrian stayed or not, I'd always have a piece of him with me and, if he did leave, I have a good job. Solid. I could provide for a baby. My mother would relish the chance to babysit and see me more often. Maybe she'd love that baby in a way I've never believed she could love me. Maybe seeing that love would change everything.

With a sigh, I push away from the building and continue my walk. For the first time since I realized how late my period is, that mantle of terror lifts away. This is not a tragedy. Plans are made to be altered, broken, transformed.

I expected to fall in love my first year of University. And I had. Connor. Next step was to marry shortly after graduation and two years later start a family. Only Connor didn't want that to be his plan. So I've lived through new plans: teaching, the Aspire group, meeting Adrian. My life is good.

A large smile greets me in my building's elevator mirrors. The woman staring back at me looks hopeful, or at least open to whatever the future reveals.

The test directions tell me to use 'first morning urine,' to get the highest concentration of 'HCG,' but seeing as I'd be a month and a half pregnant by now, I figure that's not necessary. I set my timer, resolving not to look until it beeps. I brush my teeth, clean the bathroom counter, straighten my toiletries and, at last, pick up the stick. Negative.

I stare at the results, look back to the directions, sink to the edge of the tub. What do I feel? Not relief. Not sadness. Perplexed? I look again at the box, not taking in the words. Maybe first morning urine does matter. My phone buzzes. Adrian: *This story is blowing up. My editor says even a feature spread may not be enough. We may hold it for a doc. My first commissioned doc! Need to follow a lead. Meet at 8 instead of 7? Promise I'll wine and dine you right to make up for this. :)*

My skin warms. A sense of security washes over me. It's only two in the afternoon and he's already letting me know he'll be late *and* saying he'll make up for it. Most of the men I've dated since Connor would send me a text five minutes after they were supposed to arrive. If I were lucky, five minutes before. I text back, *No problem. Get that story!* and put my phone away. Grabbing my planner, I look at my goals for the day. Finishing my portion of Aspire's first week's programming is top of the list. I sit at my desk to start. I can't concentrate. After fifteen to twenty minutes of getting nothing done, I go to the nearest pharmacy and purchase another test.

During the afternoon I slip into lesson planning then make a handful of calls to women we hope will guest speak at the summer meetings. Empowering young girls—it's a hard cause to ignore, and four out of the five women I call agree to speak. Feeling like I've done a good day's work, especially as I'm technically on vacation, I make myself a tide-me-over-till-dinner meal and settle into my comfiest armchair with a book I picked up earlier this week and my cat, Toulouse, snuggled beside me.

When Adrian arrives at eight o'clock on the dot, I'm ready and eager to put aside this morning's fears and questions for a night of fun.

"You look ravishing!" He grins. I offer him a kiss and hug, loving how broad his back feels under my hands, the way I have to rise up on tiptoe to meet his lips.

I step back, hoping the blush that rose upon seeing him has disappeared. "You look pretty ravishing yourself."

"Well," he pops his collar in a completely ironic way, "I had a successful day, thought I should look as dapper as I feel."

He does look dapper, in his slim-fit khakis and pale green dress shirt. I reach for my purse, step over the threshold, and lock the door behind me. "So you caught your leads."

"I did indeed. But before work talk, tell me about your day. Autumn's back in town, right? You had your girl's lunch?"

"I did."

"And?" He opens the lobby door for me and places his hand on the small of my back as I step through. The instant he touches me this morning's fear creeps back. What if a baby means I lose this? He looks down at me, a smile in his eyes. "Well, how was it? How is everyone? How's Autumn?"

"She's great." My voice rises. "Everyone's good. Jennifer's pregnant."

"Jennifer." He rubs his chin. "She's…"

"Autumn's cousin."

"Oh, okay. You know I need to meet these people at some point, put faces to the names. So there's Eloise, who I've met. Autumn, who lives in England with her boyfriend, Jakob. Allison, the fitness nut—"

"Owner of a fitness studio."

"Yeah, fitness nut," he grins, "so nutty for fitness she opened a studio to indulge her obsession."

"Is that how I talk about her?" I look up at him slyly, while also feeling a jolt of fear that I've misrepresented her. She's a bit fitness obsessed, but she's also so much more than that.

"No, no." He laughs. "I'm messing with you. And then there's Sheila, the workaholic lawyer."

I swat him. He raises his arms. "Hey, you have actually used the term workaholic on her."

"I guess so. I didn't mean it like that, though. She has a really important job. And she does her job well. It's demanding."

"I know. Tracey," he rests a hand on my shoulder, "relax, okay."

"I don't want you thinking I trash talk my friends, that's not what—"

"I don't think you trash talk them. You don't. I just have a habit of clinging onto labels. I need to, especially with people I've never met before. When I meet them, I'll develop other ways to keep them straight. Like Allison with the bulging muscles, who could knock me out if I ever step out of line?"

I laugh. "Not exactly. She's probably five foot three. We're about the same height. And I don't know what she weighs, but her muscles are lean, not bulging. She doesn't have a bulge on her entire body."

He directs me up the street, away from where he usually parks his car. We must be eating local tonight. I glance up at him. "Autumn's having a BBQ at her parent's place Saturday. You're welcome to come if you like."

"Oh, I like." He smiles like a schoolboy. "I'll finally learn all the dirt on you. I'll pump them for information like I'm digging for the story of a lifetime."

I shake my head, smiling, but a shot of nervousness jolts through me. I definitely don't want Adrian to know some aspects of my past: the wretched men, how pathetic they made me seem. The tingling fear quickly tapers off though. My friends are discreet, all except Allison. If I keep Adrian away from her and her tendency to reference my trail of bad boyfriends, all should be well.

"I'm joking." He wraps an arm around me. "I'll wait for you to open up. You're worth the wait."

He thinks I'm closed off. "Thanks." I loop my arm around his side and squeeze gently. It's not a crime to only show people the best parts of me, to save them from my baggage. "I'm glad you'll be meeting them."

"Me too."

Several minutes up the street we stop in front of a building with a crowd of people milling around outside. I look up at Adrian. "Dinner theatre?"

"Dinner theatre."

"Was this the plan all along?"

"Nope. I said I needed to make up for my tardiness. Good effort?"

"Good effort." I grin as he hands over our tickets. "No press pass?"

"Nah, this a real date." He leads me into the intimate room. The play is a comedic musical, half fanciful fun, half satire on the expectations society places on women. The food isn't amazing, but good. With not a lot of time for conversation, I find myself ruminating again about what is or isn't growing inside me. I look to Adrian as he laughs at the show. He's kind and funny and smart and decidedly into me. But will that be enough?

Tomorrow morning's test requires privacy, so I'll need to make sure we go home separately tonight. I try to think up a valid excuse, which isn't easy. With the exception of the Aspire Program, I'm not exactly working through the summer. I still haven't decided which made up reason sounds best when we reach my building's lobby.

"Early interview." Adrian pulls me toward him.

"Oh, really?" I sigh an inward breath of relief: no excuse needed.

He kisses me long and deep, then finishes it off with a gentle peck to my forehead. "Also, you remember I'll be out of town for the next two days at least?"

I nod.

"Even if things get drawn out, though, I'll make sure I'm back in time for the BBQ."

I fiddle with my keys. "It's not that important."

"My first invite into Tracey Sampson's inner-sanctum. Oh, it's important alright." He winks. "Sleep well, my beauty."

I smile at his corniness, then make my way toward the elevator. That's what I need to do, sleep, and when I wake I'll have my answer.

CHAPTER THREE

I hold the stick in my hand. Still negative. I'm not pregnant. Setting the test down, I sit on the tub, my shoulders resting against the shower's cool tile. *This is good,* I tell myself. *Very good.* It means Adrian and I have a chance to grow our relationship naturally. It means he's less likely to leave me or stay simply out of obligation.

I wasted a night's sleep worrying over nothing. I look at the stick again. I've been afraid to admit it to myself, afraid to let my feelings run wild, afraid to emotionally tie myself to a man who's not worthy of my respect and love. But I can't deny it: I am falling in love with Adrian. I may have already fallen. And as far as I can tell, he's worthy.

So this is good. Not being pregnant is great news. But—I calculate the dates—it's been seventy-three days since my last period. Could the test be wrong? If it isn't, something else is.

I force myself to stop ruminating, make breakfast, get dressed, then call my doctor's office. The soonest appointment is in a week and a half. I hesitate before accepting it. Most likely my period will be back by then. My mind flashes to the countless doctor's visits when I lived in the group home—the dingy waiting room walls, the itchy chairs, the office with a damp stale smell and a hairy old man. A different case worker escorted me every time. 'You need to get healthy,' the case worker would say. 'You're here so you can be healthy and find a family.'

Only memories. My doctor's office is nothing like that one. Its walls are pristine white, the chairs clean and comfortable, my doctor is a young, fit woman, and the room has no smell at all.

"I'll take it."

❧

OVER THE NEXT SEVERAL days I prep for the Aspire group, read three books, go for long walks, and try to keep my mind off the mystery of my missing monthly visitor.

On Saturday the sun shines bright and the forecast tells of a perfect day. Before I've even knocked on Autumn's parents' door it swings open. Mrs. Caparelli's smiling face greets me. "Sweetie, come in, come in!" She wraps her arms around me as she draws me into the foyer. "It's been too long. You know I told you to visit."

"I know." I let her embrace warm me a moment and imagine what it must be like for Autumn to have a mother like this, so full of love and acceptance. So unconcerned. I almost trip as I stumble over shoes in front of the door. They don't seem to bother Mrs. Caparelli a bit. Embarrassment would seep all through my mother. "Sorry, I meant to visit."

"Mean a little harder next time." She steps back, her lopsided grin stretched across her face. "I'm glad you're here now. Everything good?" She looks past me toward the driveway and her smile lessens. "Autumn told me you were bringing a new friend. He couldn't make it?"

"He'll be here." I push the door closed. "He'll be late so we came separately."

"Oh! Smart. Good to keep some independence." She nudges me and wavers slightly. "Everyone's out back." Mrs. Caparelli limps her way to the back of the house, resting heavily on her cane. It's amazing, really. Only two years ago she was in a wheelchair from a stroke that almost killed her, she couldn't eat on her own, let alone talk, and here she is, walking.

As we pass the kitchen, Mrs. Caparelli stops. "I was on my way to get something when I saw you pull up."

"You need help?"

"No, no. You go have fun."

I hesitate, how can she get anything while holding the cane? Autumn's father still works though, so she must manage on her own all the time.

"Tracey, hi!" Autumn waves from the lawn, where she and her cousin Billy set up a volleyball net.

"Hi!" I call back. Autumn's gaze darts from me to the space surrounding me, the same question on her face that was on her mother's lips, but she keeps silent. I smile, hoping to assure her everything is fine.

An arm wraps around my shoulder from behind. "Lori wants you to see the baby," says Eloise. I look to the corner of the yard where Eloise's sister and her toddler play in the shade. "I wanted to make sure you were okay before," Eloise glances over to the mother and child then back at me, "she thrusts Trisa into your arms or something."

"I'm okay."

"I just meant—"

"I know." I wave away her words. "And thank you. I'm fine."

"I've been eager to ask all week. I know I shouldn't pry…I just want you to know that I'm—"

"Looks like it was a false alarm."

Eloise shows no reaction. "And this is…"

"Good news," I keep my gaze toward the yard. "Of course good news."

Her gaze rests on me. "It doesn't sound so good."

Beyond us, Jenn and Autumn's brothers toss a frisbee. Lori chases Trisa. I lean on the porch railing. I want to relax, enjoy the view, but my mind's filled with fear; it's been creeping at the back of my mind ever since I made the doctor's appointment. What if this late period is something big? My childhood could be coming back to haunt me. I could be sick. Very sick. "A little nervous, that's all." I toss Eloise a smile. "I still haven't gotten my visitor. So I guess it's not a guarantee it's a false alarm. And if it is, it's just weird." I glance over at her. "You know?"

"How long has it been?"

"Seventy-five days."

"It's probably nothing." Eloise joins me against the railing. "I've heard of women going three months or so. Like I said before, probably just some hormonal imbalance."

"You're right." I push myself up and turn to the steps. "Probably nothing."

"And Adrian? He couldn't make it?" Eloise follows behind me.

"He should be here within the hour."

Trisa's big brown eyes light up when she sees me. Her curls bounce as she toddles over, arms outstretched. I bend down and she snuggles into my shoulder then squirms free. "How did finals go?" I ask Lori.

"Exhausting." Lori gives a tired smile. "But pretty good. I don't think I failed anything. Thanks again for helping me prep."

"My pleasure."

"It's nice having only one class for the summer term. Trisa, don't touch that. Dirty." Lori shakes a finger at the girl then draws her gaze back to me. "And teaching fewer dance classes too. The summer students are way less intense than the regulars. The regulars take their intensity to summer camp."

"Just like you did."

"Just like I did."

I spend the next several minutes playing with Trisa and chatting with the people who come to see her before filtering away. Without needing to look, I know when

Allison has arrived. After greeting several people and expressing her excitement about volleyball, she shouts, "Look who I found!" Afraid I already know the answer, I turn to see Adrian stepping onto the back porch, grinning and scanning the crowd until his gaze finds mine. His smile broadens and my stomach drops. Allison with Adrian. Exactly what I didn't want. Will she have mentioned my long dry spell before meeting him? Before that spell, the countless guy after guy who turned out to be, in some way or another, a dirt bag? There were a lot, too many, as I tried to find that security I've been longing for in a man, any man. But I'm not like that anymore. Still, will he question whether I'm the girl for him?

He waves as he's ushered down the steps where Autumn, Sheila, Jennifer, and Autumn's brother, Daniel, stand chatting. Based on the smile he sends me before drawing his attention to my friends, it doesn't seem like he's been scared off yet. I rise from my crouched position with Trisa, my gaze on Adrian. He looks at ease, not the least bit nervous. He looks like he belongs. I wait a moment more before crossing the yard.

"Interesting fella you've got here," says Daniel as Adrian drapes an arm around my shoulder and kisses my temple.

"What's he been saying?" I wrap my arm around Adrian's waist and give a little pinch.

Adrian laughs. "Just talking about the story I've been working on." He turns from me. "But I want to know about this book of yours, Jennifer. What's it about?"

SWEATY AND ENERGIZED from a surprisingly competitive game of volleyball, we gather around the BBQ and picnic table to load our plates. "Yumm." Autumn settles into the chair next to mine. "Rajeev can cook. Jennifer's always complaining about how hard keeping her weight down is with him in the kitchen. But I'd be just fine carrying a few extra pounds if I got to have food like this every night."

"You say that now," Eloise takes the chair on the other side of me, "but you'd feel different as soon as the pounds piled on."

"You're probably right." Autumn turns to me. "Adrian's nice."

I laugh. "He is."

"And quite handsome."

I grin.

Eloise looks sideways at me. "I don't see any red flags."

"You barely know him."

"True."

Autumn leans back in her chair and stretches her legs. "The important thing is that you don't see any red flags, right?"

"Not yet." I shrug.

"That's good, Tracey. Keep your eyes open. But don't look for them. Red flags generally pop up pretty early."

"I know."

Autumn leans toward me. "And I know the look of a man in love."

"He's not in love." A blush works its way up my cheeks.

"Well, if not, he's in deep like."

Adrian sits across the yard with Rajeev, Billy, Sheila, and Autumn's mom. Whatever story he's telling even makes Sheila laugh. "I hope so."

Eloise follows my gaze. "You hope so, but?"

"It's been a heavy week."

"Did you tell him what's going on?" asks Autumn.

"No. I tested negative. So I don't know what's going on. I don't think we're at the point where I should tell him about unknowns."

"I get that." Autumn takes a bite of her Shish Kebab, pausing a moment to savour it. "That's what's on your mind today, then? I thought maybe a positive result was weighing on you…and that you hadn't told him."

"Am I that transparent?"

"Just to us." Autumn winks. "I'm sure no one else notices."

"Do you have any idea what may be causing the hold-up? Stress or—"

"No. None." I pick up a carrot stick and chew heartily, my excuse to not elaborate. I decided not to look up causes online. It'd be worse to know details of all the possible degenerative diseases or genetic malfunctions that could cause a period to disappear. I swallow and turn to Autumn. "So it's been what, four days away now? How is Jakob faring without you, and how are you faring without him?"

Autumn grins a shy grin. "Good. Good in the sense that I miss him like crazy." She glances at her plate and her eyes glisten with a slight mist. "I was worried I wouldn't. I was worried being here after so long away, being in all the places Matt had been, this backyard where we had our engagement party, driving past the apartment where we first made love, would bring him back…and it does bring him back. But it's not pushing Jakob out of my mind. It's weird, very weird, to completely love two men at the same time." She picks up a Shish Kebab then sets it down again. "I was scared of both possibilities, that Jakob would lessen my love for Matt or Matt would lessen my love for Jakob. But it's like they support each other." She looks up at us. "So weird."

I put my hand on Autumn's shoulder and Eloise grins as she says the words I'm thinking. "So you love him."

Autumn's eyes widen. "Well, yeah, I…"

"You've never said that before. At least not to us."

She shrugs, then her expression kind of melts. "I do. I never thought I could. I mean when Matt died I thought the ability to feel that way for someone again was dead too. And it's not the same. It's not better or worse the way I feel about Jakob. It's just different. But," she hesitates, "I'm still frightened of the anniversary, being here on the anniversary. Going to his grave."

"We'll go with you," I say, "or be there afterwards, whatever you want."

She sighs. "I want to be alone. I saw his parents the other day. They were so sweet. Happy for me, but I could tell it hurt them, knowing I was moving on with my life, in love again, when their son was…" She shakes her head. "I had them agree on separate times to go to the grave. I think they understood."

"Of course they'd understand."

"Jakob's really good about it too. Patient. If it were up to him we'd be engaged by now. But he knows I'm not ready."

"You will be someday."

"It's stupid, but part of me is scared if we get married something horrible will happen."

"You can't think like that," says Eloise. "Follow your life as it leads you, you know? Listen to your heart and all that woo-woo stuff." She winks.

"Yeah, you need to add that, don't you.? Autumn laughs. "To think, Eloise Grant telling someone to listen to their heart."

"People change," says Eloise. "Slowly, but we change."

"Do you ever see Moses?" asks Autumn.

Eloise takes a deep breath and shakes her head. Has she told Autumn about the relationship Moses and I almost started after they broke their engagement? Of the kiss we shared? She hasn't brought it up since I assured her nothing was going to happen between him and me. I can't help seeing him daily during the school year, but Eloise and I have an unspoken agreement that his name is out of bounds. "I've run into him a few times," says Eloise, "while at the school for the Aspire program. That'll stop for the summer." She pauses. "He's getting married next month."

"Next month!" Autumn sucks in a breath.

I put my head down and pretend to concentrate on my

food. Eloise knows. I hoped she didn't.

"It's good," says Eloise. "I'm happy for him. Maybe if I'd had my little 'woo-woo' change of heart sooner it could have been us, but I didn't, and I don't regret my life."

Autumn reaches across me to squeeze Eloise's knee.

"And I've got my girls." She shoots us a smile. "And the girls at Aspire and Lori and Trisa, Junior and Dad and," she grins, "a young man in our apartment who was fairly insistent about getting me to agree to a cup of coffee."

We spend the next minute or two chatting about said guy, until Mr. Caparelli suggests a bonfire and s'mores. We move our chairs to form a circle around the fire pit.

I settle into my seat then look up to see Adrian. He gestures to the chair beside me. "May I?"

"You may."

He plops down then leans toward me and holds my head in his hands. "I've missed you."

"I missed you too." I grin, still finding it hard to believe this is real, that he's real, that he's looking at me like this.

"I like your friends." He takes four marshmallows from Mr. Caparelli's bag and passes me two.

"They seem to like you."

"And I like how much they like you."

"How much they like me?"

"Yeah. I mean I know you're this sweet, caring, thoughtful person. I've seen it with the students, I've seen it with me…though we're still new, but I like seeing it with people who've known you for years. Who've probably had the chance to see you at your worst and love you anyways"

"So this was some kind of social experiment for you?" I ask, a twinkle to my eye but a knot of fear in my heart.

"Not experiment." He reaches for two sticks, hands me one, then pauses. "It's like you've finally invited me into the outer ring of your inner circle. And I like being here."

"The outer ring of my inner circle?"

"Your family would comprise the inner ring, and then,"

he points to my chest, "really opening up to me, letting me see you with nothing else blocking my view, would be the core."

"I've let you see me." I keep my voice low. "With nothing blocking your view."

He grins, then scoots his chair closer to the fire. "That's not the type of view I'm talking about."

I hesitate before nudging my chair closer to his. This is new: a man who sees past the face I display for the world, who recognizes it as a face, and wants to delve deeper. Some of my closest friends don't realize how much I withhold. A few years ago Allison commented, 'With Tracey, what you see is what you get.' She has no idea. My barrier, my shield: necessary companions. Yet Adrian wants past that, sees that there's more beneath. "How did your research go? Did you get good interviews?"

Adrian turns from roasting. Our knees bump. "Not as good as I'd hoped, but a gem or two. Some quotable quotes. A couple more leads." He lifts his stick to display his marshmallow, perfectly golden all around. "Like riding a bike." He laughs, pulls the marshmallow off the stick, and pops the treat in his mouth.

"No chocolate and graham cracker?" asks Eloise.

"Nah, I'm all about the art of the roast."

Allison leans over, her eyes sparkling. "All about the art, eh? I'd wager my roasting skills surpass any man's. You up for the challenge?"

"I'm in," Rajeev calls from across the pit.

Adrian chuckles. "Me too. Rajeev, let's put this fiery red head in her place."

The competition begins. They definitely like him, which is good, very good. One less stress. My missing period flows back into my mind. It could be anything, like Eloise said. Worrying is foolish.

CHAPTER FOUR

On the morning of my doctor's appointment a torrential downpour falls outside my window. The clinic is three blocks away and there's never parking so, knowing the rain in this city rarely falls down, but sideways, I don my full piece rain-suit. At the clinic I peel away the sopping layer and scrunch the suit in a grocery bag. Peaceful music streams from the speakers affixed to the walls. "Tracey Sampson."

Right on time. I smile at the nurse, amazed again at my luck of finding a doctor who somehow manages to keep her patients from waiting hours.

"WHAT CAN I DO FOR you today?" asks Dr. Keer.

"Oh." Moisture gathers under my armpits and along the small of my back. It's not from the rain. "I'm wondering about my period."

"What's it been like?" She looks at me, not her notes, another characteristic I appreciate.

"Well, it hasn't been."

"You've missed your period?"

"Yes."

"And you've taken a pregnancy test."

"Yes."

"How late?"

"Uh…" I try to calculate but am too nervous to do the math. "It's been eighty-three days since my last one."

Her expression remains unchanged except for a tightening of her lips. She glances at my file. "You went off of birth control a little over a year ago. So, you have been getting periods since then? Regular ones?"

"Pretty regular. I think."

"You think?"

"I wasn't keeping track too closely. There really wasn't a reason to."

"But you have a reason now? Have you been active?"

"Yes."

"And using an alternate form of protection?"

"Condoms."

"Okay. First thing, let's get you a urine test and then come back in here and we'll talk possibilities."

Several minutes later I'm back in Dr. Keer's office. "You're not pregnant. Were you regular before you started birth control?"

"I started when I was nineteen. I don't remember too well. I don't think I was very regular. Actually, no. I wasn't. Sometimes a few weeks, sometimes a few months."

She writes in my file. "Suffered any depression recently?"

"I'm happier than I've been in months…though this is worrying me."

"Have you changed your exercise regime? Any intense workouts, training for a marathon?"

"No."

"Change in diet?"

"No."

"Drugs, prescription or otherwise?"

"No."

"Sexually transmitted diseases?"

"No."

Dr. Keer taps her pen on the table. "When's the last time you were tested?"

"After my last partner."

"And since your current one?"

"No."

She writes again. "Have you gained or lost any noticeable amount of weight recently?"

"Still battling that unshakable last ten pounds."

She looks up from my file. "Your weight is perfectly healthy. You don't need to be a model."

"I know, I—"

She looks back to the chart. "Have you been experiencing dizziness, nausea, sleep disturbances?"

"No, no, and no. Well, maybe a little dizzy and nauseated right now."

She looks up again. "I'm sorry. I know this is a lot."

"It's okay." I shift in my seat. "I guess sometimes I find it hard to sleep, but that's nothing new."

"Night sweats?"

"It's happened, but rarely."

She nods. "Any history of thyroid problems?"

"With me? I don't—"

"In your family?"

"My birth family?"

She sets her pen down. "I'm sorry. It slipped my mind."

"You don't have to apologize." Twenty-six years and I still hate people's tendency to apologize about my adoption.

"Any unusual hair growth? So on your chin, upper lip, breasts?"

"Uh…I rub my hand across my chin. Not anymore."

She looks at me, a question on her face.

"Hundreds of dollars of laser treatments have taken care of that, well, at least the more noticeable hair."

She makes a noise of acknowledgement and jots a note.

"What do you think is wrong?"

Her gaze is back on me. "I can't say. It could be as simple as an ovarian cyst that will likely pop, allowing your cycle to normalize."

"Or it could be?"

"It would be helpful if we had some sort of medical history for you. Was the adoption closed? Can you access your birth parents?"

My body tenses. "I can. I just haven't. Well, my mother. I have access to my mother's contact information. My father isn't listed."

"The mother is more important in this case."

I stare at her.

"Okay, usually we don't express too much concern unless your period is absent more than three months but you're close enough to that point that I don't see the sense of having you come in a week from now."

"Okay."

"So I'll send you for some blood tests and an STD test, see what we can rule out. If your period comes back in the meantime, it's more likely this was a one-off, something innocuous."

"Okay."

A paper streams out of her printer. Dr. Keer hands it to me. "This clinic is closest. You know it?"

I nod. "Do I still go if my period comes back?"

"You might as well."

I hold the sheet in my hand, the moisture along my arm its and back thoroughly uncomfortable by now. "Should I be concerned?"

"I don't think so. You're a healthy young woman. And you're not trying to conceive right now?"

"No. No, I'm not."

"There's no point in worrying. We'll figure it out."

Standing, I thank her then make my way through the waiting room. The rain has cleared and I'm relieved not to put my soggy rain suit back on. Her question—*you're not trying to conceive right now*—wriggles around in my brain. I'm not, but would whatever she thinks is wrong be an issue if I were? No period in almost three months. How could it not?

✌

FIFTEEN MINUTES LATER I'm standing with Eloise in the space we've rented for the Aspire summer program. "Over fifty teenage girls for three hours a week." She smiles at me. "Think we can handle it?"

"Can't Eloise Grant handle anything?"

"Oh right," she smacks her hand against the side of her face as if she's been absentminded, "how could I forget?"

"This is really something, isn't it?" Two rows of new computers line one side of the space. Three glass-walled rooms house conference style tables. A podium stands before a large open space, suitable for activities or to set up chairs.

"It's what it should be." Eloise folds her arms across her chest. "Professional. Sleek. It'll show the girls we take them seriously, so they'll take themselves seriously." She grins back at me. "Oh, the wonders of corporate sponsorship."

"The wonders of your connections and smooth-talking." I laugh. "Have I told you lately how thankful I am that you've come on board with this—taken it over, basically?"

Eloise surveys the room then turns to me. "It's me who's thankful. Who knows where I'd be without this? I probably would have slid back into the role of PR guru extraordinaire or tried to redesign some company whose sole goal was riches."

"You wouldn't have. But even if you had, there's good in that too."

"Not like this. The flexibility, the knowledge that what I'm doing actually matters?" Eloise hesitates. "Well, no, what I was doing before mattered. But the way I had to do it…I wasn't the person I wanted to be."

"And you are now?"

She shrugs. "I'm getting there. I miss some pricier pleasures my life can no longer afford, but I don't miss the constant pressure to always be better, to always take the lead, to let no man or woman surpass me."

"I don't think that has changed so much." I extend my arm. "I'm not sure many people could have achieved this, and in such a short time."

She nods. "Maybe. But there wasn't that pressure, you know? That single-mindedness. I did this because I wanted to, not because I felt I had to. I achieved it through partnerships, collaboration. It's different."

"El?" I hesitate, not sure if I should ask the question.

"Yeah."

"How are you doing, really? With the news about Moses?"

She takes a deep breath and looks to the ceiling before meeting my gaze. "I'm happy for him."

Silence floats around us.

She strides to the large window looking out on the downtown skyline. "I guess I'm sad for me." She turns back. "He's a good guy, and I don't think I should have let him get away." She wraps her arms around her middle. "But I did. And it's too late to change that. It's been too late for a long time. So I'm glad he's happy."

Not sure what to say, I nod.

"It's so ironic, you know? What he wanted from me, I resisted—a family, a more balanced life. And now that's what I have. And what I want. Being around Trisa…even when it's rough and tiring, I just think, I want this. For me." She steps toward me. "For the most part I'm happy. I hope to find the guy I can fulfil those dreams with sooner than later, but still, my life is," she grins, "back to the woo-woo talk, very full. Being a live-in Aunt is probably the next best thing."

I nod again, wondering if I hadn't been in the way, there to comfort Moses, to let his feelings transfer from Eloise toward me, would he have taken her back when she came to his door asking for forgiveness and another chance. It's impossible to know and pointless to dwell on...just like what's going on inside me—for now, impossible to know and pointless to dwell on.

"And the coffee guy?"

A smile lights Eloise's face as she set up the chairs. "The coffee guy is promising. Very promising."

A FEW DAYS LATER I meet Adrian at one of my favourite restaurants. All you can eat sushi that actually tastes fresh. Adrian smiles large when he sees me, almost awkwardly so. He jumps when the hostess calls our name. When he pulls out my chair, he bangs his shins in the process. He grins and grits his teeth, denying the pain.

"You all right?" I ask.

"Perfect. Swell."

"Swell?"

"Yeah." He laughs. "It's old newspaper man talk, see."

I shake my head and chuckle. "What's with you today?" Inside I'm not smiling. Shifty behaviour from men isn't new to me and it's rarely a good thing. My favourite restaurant. Acute attentiveness, though Adrian is always attentive. And all of this initiated by a message saying he wants to have a talk. I sense a breakup speech.

"How's your week been so far?" He looks at me, not his menu.

"Great. Fabulous." *Get on with it!* I sigh inwardly. At least I won't have to worry about what to tell him if those tests come back with answers I don't want to hear. At least I'll know now, before it's really serious, before—

"What was fabulous about it?"

"Huh?" His words bring me back to focus. "Oh, uh...I spent some time resting, reading. And then the Aspire group, of course. The summer program's first meeting is next week."

"I know." He grins again. "Are you excited?"

"Uh…" I hadn't really thought about it. With my mind so consumed I've had little time for anything else, even, I realize, for Adrian. When's the last time I initiated contact? When's the last time I planned a fun date for us? He's had a bunch of work commitments lately, but still, I could definitely be a more proactive girlfriend. Maybe this speech he's planned is actually about me, about how distant I've been. Tonight I'll be present, and if we last past tonight, I'll do better. I take a moment to think about his question. Am I excited about the summer program? Absolutely. All Eloise and I have done to make it fabulous, will burst into fruition in the next few days. "Yes, I'm really excited. This program is going to transform girls' lives, help them see life can give them so much more than they may have ever imagined." I grin. "Outside of the conference it's the first time all the girls will be working together. I think that will stretch them. Get them out of their comfort zones, give them a better idea of what it'll be like once they leave high school and start interacting in the real world. There'll be modules on marketing, public relations, business management, and then more general ones: nailing the job interview, exam prep, discovering your passion."

"Wonderful." Adrian leans forward. "It's so amazing what you've done with that, Tracey. So amazing."

"Eloise was a big part of it. Without her—"

"And without you there'd be nothing."

Accept the compliment. Don't divert. "Thank you."

He leans back in his chair. "I really enjoyed meeting your friends. I like them."

"They liked you too."

"Did they say much about me? Offer their thoughts and opinions?"

"Oh," I smile coyly. "I would never repeat anything they said." Would a man about to leave me care?

"Good or bad?"

I hesitate, then drop the facade. "Not a word of bad."

He looks relieved. "I was nervous."

Nervous? I would have guessed Adrian had never felt nervous in his life. "Why?"

"You're obviously close to them. From the way you talk about them maybe even closer than to your family..." He pauses. "And so I figured if any of them had an issue with me, you might have an issue with me."

I smooth my hands across my skirt. "No, no issue."

He looks toward the ceiling, as if searching for something, then draws his gaze back to me. "You can be very distant, Tracey. I've wanted to meet your family for weeks now."

Ahh, so this is the route he's taking; It is a breakup speech. I didn't let him in. I held too much back. It's always one or the other. Too distant or too clingy.

"So meeting your friends, it was a big step. But not enough."

My lips purse.

"Not nearly enough." He sits up straight. "What I wanted to say was—"

"You ready to order?" Our heads snap toward the waiter.

"Yes," I say as Adrian says, "No."

"I know what I want. You need more time?"

He shrugs. "You just order the first round."

I place our order then excuse myself to the bathroom, my arms and legs tingling. This is ridiculous. Why jump to conclusions? Why assume the worst, assume anyone new to my life is always on the verge of leaving it? With my hands resting on the counter, I stare at my reflection. I know exactly why. And it didn't start with the slew of men that haven't worked out in the past decade. I left more of them than left me. It didn't start out with Connor either. It goes further back than that. It may be stupid, irrational, to let an event that happened almost thirty years ago affect me today, but I can't help it.

I drop my head so I'm staring at the sink and try to reason away my fear. My adoptive parents never gave me back. They never once implied they no longer wanted me. Rather, they implied I was as perfect as I could be. They kept me. But it wasn't enough. It's never enough. And now Adrian sees something that isn't perfect. Just like my mother, just like all the potential parents who decided they wanted a better child, a healthier, more adjusted child.

I snap my head up, pleased not a tear has fallen. At least I have control over that. I make my way back to our table. The food arrives just as I do.

"The Nigiri's great," I say after the first bite.

"Yeah." Adrian picks up his chopsticks. "I'm glad you introduced me to this place. I've taken a few of my fellow journalists here. They love it."

"Oh, yeah?" My attention perks. Is this what it's about? Another journalist. A female journalist? Not what I expected. "Who'd you bring?"

He waves off my answer. "I don't know. A bunch of people."

How can he not know? I swallow and reach for my tea. My skin seems to tighten against my body. My smile is sweet. My stomach twists. It hasn't been long. A little over five months. Five of the best months I've ever had with a man, which makes the thought of my life without Adrian a thought I'd rather not consider. "Who, though? Anyone I know?"

"Umm," he hesitates, "you've met Parker, right? He and me and some others I don't think you know. Oh, you'd recognize that newscaster from channel five. She was with us."

The one with the luscious black hair, big brown eyes, and curves that go for miles. A rock lands on my twisted insides. "Oh yeah," my smile grows as if I'm excited, "is she as nice as she seems?"

"Definitely." He lights up. "Maesa is really sweet. One of those people who would do anything for her friends."

"Maesa. That's a different name."

"Yeah. Ancient Assyrian."

"Ancient Assyrian?"

"Her father's Assyrian by ancestry, so they wanted to honour that. And her mother is Swedish. So her middle name is Evelina. In full, Maesa Evelina Arikan. She had a time explaining herself in middle school."

"Sounds it." I take another sip of tea. "You know a lot about her."

"Oh, well, we've chatted. Both ethnic mutts, you know. We've compared notes."

"Of course."

He plops a piece of California roll in his mouth, smiling. He's so handsome. So cute, with his green eyes and his dark brown hair. Who else could look this good with his mouth full of sushi? His gaze seems intent on me. He swallows. "What's your ancestry? A little Mediterranean in there, your skin has that olive hue, or even South East Asian…the shape of your eyes."

"I'm just me." I reach for a piece of California roll and dip it in my wasabi/soy sauce mix.

"Nah." He reaches for the spicy salmon. "You're not plain old Caucasian. You can't be. There's something else there."

"Plain old Caucasian can have a lot of mixes in it too."

"That's true." He pauses, chopsticks mid-air. "You've never asked your parents about it?"

"No."

"Never done a family tree project at school?"

"My father's family is from England and Ireland. My mother's from France—if you go back several generations."

"That doesn't necessarily explain the eyes or the colouring. There's probably a story there. Aren't you interes—"

"No."

His eyes widen.

"Sorry." I smile and hate myself for this stupid deception. "I guess I'm happy being me. We're all one, essentially, right? So why does it matter where we came from? Race isn't even a thing. Not scientifically, anyway."

"Ahh, but culture. Culture is very much a thing, and history."

"Well," I pull the edge from my voice as best I can, while making it clear this is not a conversational trail I'm interested in following, "my family's culture isn't connected to any of those places. As I said, they've been here for generations."

"Okay, okay." He stops, looks down, then up again. "Maybe when I finally get to meet those parents of yours, I'll ask them myself."

He still wants to meet my parents? I shift and take another sip of tea. "What was it you wanted to say earlier?"

His Adam's apple bobs as he swallows. He laughs. "I didn't exactly want my mouth to be full of food."

"Okay?"

"We've been together now, what? Five months, almost six?"

"Yes."

"That's not that long."

"No."

"But it's long enough to know that as much as I already know about you, I want to know more."

I lean back. "Okay."

"I'm not saying anything has to be decided today. Absolutely not. It's just a thought I want to put out there and maybe start thinking about—together." He pauses.

"I'm listening."

"Because it's something that could take some planning. It's not a jump into it kind of thing."

"Adrian. Please."

"Sorry, sorry. So circuitous, I know. I'm nervous."

"Why?"

"In case you say no."

"No to what?"

"I want to…well, I want you to consider, to think about the possibility…of" he takes a deep breath, "moving in with me."

The room seems to go silent, the breath within me halts mid-inhalation. His seems to as well. "Move in with you?"

"Yes."

"Move in with you." I sit in wonder.

"It's too soon, isn't it? I'm sorry." He shifts away from me. "I didn't want to rush you. Don't freak out or anything, okay? You can forget I said it if you want…well, forget it for a while, for a few months. I didn't mean tomorrow or anything but—" he reaches for my hand, "I like you, Tracey. A lot. I love you."

My vision blurs. I've wondered. I've hoped. I'm not even sure how I feel myself, but—"You love me?"

"Of course." He smiles and reaches forward with his other hand, so he's grasping both of mine. "I miss you when I don't see you and with my hours, and your hours during the school year, sometimes days pass. Two or three. Not forever, I know. But it's more than I want to pass. I want to see you every day. I want to be there when you're sick, or just not in the mood to go out. We've been dating, and it's great, but I want more. I want to know this is going somewhere."

"Where?" I ask, stunned…and happy. Deliriously happy. And scared. And uncertain. And like I'm about to puke because what if what he wants is what I want—a family and children and that whole ideal life? And what if I can't give it to him?

"Building a life together. Really getting to know each other. Letting us see each other—the good, the bad, and the ugly."

"A life?"

"Yeah. A life. The first step to a life, but just an exploration, you know? No pressure. See what happens."

I let my gaze fall to the table. And if he doesn't like the life he sees with me? If I can't open up the way he wants? My insecurities, fears, scars—the past I can't seem to let go of—he's barely seen the surface. "This is big." I smile, a mask for the roiling emotions inside of me. "Very big."

"Yeah." He nods. "It is." We're both silent. "Well, what do you think?"

A half-sigh, half-laugh escapes my throat. "I don't know. Like you said, it's something to think about."

He nods. "Yeah, of course. Absolutely. I've been thinking about this for a couple of weeks now. You need time to think about it too." He pauses, I've never seen him like this: Scared. Vulnerable. I want to scream out 'Yes'! and take that expression off his face.

"You're not completely freaked out though, right? Not thinking of running for the hills?"

"No. Not at all."

"Okay. Good." He palms his fist, which turns into a kind of rubbing of his hand. "That's good."

My thoughts travel to another place, a place we've barely been to together, but I ask the question anyway. "Have you lived with anyone since your wife?"

His shoulders tense. "No."

"And was she the only person you've lived with?"

"My family. My college roomies." He offers a half-grin. "The only woman."

"You two lived together before you got married?"

"No, actually, we didn't."

The next question: is this what this is then, a test? A chance to see if you'd marry me? Or, the other question we've never broached: would he marry again? I keep my mouth shut.

"You're thinking this is a test," he says.

"I—"

"Nah, it's okay. I see that. And maybe it is…kind of. But mostly it's that I want to see you more, spend time with you, know that when I go to sleep at night and wake up in the morning, you'll be the one beside me."

I close my eyes, letting his words wash over me. This is what I've wanted, but not how I wanted it. "I never thought I'd move in with someone before I got married."

"Tracey," he leans back, "marriage is a big commitment."

"I know. Of course, I know. I'm not saying," I search for the words, the heat rising to my cheeks—blast my wretched cheeks! "I just. For me, I mean it's huge to think about." I shrug, try to brush off my obvious discomfort. "I've done a lot of things I never thought I would do."

The waiter comes and we put in our next order.

"Adrian."

"Yeah?"

"What happened between you and your wife? Why didn't it work out? How do you know we'll be different?"

His expression clouds and immediately I regret my words.

"I'm sorry. That's inappropriate. You don't have to answer. I shouldn't have asked."

He inhales deeply, his chest expanding. "I can understand how you would have that question. But you've had relationships too, right? And they didn't work out. That doesn't mean every other relationship won't work out—"

"That's not what I meant. I just thought—"

He holds up his hand. "Listen. I was young. We both were. Too young. And…" he pauses, as if struggling with something, "she wasn't the person I thought she was."

Would you ever get married again? The question turns over and over in my mind, but I can't ask it because what about the next questions—do you want children? Is that one of your dreams? What if I can't be the one to give them to you? "I'm sorry."

"Me too." He smiles. "But that's a long way in my past. I want to think about the future."

"There's still about five months left on my lease."

"Don't think about that kind of thing yet." He reaches out and grasps my hand. "Think about whether you want my home and your home to be our home. Think about whether you see me as…well, someone you're willing to make that big of a life shift with. No pressure. I'm not asking for this now. I'm just asking for your thoughts, and then we can take it from there."

"Okay."

He squeezes my hand then releases it as the next round of sushi arrives. I can hardly taste my food. Our positions have switched. He's calm and composed. I'm nervous and jumpy. More than once my sushi slips out of my chopsticks. The second time it splashes in the soy sauce, sending little brownish green specs across the table.

Adrian stares at me. "I didn't mean to drop this on you. Though I'm not sure how else I could have done it." He sets down his chopsticks. "It's okay if you're not ready. I'll understand. Obviously I hope we'll move forward some day. But we don't need to rush." He stops again. My heart palpitates in a way it never has before. I try to ignore it and focus on Adrian's words. "I'm not asking for forever. I just know I want you in my life and more than you are right now. That's what this is about."

I bite my lip and nod as a wave of what must be love washes over me.

CHAPTER FIVE

The following week, after the Aspire Summer Program's first session, Eloise and I meet for lunch in a spunky little restaurant with vines on the walls and eccentric sounding menu items. Once we've gone over all of our Aspire business: the need to draw out the shyer girls, not let the 'Type A' ones dominate the group; the way too high air conditioning; and how to handle one girl's perception that she's a co-leader of this endeavour, we eat in companionable silence, or at least what I think is companionable silence. Eventually I realize Eloise is watching me. Every time I look up from my meal her gaze darts away from mine.

I set down my sandwich. "What?"

She rests her spoon in her near-empty bowl. "I don't want to pry. I know you talk when you're ready."

"What do you expect me to say?"

"Have you gotten your period?"

"Two days ago, and I was at the doctor's this morning."

"Good." She pauses. "But still you have nothing to say?"

"I had tests. They're all clear." Which means the problem is most likely something simple, something easily fixable or that will go away on its own, maybe that already has.

"So, that's good. Just a one-off most likely?"

"Most likely." Except it wasn't a one-off. I generally mark an x on my calendar the day I start but rarely look back to see when my next period is due. The debilitating cramps I get several days before are warning enough. But I went back through the calendar. The first few months off of birth control were twenty-nine, thirty, and thirty-two days, but then it was forty-two, fifty-one, twenty-two…back again to what seemed somewhat close enough to normal, thirty-three. This carried on until my last cycle, eighty-eight days, which, according to Dr. Keer, doesn't even qualify as a cycle. Not a period, but something called anovulatory bleeding. No egg released.

"What else could it be?" asks Eloise.

Fibroids. Poly-Cystic Ovarian Syndrome (PCOS for short, which sounds cute, but isn't). Endometriosis. Something worse. A combination of things. "An ovarian cyst, maybe. That could cause a delay. No big deal." But that wouldn't explain the consistent irregularity. "Or a benign cyst."

"Well, that's good news. And not the end of the world to go a couple of months without your period, right?"

"Right." I smile and take a bite of my sandwich. Except it could be the end of the world. The end of my world as I know it, anyway. The end of my chance to have a family, my own family. To know unconditional love.

A few moments pass as I take several bites of my sandwich. Eloise keeps her gaze on me. "What aren't you saying?"

"Nothing."

"Trace." Her voice is soft.

I shrug. "It could be something worse."

"Worse?"

"Cancer." Eloise's eyes widen. "Though my doctor doesn't think that's the case. She's scheduled a test but says it's unlikely as I had a pap test four or five months ago," when my irregularity had already started, "and everything was fine. She did a physical exam too and couldn't find anything that seemed to explain my problems." I take a breath. "There are these diseases that women get, though, the other possibilities. They often cause irregularity." Eloise nods, urging me to continue. "They often also cause infertility. Not always, but…"

"Oh, Tracey."

I shake my head and look down at my plate. "This doesn't mean I have a disease." My eyes mist. "It's just a possibility." I blink the tears away, put forward another smile. "It's silly to worry. I'm being paranoid. It's stupid, I'm—"

"No." Eloise's voice is firm. "Tracey, don't do that. Don't dismiss this. You have a right to be scared. It's not stupid. Having a baby…well, more than anyone I know, that's your dream, isn't it?"

"I have other dreams."

"I know but—" the waiter heads toward our table and Eloise waves him away. "When will you find out? How soon will you know?"

"That's the thing. Some of the possible diseases, the ones that cause infertility, there's not such an easy way to diagnose them, without surgery that is."

"Surgery?"

"Yeah, and since I'm not trying to conceive yet, the doctor thinks it's best to wait it out for now, see if things go back to normal. She said a healthy diet could help, exercise."

"You work out, what, three to four times a week? And you eat healthy, don't you?"

"I think so." My genetic history could make things clearer, suggest possibilities. Though I already have a strong contender. That pain that came around shortly after I stopped birth control, that cut through me like a knife and had me popping painkillers like they're candy—endometriosis could be the culprit, and if my mother had it…

"So, surgery, will you have it?"

"No. Not yet." I look to my near empty plate. It was stupid of me, really, to not think something was wrong. But

I remembered having painful periods as a teenager and knew birth control made PMS symptoms less. Besides, everyone complains about period cramping. But according to Dr. Keer, not everyone tends to start that cramping a week before they bleed, which also probably means not everyone finds themselves curled up on the floor, feeling death would be a relief...I offer Eloise a smile. "Surgery brings complications of its own. It could diagnose my condition but could also make it worse. It's complicated."

Eloise waves the waiter away again. "I'll call you when we're ready." She turns her attention back to me.

"The doctor referred me for an ultrasound. That could tell us something. It will probably be a four to seven month wait."

"Trace."

"Until I'm ready to conceive...until I find out I can't conceive, she doesn't want to risk surgery."

"So you have to wait?"

I rub my hand across my forearm and squeeze tight. "I have to wait." This isn't entirely true, Dr. Keer gave me another option: go back on birth control. It'd help with the pain, regulate my cycle, and if this is endometriosis, slow the disease's growth. I turned down that option. Besides the fact that I've felt like a different person since stopping the drugs, a better person, I want to know if something is wrong with me. I don't want it to be masked. I want to know.

"I'm really sorry." We're both silent. The sounds of the other diners, of the cars outside the open windows, of a little girl laughing, fill my ears. Eloise sits up straighter. "I'm sure it's nothing. A cyst, something benign. Maybe you've been more stressed about starting this Aspire program than you've realized. This is supposed to be your summer holiday and you're still doing a fair amount of work."

"Hardly."

"It's going to be fine, Tracey. Just fine. Your life is going to be fabulous. This is a bump in the road, nothing more than that." Her voice falters. She's probably thinking what I'm thinking: she can't be sure of anything. She's just saying what she thinks I want to hear, though I don't want to hear it. "And you've got Adrian. Focus on him. Enjoy yourself and try not to worry." She pauses again. "Just try."

I nod.

"How is Adrian's story going? The investigative piece?" She waves over the waiter.

"It's on a bit of standstill right now. He's working on something else for the time being."

The waiter shows up with one bill and Eloise hands him her card. She shakes her head when I try to protest. "You're the one who created this fabulous new job I have. It's on me."

I acquiesce and finish the last of my water. "Adrian and I are good." We stand and sling our purses over our shoulders. I focus on not letting my voice shake. "He could be the one."

Eloise stays where she's standing. I turn back to look at her. "You don't sound happy about that."

"I am."

She doesn't move.

"We haven't talked about children yet…obviously. But if I can't…"

Eloise leads me out of the restaurant and stops under the awning, away from the line that's formed along the street. "Don't go there, Tracey. This may be nothing. Probably is nothing. This is a good guy, okay? He could be the guy you've been waiting for. Don't sabotage it."

"I might not be right for him."

"You are. Or at least if you are, this won't ruin it. Even if…well, there are other options. Adoption."

I inhale sharply. Adoption is not an answer I would consider, but I can't explain that to Eloise.

"Not that you even need to think about that yet." Eloise lowers her voice. "Give it time. Let the relationship develop naturally."

"I think I'm falling in love with him."

"In love?" Eloise turns and leans against the wall. "Really?"

I draw my gaze to her. "Actually, I think I've already fallen. How do you know?"

"I'm not sure. Maybe sometimes you just know, and sometimes it takes time. It grows."

"He told me he loves me."

"Wow." Eloise's smile erupts. "Tracey, that's amazing. Why don't you look happier?"

"I am happy. Too happy. It's terrifying."

"Listen." She turns toward the street. "I know it's scary. I spent years not letting anyone get close, and when I finally found love I think part of me was still scared, I don't know, to give into it. But if you think this is love, do whatever you can to find out. And if you find out, fight to keep it." She tilts her head toward me. "How did he say it, did it just come out or—"

I let out a puff of air, a sheepish smile covers my face. "He asked me to move in with him."

Eloise shakes her head and grins. "Aren't you full of surprises."

"But what if—"

"Let go of the buts."

I really want to. "El?"

"Yeah?"

"You weren't clear with Moses about what you wanted, what your future would hold. It wasn't the best idea, was it?"

She tenses, then turns to me. "That was different. That would have been my choice. This is you maybe having a disease or...problems. It's not you choosing. And you don't even know. Nothing may be wrong."

"But the end result is the same. I could be letting him imagine a life with me that I may never be able to give him.

Don't you think that's something he should be aware of?"

She opens her mouth then closes it again. She looks to the sidewalk then back at me. "I see what you're saying."

"And it makes sense?"

"It makes sense...have you decided if you want to move in with him yet? Didn't you always say you'd never move in with a man until you were married?"

"Yes." I cross my arms over my middle. "In undergrad with Connor I said it all the time. And I meant it. But I never thought eleven years later I wouldn't be married. I never thought Connor wouldn't be the one I was married to." I tilt my head to the sky. "Maybe this makes sense, get to know each other on a deeper level, see how compatible we are before making an even bigger commitment." I uncross my arms and turn so my side's against the wall and I'm looking directly at Eloise. "It does makes sense, especially for Adrian. He's been married before. He'll want to know it's right."

"So you don't know why—"

"No. No details."

Eloise nods and pushes herself from the wall. "If you tell him and it's a problem, I guess it's good to know now. It would be awful. But more awful a year from now."

"Part of me wants to have surgery. Know for sure."

"But your doctor doesn't recommend it?"

"Very vehemently not."

"Listen to her."

I nod.

"Have you talked to your family about this? What do they think?"

I shake my head and laugh. "El."

"They're your family, Trace. And who knows, maybe your mom has gone through similar things. A lot of diseases are genetic, so if your mom didn't have them, couldn't that rule things out?"

"She did have it, actually." My adoptive mother, that is. I

close my eyes. Guilt for never telling Eloise passes through me.

"Well, there you go, and she had two healthy children." She puts a hand on my shoulder. "All is not lost."

One healthy child, after fifteen years of trying and five miscarriages. And that one healthy child wasn't a healthy pregnancy. It almost killed her.

"Trace?"

"Yeah. You're right. All is not lost. There's hope." I push myself away from the wall.

"You should talk to her about this."

"Yeah." But I won't. I know what her opinion would be: if anything's wrong, just adopt, don't put myself through the years of trying, the years of heartache. And she won't understand why that's not a solution.

Eloise's phone buzzes. "Arghh. Sorry, I gotta go. If I'm late to watch Trisa, there'll be an instructor-less room of ten-year-old girls eager to dance." We hug goodbye.

On the walk to my apartment I replay our conversation. By the time I get home I've concluded two things. One, if I decide to move in with Adrian I need to tell him about the possibility of not being able to conceive, which may also mean telling him the family he hasn't yet met is not my real family, and two…well, no, maybe I haven't decided on two yet.

CHAPTER SIX

I pace back and forth, check the clock for probably the fifth time. Adrian isn't late. He has eight minutes before he'd be late. At the window I scan the street below. His green Toyota is nowhere in sight. I need to think of something else. The party. It's the perfect event. My niece and nephew are turning four this weekend and two weeks after that is my father's seventy-fourth. The week in between we'll all be together, celebrating, and if all goes well tonight, if my potentially defective reproductive organs don't scare him away, I'll be inviting Adrian into that inner sanctum he's been wanting to see. A car door slams and my head turns to the noise. Not him.

I glance around my apartment. Everything is in order. It's not like Adrian's never been here before, and not like he hasn't seen my place when it wasn't perfectly in order, but I want it to be perfectly in order today. Another door slams. I dash to the window. Him.

A glance in the mirror reveals a reflection I'm pleased with. Everything visible about my life right now is as perfect as I can make it. A triple knock on the door. I turn the handle.

"I love that dress." He scoops me into his arms. Our eyes lock. My lips part. For a moment, all worries melt away. If he's the only man I ever kiss again, I could be happy.

"So." He makes his way deeper into my apartment. Toulouse nuzzles up to his legs, and he crouches to give the cat a quick rub. "What's the plan? You were so vague."

"An evening in. A chicken's in the oven. I made roasted bacon and asparagus and a homemade Caesar salad."

"Wow." He grins. "That's your idea of relaxing. Cooking an amazing meal?"

"I wanted to do something special for you."

"I like." He pulls me to him again, drawing my torso against his. The kiss is deeper this time. It leaves me breathless.

"You're feeling affectionate tonight." I laugh.

"I've missed you."

I swallow and stare at him. If the answer's no, if he runs away after the conversation we have to have, I want him gone as soon as possible. Ever since the thought became a feeling—I'm falling in love, maybe I'm already in love—my fear of losing him has exploded. "Let's sit."

His brow furrows. "Okay. Don't scare me."

I'm doing to him what he did to me at the sushi restaurant…only my news isn't good. "Sorry. Just sit." He lowers. I settle on the couch angled toward him—close enough to reach for his hand, far enough away that not even our knees touch. I rest my hands in my lap. "I've had a lot on my mind lately and you asking me to move in, uh, amplified it. I'm sorry I haven't given you an answer yet."

"Take your time, remember. No rush." He flashes his little boy grin. "Just promise me you're not breaking up with me because of it." He raises his hands. "I'll take it back."

"No, no. I'm not." My hand lands on his thigh. "It's just, if we're taking this next step, you need to know—"

He grasps my shoulders. "You're saying yes?" He chuckles and releases me. "Sorry, you speak."

He's so excited. That wonderful feeling of loving, of being loved, washes over me. It's short-lived. "I've been having some medical issues lately."

"Oh, yeah?" He shifts to the edge of the seat cushion.

"I'm not dying or anything." His shoulders relax. "I went

about three months without a period. I thought I was pregnant."

He stares and rubs a hand across the back of his neck. "But you're not."

I shake my head. "It could be the opposite, actually. Well, I mean, it could be that I can't get pregnant."

"Could be?"

"I don't know yet. My doctor thinks it could be any number of things, and several of those things could cause infertility." I explain the possible scenarios, the unknowns, the interminable wait before even a chance for answers. He leans toward me. His eyes are soft and focused, his jawline hard.

When I stop talking, he stays in that position. Stiff. "And you're telling me all of this because…"

I blink. "Because you need to know. Because moving in together is one step closer to maybe forever. Our lives will meld, and if the life you want involves children of your own, you need to know I might not be able to give you them."

"Yeah, yes. Of course." He looks down. The ticking clock might as well be a gong. His gaze meets mine. "But you don't know, right? You have no idea? This could be nothing. You could be perfectly fine."

"I could be."

"And you're telling me this because you're what? Worried I'll leave you if I know?" He rubs his hands through his hair. "You think I'd walk away because of this huge unknown that may not be anything at all?" His hand slams into his thigh. "We've never even discussed whether we wanted kids, and certainly not together."

I shift away. "That's it exactly. We've never discussed it and what if one of your biggest dreams is to have children, a family, and here I am with this knowledge that I may not be able to give it to you. Don't you think you deserve to know?" I snap the words. "Now, not a year or two or three from now?"

His eyes widen as if he's just been shaken. "Yeah. Yeah, of course." The Adrian I know sits before me again. "Sorry. I just, I mean, I respect that you're telling me this. Thank you for telling me this. It was shocking." He smiles. "I didn't think we were there yet."

"You want me to move in."

"I know. And what you're saying is completely legitimate. I just…at first I was hearing that you wanted us to start trying, so you could find out. But you're not saying that."

"Of course I'm not saying that!" I lean against the couch. "I'm just letting you know. That's all."

He nods. "Yeah. I get it. Thank you."

Several moments pass. I break the silence. "So?"

"Yeah, well. Thank you for telling me."

"But what do you think? Does this—"

He shifts toward me. "I'd like a family, Tracey. I really would. Some day. One day. I bet we'd make great kids." He reaches out and jostles my knee. "But it's not the be all and end all. And there are always other options if you're not…if you can't…but you probably can."

My gaze travels to Toulouse, curled up against Adrian's thigh, content.

"Didn't you say something about some of the possible issues being genetic? Won't that give some indication of what your chances are, based on your family? What's the situation there?"

My pulse races and my mouth grows dry. With all certainty, my previous news was more substantial, tougher to tell, but these reactions are visceral. "That's the other thing I wanted to talk to you about." I look up with a smile. "If we move in together, if I let you into that much of my life, I want to let you into all of it. And that means meeting my family."

"They outlaws or something?"

I laugh, thankful he's broken some of the tension I'm

carrying. "No, no. They're really nice. They're just not my real family, hence no genetic information provided. I'm adopted."

He nods as if expecting me to go on. His expression remains blank. No sympathy. No awkwardness. No slew of questions. Outside of my doctor, he is the first person I've shared this information with in fourteen years. No reaction is not the reaction I expect.

When it's clear I have nothing more to say, he speaks. "So, that's rough then, that you can't get a family history. Was it a closed adoption or something? No medical records?"

I stare at him, unnerved by this nonchalance. "I've had an option for contact since I was eighteen. I never took advantage of it." I pause. "I called once about medical records but the organization didn't have any. They said I would have to contact my birth mother directly."

"And you don't want to do that?"

"I've never had a reason to."

"Well," he gives my arm a squeeze, "at least that option is there if you want to use it. But a genetic history wouldn't give you a definitive answer. You'd still have to wait for that ultrasound, try for a while?"

"Yeah."

He reaches for my hand. "Life is full of uncertainties. This isn't such a big one."

Not such a big one? I want to yell. I want to push his hand away. It's a huge one. I smile back and shrug, tuck away my anger, try to be thankful he's holding my hand, not walking away. "I guess not."

He pauses. "It could be. I recognize it could be. You want kids quite a lot, don't you?"

"Mm-hmm."

"If we get to that juncture we'll figure it out. You should know better than anyone if it turns out you can't have your own children that doesn't mean you can't have a child."

I purse my lips. Enough for one day.

"So," he pulls out his phone, "I finally get to meet your family. Give me a date, I'm locking this in."

"A family birthday party. The weekend after this one. Saturday afternoon."

He makes several swipes on his phone then looks up. "Done." A broad grin. "That chicken is smelling pretty good."

⁂

ADRIAN CRAWLS OUT OF bed when the sun is still low in the sky. I lay curled in the sheets, enjoying the faint scent of cinnamon he leaves behind, and watch, my eyes scarcely open, as he gathers his clothing and tiptoes out of the room. It's my first moment to think. I should be happy. I should be relieved. And I am. The possibility of infertility didn't scare him away…yet. It's that 'yet' that prevents me from feeling peace. Nothing has been figured out. Nothing has been decided. Like he said, like I know—all these possibilities I'm worrying about are nothing more than possibilities, and where he is right now, where we are, 'maybes' aren't overly important. But what if one year down the road, two, three, those possibilities are more than possible? Will he stay? Decide he wants a broken woman? And what if adoption is our only chance and I refuse?

These thoughts are useless, destructive, but I can't seem to stop them. I peel myself out of bed and step onto the balcony. The world hurries on below me. I turn from the window, in need of answers. There's only one doctor recommended way to get them, or at least to get closer to them. It's that second thing I couldn't decide on, a route I'm not ready to take.

One task at a time. One fear conquered. Next task, tell my mom to set one more place for dinner. I pick up the phone, ashamed at how long it's been since I called her. The line rings three times.

"Tracey, is everything all right?"

"Yeah, Mom. It's fine."

"Oh, good." She lets out a little sigh. "You so rarely call." She laughs, not knowing she's rubbing my guilt. "It made my heart pulse."

"Sorry."

"No, no." She laughs again. "Don't you apologize. How are you? Enjoying summer vacation? Did you get my voice mail? I saw that article about your girls' group in the paper. We were so proud."

An image of my mother pops into my mind. Sweet and kind, every hair in place and, always, *always* perfectly accessorized. She's probably standing in the kitchen, delicious smells wafting from the oven or pancakes sizzling on the griddle. "Thanks. It's going really well. Both my vacation and the Aspire group. The girls are thriving."

"That's wonderful, dear."

"How are you?"

"Oh, pretty good." She pauses. "Your father decided to redo the basement. He's turning it into a workroom and game area. Taking out a wall! I just pray the house doesn't collapse."

I laugh. Dad spent his whole life in construction. It's the mess, not fear of destruction, that's stressing my mother. "I'm calling about the party."

She lets out a stifled little gasp. "You're coming, aren't you?"

"Yeah. I wouldn't miss it." It's true, I wouldn't. I've never missed any major family days. Birthdays, anniversaries, the 'Big Three' holidays, I always make an appearance. How could I not? In recent years, though, those are about the only appearances I make. It's too hard: the obligation I've felt my whole life to be thankful, the debt of being given a stable home one I can never fully repay. The weight of it is exhausting and then living with the pretense we're something we're not, knowing, essentially, I was a consolation prize that ended up being unnecessary. But she is my mother, and I am thankful. I ensure my voice is pleasant. "I'm actually bringing someone."

"A friend?" Her voice fills with hope.

"More than a friend."

"Oh, Tracey!" I pull the phone from my ear as she squeals. "You haven't brought anyone home since Connor. He's special, isn't he?"

I lean against my living room wall; the feel of Adrian's heavy arm resting on my torso, the way he pulled me against him before crawling out of bed, comes back to me. "I think so."

"That's wonderful. What's his name? What does he do? Where did you meet him? How long have you—"

"Mom." I laugh again, touched and humbled by her excitement. I'm more than a consolation prize. I know this. "His name's Adrian. How about we leave those other questions for when you meet him?"

"But he'll think you never talk about him."

"I don't."

"Oh, Tracey. You're such a sweet girl, pretty and smart. I could never understand why—"

"Mom."

"I'm sorry, dear." She pauses. "I'll save my questions."

"Don't interrogate him either, though, okay?"

"I won't." Her voice dances with glee. "Just tell me, how serious? Should I expect more grandbabies in a few years?"

"Mom."

"Sorry, sorry." The oven timer chimes in the background. "This is great!"

"Sounds like something's done."

"Yes, but I can still chat. I bought a headset."

"No, I'll let you go. See you Saturday."

Her voice drops an octave. "Okay. See you Saturday." It

raises again. "But Adrian. Tell me what he looks like? Is he tall? What does he do?"

I smile into the phone, my chest full of tenderness and dread. "Saturday."

CHAPTER SEVEN

The door opens to reveal my mother's huge smile. "Come in! Come in!" Mom gives me a quick hug then turns to Adrian. She rests her hands on the side of his shoulders, arms outstretched, staring at him like he's a long-lost child she finally has back in her arms. After a moment she pulls him toward her and hugs him tighter than she's hugged me in years. He hugs her back and glances over her shoulder at me, grinning. "Come in, come in," she repeats while waving us into the foyer. My parents' house is large, more because it's in the middle of nowhere than because of excessive wealth. Stepping into their home, I feel like a stranger. The house I grew up in was smaller, with lower ceilings and less space between the walls. I liked it.

As we're about to descend into the large, oval living room, a masked child dashes past us. We jump back in time for the second runner. This one screams a deathly roar.

"Lulu and Reggie?" Adrian turns to Mom.

"You know their names." Based on Mom's face, you'd think she was staring at a knight in shining armour.

Adrian nods then winks at me. All that grilling me for names, faces and personality descriptions he put me through during the drive up here paid off. Now it's Adrian's turn. Mom doesn't waste any time asking him about his parents, siblings and graduate status. Tuning out, I study her. Her hair is different, lightened by several shades. Twenty years of religiously dyeing away rogue strands and is she now starting the transition to white? My perfectly presented mother, at fifty-nine, surrendering to age. Or, surrendering her need to be perfectly perfect?

Friends have always told me how alike we are. The familiar look, though, is about much more than appearance. We have the same build, petite and curvy, but as far as seeming genetic similarities go, the resemblance ends there. Where my mother's lips are thin and straight, mine are wide and plump. Her hair, naturally, is dark brown, almost black. Mine is light auburn. Her eyes are a striking blue, mine a bright green. Her skin is alabaster, mine a tan that never fades. But, like her, because of her, my hair is always well-styled, my nails manicured, my outfits properly fitted. I found my first grey hair a couple of months ago and, I'm sure, as more start popping up, like her, my roots will never show. These habits came early: A simple way to ensure I didn't disappoint.

My sister, Jojo, walks into the room: her damp orange peasant top and long flowing white pants moving as if a perpetual breeze surrounds her, her hair thrown back in a messy bun, her body encased in one of those cloth baby carriers. She actually is just like Mom in genetic appearance, but that's where the resemblance ends. The lacing on her top is undone and my niece, Neveah, suckles at her exposed breast. "Tracey." Jojo smiles, her expression tired but with an almost placid look of contentment. It unnerves me. The Jojo I grew up with never wore that look. It looks false on her face. "As soon as this one's done, would you like to take her off my hands?"

"Sure." I accept the feather-light hug she offers and bend to kiss Neveah's forehead.

Jojo puts her hand on her hip and looks Adrian up and down. He turns to her and she glances at me with a look that says, 'nice.' This is the Jojo I know.

He extends his hand, but she waves it away and draws him into a hug. He keeps his body far from her baby and gleaming white flesh. "It's nice to meet you. Jojo? And Neveah?"

"You studied." Jojo raises an eyebrow. "Impressive. But really all you had to do was show up to impress. It's been what, a decade since Tracey's brought a boy home…" She grins. "My apologies, a man. The last one was a boy."

I purse my lips, just as Mom would, not wanting to make a ruffle while company is present, and refrain from shooting darts at Jojo with my eyes. We've never been close. Me, the obedient daughter, her the rebellious, angst-ridden teen. She rebelled against my parents and their conventional lifestyle, and against me for adhering to it. Now, though, she's discovered 'peace and flow' and our relationship is less like pulled taffy; more because she's less likely to engage in a fight than because we suddenly get along.

She adjusts Neveah, whispering sweetness in her ear. This too is a Jojo that never ceases to surprise and awe me. Pregnant at twenty, she still seemed a baby to me as she held the twins in her arms. She was. A baby who'd found inner peace with the man who'd impregnated her.

Next came Neveah, the result of a Cambodian 'soul journey' once the twins were potty trained. The peace seemed real at first. Today, Jojo flinches as the twins run by. Her shoulders slump as if the weight of Neveah, conceived under the stars during the night Jojo dreamt of a butterfly landing on her belly, is pulling her down.

"Where's Damien?"

Jojo turns from Adrian to me. "He'll be late." She shrugs. "But he'll be here for dinner."

I nod. My whole life I've been envious of Jojo—the legitimate daughter. The free spirit. Blessed with three children, even if that blessing came much sooner than she would have wanted—but as I watch her, I can't help but wonder. What is my sister's life really like? Under the veil of spirituality, there's pain in her eyes, her voice, her stance.

The twins burst into the room with my father, hunched

over and stomping like a monster, behind them. He stops, his face lighting up as he stands to his full six feet and five inches. "Tracey!"

He weaves around the twins, who collapse in a pile of arms and legs and tickles, then scoops me into a hug. His lips land on my forehead. "The only present I want is for you to visit more. Agreed?"

I stay in his arms, one of my favourite places to be. "Sorry, Dad. I know I haven't been up recently." My eyes mist. I blink. It has been too long. A distance exists between Mom and me, like neither of us are what the other expected or wanted, but with Dad it's different.

He turns to Adrian. This time it's my father who extends his hand. Adrian takes it. He stands tall, at ease. He said he was nervous to meet my friends, wouldn't meeting my family be more nerve-wracking? But from all appearances, he's as relaxed as can be.

The twins, realizing I exist, push off their masks and each grab hold of one of my legs. "We had a birthday party—" Lulu

"With all of my friends—" Reggie

"And more of my friends—" Lulu

"And we got lots of presents—"

"Almost hundreds of presents—"

"And mommy says we don't need more—"

Lulu looks up, her eyes bright. "But we'd like presents. Do you have presents?"

I crouch before them. "One for each."

They squeal and laugh, then notice Adrian. More squeals when this strange man knows who they are without being told. Lulu sticks her tongue between the gap in her front teeth, her brown eyes glowing with pride. Adrian marvels. Among questions and tales, he's taken captive and dragged away to some wonder in the backyard. Dad and Jojo follow. Mom returns to the kitchen. Left alone, I step into the living room.

Snapshots of my life—my recorded life—are spotted throughout the room. I look happy. In the room's oldest picture, I am four years old. I sit in a white, frilly dress, propped up on my father's hip, smiling broadly for the camera. My mother stands under the crook of my father's arm…a full foot shorter than him, and gazes up at me, a look on her face that any casual observer would label pure love. We look like a family. We look like we belong.

The years before this picture are like a vast hole. Only one baby picture exists, proving I didn't materialize out of thin air. It sits on my mother's dressing table upstairs. A baby picture, the type taken in the hospital during the first hours of life. I'm surprised she has it so close. From all my mother will say about the years before I came to her, this picture on the mantle, taken the day my parents adopted me, is the day my life began.

I know different. Most people remember almost nothing from their early years, five or six being the typical age for recalling drawn out memories. The time before exists in vague flashes. The twins will probably not remember this day, but my fourth year is as clear as last year, clearer than many of the years that came afterwards. Exactly one month after my fourth birthday my caseworker took me into the counselling room. When children went into that room they usually came out with news of a family. A real family. In two years I'd been taken in three times, but only for transfer to foster homes. Foster homes didn't mean a thing. Every child who lived at the group home when I arrived had found their family. Every one, but not me. Each time a new child went in, I knew it was less likely my day would ever come.

I shook as I followed the caseworker in, hoping, terrified. Would this be the day? The *real* day? I wished and wished. I said the words like a prayer. A family. A family. A family. I hadn't been to the doctor in two months. I knew that was my problem. No one wanted a sick kid.

The caseworker sat me down on a big blue chair. She

asked if I wanted one of the candies on her desk. I shook my head. She pulled her desk chair in front of me, so our faces were close. 'Do you remember the Sampson's, the tall man who made animal voices and the woman with the dark hair and pretty flowered dress? You drew a picture of them, and the woman thought you were so talented.'

I nodded.

'They're going to take you home with them,' the caseworker explained. 'You're going to be their daughter. Do you understand that?'

'They'll be my mommy and daddy?' I half asked, half confirmed in wonderment.

'They'll be your mommy and daddy.'

'I never even had a daddy before.'

The case worker smiled.

I scrunched up my face. 'Forever?' Children could come back after getting their new mommies and daddies. It was possible.

'That's what they said.' The caseworker squeezed my knee.

'If I'm good.'

She hesitated.

'And healthy?' I added before she could respond.

'They're promising to be your mommy and daddy forever. But it's always a good idea to try to be good. We should all try to be good.'

A hand on my shoulder breaks me out of these memories. I turn to my father's smiling face, the face that made me believe I'd finally have a home. "He seems like a nice young man."

"He is."

He pulls me to his side. "How've you been, sweetie?"

"Good."

"Happy?"

"Pretty happy. Happy enough."

He tuts. "Is there ever such a thing?"

I shrug.

He pulls the frame in front of us off the mantel. "One of the three best days of my life. Do you remember?"

"Of course."

He looks at me, his head tilted. "You were pretty young."

"I remember."

"From the first moment I saw you in that room, sitting with a crayon in your hand, your brow furrowed in concentration, those green eyes so focused, I knew you were my daughter."

"Henry!" My mother's voice carries through the room. "I need some help, darling."

A high-pitched scream cuts through the air in the same instant my father turns to the kitchen. Jojo dashes into the room and thrusts a gurgling Neveah into my arms before fleeing again. I follow Jojo's dash to the porch and stand at the door. Jojo stands several feet in front of me. Lulu's screams have stopped, and Adrian is crouched down beside her. A hand rests on her shoulder and she looks up at him, her lip trembling and her eyes moist. Adrian smiles. Reggie stands a few feet away from them with arms crossed, looking scared yet defiant. Adrian whispers something in Lulu's ear and her tinkling laugh travels across the breeze. He bends down and kisses her knee. Lulu's face erupts into a smile. Just then she catches sight of Jojo and her arms reach out. "Mommy."

Adrian stands, brushes off his pants, and makes way for Jojo to comfort her daughter.

He walks toward me, a smile on his face, and I step back so he can enter the house. "You hurting my niece?" I ask.

"Not at all."

He stuffs his hands in his pocket and glances down at Neveah before bringing his gaze back to me. "Reggie stuffed Lulu's doll in the dirt head first. Lulu tried to grab it from him. She tripped and banged her knee."

I smile. "You were good with her."

He drapes an arm across my shoulder. "Lots of practice. You've met my brothers and sister's herd of kids."

"I have."

"That Lulu, though," he turns his head toward the window where Jojo is lifting Lulu off the ground, "what a sweetie."

"Yeah." I jostle Neveah in my arms and smile as she reaches her hand up to bat it at my chin. I love these children. I definitely do, but is it at all the way Adrian loves his nieces and nephews? How Eloise loves Trisa? The way my mother looks at Jojo is not the way she looks at me. People say love is love, but it's not. Love has levels. I was six when I learned this. My father held my hand as we walked through the corridors of the hospital. 'Is Mommy sick?'

'No.'

Hospitals were for sick people. I knew. And when people were sick, you didn't want them anymore. If Mom wasn't sick that meant the baby was, which meant I wouldn't get a little sister like they promised. Nobody wanted a sick baby. I pulled back on Dad's arm as we approached the hospital room. I didn't want to see a sister we couldn't keep. He pushed me through the door. My mom's head tilted up as we walked in the room, but her gaze fell right back to the bundle in her arms. She angled it toward me and, still looking at the face inside those cloths, told me to come meet my sister. I didn't even look at Jojo. I looked at Mom's face, at the look I'd seen on other Mommies but until this moment had never seen on mine. The baby wasn't going anywhere and never would. 'She's your baby?'

She glanced up, briefly. 'She's my baby.' Then what was I?

※

I WANT NEVEAH OUT of my arms. The fear that I'll never hold my own child, never look at a baby the way Mom looked at Jojo, the way Jojo looks at her children, the way I hope Adrian will one day look at his, washes over me stronger than it ever has. But there's nowhere to put Neveah, nothing to do. I can't just thrust her at Adrian. Jojo is outside with the twins and, from the sound of Reggie's yells, the issue is not resolved. Mom and Dad are in the kitchen.

"So, Damien," Adrian whispers. "Some tension there?"

"Tension?" I jostle Neveah, each pound of her reminding me what I may never have, what, if Adrian stays with me, he may never have either.

"Yeah. Trouble in paradise? Things not going too well?"

"Oh, I…" My mind searches for whatever made him think this. "That he's not here? He had to work."

Adrian's eyebrows raise as if he expected me to be more in tune with my family. "Maybe."

Mom and Dad reappear, Mom carrying a tray filled with hors d'oeuvres. Family dinners are always an affair at the Sampson household, but from this array, it's clear my mom is trying to impress.

Adrian takes a couple of bites and makes appropriate noises of pleasure. The moment Mom sets the tray on the coffee table, I offer Neveah to her. Jojo returns, the twins trailing behind her, dirt smothered and smiling. They attack the plate of hors d'oeuvres. I don't have to look to know Mom is struggling not to say anything—in regards to both their behaviour and the mud they're sure to be smudging into her couch.

Adrian and my father stay standing as Adrian asks him about the living room's ornate beam structure. Concave, it's more what you'd expect in an ancient country church, not someone's living room.

"That's one of the first things that drew me to this house." Dad grins. "It reminded me of the chapel I grew up attending." He launches into one of his stories of hometown life. Adrian listens attentively and laughs at the appropriate places.

When Dad finishes, Adrian continues his exploration. He reaches for the same photo my father held just minutes before and turns to me. "That you?"

I nod.

"What a sweetie you were." He winks.

"That's the day Auntie Tracey got adopted," shouts Reggie.

"Oh, yeah?" Adrian turns to the boy.

"Yes, it was." Mom pats her hand on Reggie's knee. "Who wants a drink?"

"So, you were what, three? Four?" Adrian holds the picture in his hands but looks at me.

"She was four. Like us." Lulu smiles. "Mommy told us on our birthday."

I glance to Jojo, surprised she's talked about my adoption with the twins. Today is the first time I've heard either of them mention it. Mom stands near the steps to the living room. "We have Perrier, Pineapple Juice, Pinot Grigio, an assortment of—"

Adrian pulls his gaze from the photo. "Do you remember your real family?"

"We're her real family," Mom snaps.

"Oh, I..." he puts the picture on the mantel. "Of course. I'm sorry. That's not what I meant." He looks to me. "Do you remember your birth family?"

My gaze travels from Adrian to my mother, my father, and back to Adrian. As far as I can recall, they've never asked this question, so I've never had to answer. I talked to Jojo about it, once.

"Uh...yes." My voice comes out soft. "Moments.

Almost more like flashes, impressions. But I remember her."

My mother makes a soft choking sound. My father leans forward. "You remember her? But you were barely two."

"Two. I thought—" says Adrian in the same instant my mother scoffs. "It must have been someone in the group home, your—"

I cut them both off. "I was given up for adoption at two. I was adopted at four."

"You can't remember." Mom steps back into the living room and straightens a seat cushion. "You were too young. They told us that life would mean nothing to you. They told us you probably wouldn't even remember your time in the home, a moment here or there, but nothing more. You're our daughter. Your life started when—"

"Joanna." My father's voice is firm, a rare occurrence. "Tracey would know what she remembers and what she doesn't." He looks to me. "Why have you never told us?"

My gaze darts back and forth between the eyes staring at me. "You never asked."

"What do you remember?"

"I don't know." Sweat creeps down the small of my back and dampens my armpits, just like at the doctor's office. I look to my mother, so often a mystery, then to my father—open and curious. "I don't remember a lot of my birth mother. Just…" my voice trails off. "I remember the group home. Arriving. Feeling confused. Wondering where my mother was, missing her, not understanding why she wasn't with me, why she never came back, why I was with those people." I pause. "I remember."

"We're not going to talk about this right now." Mom takes two steps forward. "It's upsetting. Isn't it? I can see." She sits on the couch, the drinks apparently forgotten, and takes my hand. "You feel upset talking about this, don't you? Besides, they're probably…" she hesitates, "created memories. Is that what they call it? Memories you create and believe to be real because you heard something or read something, like about how group homes are damaging or something or—"

"I didn't say it was damaging. I just—"

"Your real life started when you came home with us. Isn't that right? That's what matters. Now let's focus on the birthdays!" An octave higher. "Lulu, Reggie, tell me about the party with your preschool friends."

I smile at Mom and nod, then turn my attention to Lulu, who speaks so quickly it takes laser focus to catch every word. Adrian's gaze is on me. For us, this conversation isn't over. I glance to my father. He doesn't want it to be over either. Is he even hearing Lulu? His laser focus is on me.

CHAPTER EIGHT

We delay dinner a half hour waiting for Damien. When at last we sit to eat, he walks through the door, smiling and at ease.

"Hi, everyone." Damien steps around the table. He hugs both Mom and Dad, an act that always leaves my father looking awkward and uncertain where to put his hands. "What a wondrous day at the shop." He scoops the twins' heads toward chim and attacks their faces with a flurry of kisses. "So many people will be helped."

"Well, isn't that wonderful." Jojo's smile is broad. The two look perfectly matched. His cotton shirt is a dark green, his flowing pants a light brown, he walks with that same perpetual breeze. Damien's whole body seems at ease as he leans down to give Jojo a kiss, yet she remains rigid. Could Adrian be right?

Mom motions for Damien to sit, her lips pressed tight together. Is this coolness over the fact that her casserole may have dried out from his lateness or something more—an awareness of trouble in paradise, as Adrian suggested? Not that Mom has ever had huge love for Damien. How could she? He led her precious daughter down the path of what Mom refers to as Hippy Dippy New Ageism and impregnated that daughter at nineteen.

Damien hugs me next and comments on my pallor. His head tilts as he seems to examine me. "You're more blocked than usual." He waves a hand in front of me, indicating my aura I assume. "I have some herbs that could really help clear you out, get that glow back, or," he pauses, his hand holding his chin, "we have a meditation seminar coming up. The focus is on realignment."

I thank him, tell him as nicely as possible that I'm fine, and then introduce him to Adrian. Adrian grins. I can tell he's holding back the intense smile he wants to release.

Dinner is intense. It rarely isn't when the twins are present. They story-tell constantly: Lulu's sudden fear that meat is in the casserole (which it isn't, Mom wouldn't make that mistake again), sends her into screeching howls of terror, and Reggie's subsequent decision to act out the death of a lamb, heightens his sister's general hysteria.

Between dinner and dessert Dad rises from the table. He ushers Adrian and me to come with him. "Everyone else has seen my plans for the basement." He lets out a proud smile. "Your turn." We follow him down the stairs and step into a disaster zone. Rather than getting rid of one wall at a time, Dad has blasted holes through two, leaving the ragged edges of plaster and drywall and a pile of dust and debris on the floor. He turns to me, and I expect an elaborate description of his vision. Instead, he puts his hand on my shoulder. "I didn't know you remembered. I wondered, but I didn't know."

"What?"

His brow crinkles. "Your mother. Your birth mother. You remember her?"

I swallow, a sudden tightness enters my chest. "Dad, we don't have to talk about this. It's okay."

"You want me to leave?" Adrian glances between us.

"No, no, stay," I say. "We don't need to—"

Dad drops his hand. "It's not right, Tracey. I've known all along we should have been asking you about your experience, talking about it openly, but your mother...do you want to meet your birth mother? I can help you."

"Dad, really, it's—"

"I can't imagine. I mean you're my daughter, fully. But at the same time, if I were you I'd want to know where I came from. I'd want to understand."

I'm frozen, shocked he's thought about this, tried to see the situation from my perspective. "I don't want to know." I take a step away from him. "You and Mom are my parents."

He runs his hand through his salt and pepper hair, still as thick as the day I first went home with him. "You've never thought about it? Meeting her? Them?"

I inhale deeply, letting words I've never spoken aloud escape. "She abandoned me. She didn't want me. Why should I want her?"

He nods, his face wearing an expression I'm not sure I've ever seen before. Sorrow? "There must have been a reason, though. A good reason and—"

"What good reason could there be for throwing away your child?" I snap, then lower my gaze, shocked by the anger in my voice.

He frowns. "Is that what you think? That she threw you away?"

"Didn't she?"

"No."

"She left me at a group home, sick, not knowing whether I'd ever find a family."

"That's not true."

"Of course it's true! That's exactly what—"

"No. Your birth mother chose a family. You were only supposed to be at the group home for a week, during the transition phase." My father pauses. "There was an accident, a car accident. The woman who was supposed to be your adoptive mother was badly hurt. She was going to be in the hospital for weeks, and not fully recovered for months. She and her husband, they pulled out of the adoption."

I take another step back, trying to remember talk of this, awareness, but there's nothing.

"It was a closed adoption, so once you were in the

system—" He stops again. "They didn't contact your mother. Policy, I guess. No contact allowed until your eighteenth birthday." His shoulders slump. "We should have told you. I can't believe you thought…all these years." Dad looks up and puts his hand back on my shoulder. "She thought you were going to a good family. She thought…" A large breath pours out of him. "Well, hopefully you think you did go to a good family. It just took longer than expected."

Longer than expected. Two years longer than expected. Two years of no one wanting me. Two years of feeling like I was garbage. "Yes, of course." I reach up to Dad's hand and give a quick squeeze. My vision blurs. "A great family."

"We only mentioned it to you once, on your eighteenth birthday, about finding your birth mother. But the way we did it." He shakes his head again. "I felt like your mother was guilting you into not searching. I wanted to say something," he pauses, "I was scared."

"Of Mom?"

He chuckles. "A little. But also that you'd find her and not want us anymore. It was selfish. I should have—"

"I did find her."

"What?" Adrian and Dad say in unison.

"I mean, I didn't *find* her. I found out about her. I know her address, her name, her phone number. She's less than a day's drive away." I pause. "At least she was when I turned eighteen. The people at the agency said she had updated the information a few months earlier."

"You didn't use it?" asks Adrian. I shake my head.

Dad steps toward me. "Why?"

I wrap my arms around my middle. "I didn't want to use it. I didn't care about meeting her. I just wanted to know…I'd always wondered if maybe she'd died and that's why I was put up for adoption. I almost wanted her to be dead. But she's alive. She spent the first two years of my life with me, then decided I wasn't worth the effort."

Silence fills the room, nothing but the twins' footsteps overhead breaking it. Adrian is the first to speak. "So you didn't find out anything more about her? You didn't—"

I cut him off. "No." I smile at Dad, hoping he doesn't see that, to a degree, it's a forced motion. "This is my family."

Dad draws me against his chest, squeezing me in. He pulls away and the flesh around his eyes crinkle. "If you want to find her, though, even at all, even a little, you should. Don't worry about your mother, or about me. It's not about us. If you want to meet her, do it."

"Dad, no, I—"

"You don't even have to tell us. But if you do, it won't change anything. You'll always be our daughter, even if you're hers too."

Not knowing what to say, not wanting to explain the myriad of reasons I want nothing to do with that woman, I say the one thing guaranteed to end this conversation. "Mom will be worried about dessert. You know she'll want the pie served as soon as it's ready."

Dad stares at me, a look on his face like he wants to say more, then heads upstairs.

ON THE CAR RIDE HOME I wait for Adrian to question me. We're an hour in before he does. "Interesting day."

"Mmm-mm."

"I like your family. They're…sweet."

I let out a little laugh. "They're good people."

"But you don't feel you belong."

My head swivels in his direction. "What do you mean?"

"I mean," he taps the wheel, "it's like you're on display with them. More than normal. Like you're a guest, not their daughter. Like you," he casts a grin, "forgive the cliché, my editor would shoot me, don't want to ruffle any feathers."

"More than normal?" I ignore that he's just told me I behave like a guest with my family. I know, to an extent, that's true.

He glances over again. "Well, yeah. I mean not always, but you do kind of seem like you're walking around broken glass with people. It's not entirely a bad thing. It's nice. It's considerate. But I've wondered about it, why you seem so rarely to just relax, let yourself just be, you know?"

"Let myself just be?"

He lets out a half sigh/half groan. "You sometimes come across as…as, well, now that I have a context, as if you think if you don't act a certain way people will give you away, not want you. Something like that."

I keep my gaze on the dashboard.

"Look, Trace. I don't mean to offend. Not at all. I just…is that how you feel? Are you scared if you're not perfect or something or if you…I don't know, don't fulfil people's expectations they'll not want you in their lives?"

My gaze stays steady. "Doesn't everyone feel like that?"

He pats the steering wheel again, then flips on his indicator to take the highway on-ramp. "Not the way you seem to."

I consider explaining it all, spilling myself to him the way I've never spilled to anyone. But, no. He's talking like there's something abnormal about me, something that needs to be fixed. But this way of life is fine. It's working for me. I'm fine.

He glances over again. I turn away. But…is this the problem? Will the way I'm being right now, the distance my body creates, push him away?

"Is that true what you said?" he asks. "You didn't want to meet or know about your birth family because your adoptive family is your real family?"

I let several breaths pass before replying. "Not really."

"So you do want to meet her."

"No. She didn't want me. She just tossed—" I stop, remembering my father's words, the family I was supposed to go with. "Well, even if she thought she was putting me into a good family, she still didn't want me. So why should I want her? Besides, it goes both ways. She could have contacted me. I didn't give the agency any of my updated information, but she would have had my parents' names once I turned eighteen. And more that that, my parents, they were good to me. As good as they knew how." I pause. "If I met her—if I searched for her, it's like I'd be cheating on them."

"Your dad doesn't seem to think that."

At last I look to Adrian. He meets my gaze. "I guess he doesn't." I fold my hands across my torso and rub my upper arms. Adrian turns down the A/C instantly. A tremor of the most intense affection I've ever experienced bubbles up again. This has to be love. I want to say it. I should say it. But I can't get the words out.

"You know, I assumed when you said you were adopted that you'd been adopted as a baby. That it was the only life you ever knew. I never thought you would have been old enough to remember your birth mother, that you lived in…what did you call it? A group home?"

"Yeah. A lot of adoptions happen that way. Especially domestic adoptions. I was lucky. Really lucky. Many kids past age two spend their lives travelling through a slew of foster and group homes."

"What's the difference?"

"A foster home is with a family. They may take one kid or two or three. The group home was more like a centre or facility, a modern-day orphanage I guess, but with smaller numbers. I think there was never more than twelve to fifteen of us. We all had our meals together, were separated into ages, and there were staff. None of them lived there. Just us." I look away, remembering. "I rotated through three foster homes before becoming a permanent fixture in the group home. I'd get sick and then back they'd send me." I pause. "I guess taking on any child is a lot, but taking on a sick child…" My words trail off as I stare out the window.

"That sounds awful."

"A lot of it is a blur, just, I don't know. I remember the group home much better. They didn't send me away when I was sick, except to the hospital a few times."

Adrian flicks his indicator again and slows the car. He pulls into the entrance of a dirt road.

"What are you doing?"

He turns off the ignition and shifts toward me. "What was it like?"

"What was what like?" My body tenses as my mind travels back to the endless questions, the insipid curiosity, the reason I decided, years ago, to keep my adoption a secret. Adrian's expression, though, is one I've not seen before.

"Everything."

I bite my lip, vulnerability washing over me, then do my best to swallow it away. "I always felt I had to be this perfect child. This perfect…specimen of a human being. My parents never said this. No one ever said it. I don't even know if their actions really implied it or—" I look away, rub my forearm this time, vigorously. "My mom exudes perfection, a certain way of being, a way you present yourself to the world. She expected it from me…but I don't know that it had anything to do with being adopted. She expected it from Jojo too. Jojo just didn't care. I did." I look to Adrian. He gestures for me to continue. "It may be partly from how I was expected to act in the group home. We all knew we had to be good, we had to smile, that if we were bad, if our hair wasn't nice and our clothes clean, if we were sick too often, and therefore a burden, nobody would want us. I was sick a lot."

My eyes close, child after child were taken away, promised a home, a life, yet no one wanted me. "That's why

I wasn't adopted sooner. I should have been. People want babies and a two-year-old? That's not too bad. But I was sick all the time—snotty nose, hospital trips, puking on myself, fevers. Weak. I couldn't play outside with the other kids most of the time. I doubt I looked that appealing."

"What was wrong with you?"

"I don't know," I snap, then soften my voice. "I was sick."

"Okay." His voice is soothing and immediately I feel rotten. I smile, hoping he sees my apology in it.

"People only want a healthy little girl. My parents loved me. I know they loved me. But I was always so scared to be sick. I would hide it as best I could. If I had a headache, I'd ignore the pain. Smile. A cold was hard to hide, but with a fever or flu I'd push through the discomfort. I never wanted them to know and any time it was so bad I couldn't hide my sickness I feared they'd send me away—back to the group home I'd go. I couldn't get the idea out of my head: people only want a healthy little girl."

Adrian sits silently for an uncomfortably long time, both hands gripping the steering wheel. He exhales loudly. "And now you're scared you're sick again."

"What?"

"This issue with your period. Your fertility. How scared you were to tell me about it, how it seemed like you almost expected me to walk away, like you thought I wouldn't want you."

"Well, I mean…" I twist my purse straps, drop my hands, lift and twist again. "It's different. It's not just sick. I could be sick. I could have…" I plop the purse onto the car floor, smooth my hands along my thighs. "But it's reasonable, right? I mean if you wanted children and I couldn't give you them."

"Tracey," he shakes his head, "if we don't work out, if you and me aren't forever, it won't be because of that. I promise you. I'm not going to push you away because your body may not be perfect." He stops. "Not that perfect even exists. That's not what I mean. Whether or not you have a disease that prevents you from having kids, whether you get the flu or mono, or anything else, it won't scare me away. Okay?"

I bite my lip and clench back the tears struggling to push through. I want to believe him.

He turns from me, his gaze focused on something outside the vehicle. "Have you ever thought maybe meeting your birth mom could help you out with some of these...concerns? Like if you could confront her, find out why she gave you up it could help you heal? Maybe she has a really good reason. Maybe it was her only option."

"I'm not sure any reason could be good enough."

"Even if she honestly believed it would be giving you a better life? Maybe she was sick herself, thought she'd be dying, and wanted to make sure you were taken care of. I mean—"

"Adrian."

He grins. "Besides, it'd make a great human-interest piece."

I laugh and shake my head. "No way."

"All right, all right." He smiles. "Come here." I lean toward him and he kisses me. After pulling away, he places his hand on the ignition. "Enough prying for today?"

"Enough."

"I don't promise there won't be more. If you and I want to work, you need to trust me enough to be real, to know you won't scare me away."

I rest my hand on his leg. He turns the car on and pulls back into traffic. As the noisy silence surrounds us, I'm taken back to the basement with Dad. It doesn't change much, but the knowledge he gave me does change one thing. She didn't just drop me off. She didn't get rid of me like some unwanted trash. She took the time to set me up with what she believed was a good family. I don't want her in my life, that isn't changing, but if she cared enough to arrange a home for me, and even now, to update her contact information, giving me the chance to reach out to her, maybe she'll care enough to give me access to her medical history. Maybe I could at least learn that.

CHAPTER NINE

Alone and back in my cozy apartment, I settle in to watch a movie. My thoughts are so loud I turn the film off. I can't hear what's going on, anyway. Adrian's suggestion that meeting my mother could provide some form of emotional healing filters through my mind, but it's the idea that she could provide medical answers that really consumes me.

Feeling a chill, I reach for a blanket and wrap myself. The fuzzy texture gives me the false sense of a hug, soft and comforting against my skin. Toulouse slinks over and settles against me, adding to this cozy feeling. But the comfort is only physical. Inside a tornado whirls. I wasn't simply thrown away. She tried to secure my future. But she still let me go. She cared. But not enough. Not nearly enough. Why?

Tossing the blanket aside, I nudge Toulouse off of my lap, rise from the couch, and make my way to the bedroom. The closet looks foreign, terrifying. But it's not. It's just a closet, and what I'm looking for, just a box. I pull open the door. Everything is as it should be. Shirts piled neatly, dresses and pants hung in coloured sections, boxes piled in even rows. I know exactly where to look. Three boxes down. In the bottom of that box, another, the label scrawled in my large teenage script: 'Keepsakes.'

Passing by the other items I have to rifle through—first-love notes, movie and concert ticket stubs, a pile of report cards—I reach for the one tangible thing I have from my mother, from the life I led with her. The teddy bear is old and ragged. It's hard to know exactly what colour it once was, but my guess is white. I know its neck has been re-stitched, though my mom's needlework was so good it's hard to tell...my adoptive mom's needlework.

My hands tremble as I reach for the bear. As much as I loved this teddy, sleeping with it every night for years, dragging it around with me, my substitute security blanket, it always confused me. If she didn't care, if I meant nothing to her, why had she thought to leave me with it? Why had she made sure this was the one thing I kept?

One of the few memories of her, the last, flows back: she stares at me, tells me to keep the bear always, to hold it when I'm sad, and think of her. I can't actually remember if those were the words, but that's the feeling her words gave me. Hold the bear, think of her, be less sad. It never worked. That last hug, it was all three of us: my mommy, the bear, and me. When she turned and walked out of the room, it was just me and the bear. I clung to it.

I spent hours contemplating this bear during my prepubescent years. Had my mother bought it for me? Had we picked it out in a store together? Was it a birthday present, a Christmas present, a just-because present? Or, had it come from someone else—an aunt, a friend, a grandmother? Did I have a grandmother? If I did, and if she cared enough to buy me presents, why hadn't she cared enough to take me herself? Why had she let my mother give me away? Why hadn't she done something?

I squeeze the animal so hard my hand aches. Dozens of times I resolved to throw this toy away. Tomorrow. The next day. The next week. I never did. I drop the bear back into the box. My hands navigate to my belly—the all too familiar clenching that, perhaps, signals something awful. Maybe if I'd known something was wrong earlier, or likely to be wrong, maybe I could have done something, anticipated or managed whatever is self-destructing inside of me. A shiver runs up my spine and out to my fingertips. And what if there are other time bombs? Early onset Alzheimer's, heart disease, that one in one-hundred million disease I read about in a book last month: Fatal Familial Insomnia.

I have a right to know my genetic history. Everyone does. I have a right to look her in the face and ask. Resolve settles over me slowly, the way a leaf drifts over a puddle of water until it becomes saturated: I'm going to meet my mother.

THE AGENCY'S WALLS ARE the colour of a Caribbean Sea. Photos of happy families hang in crisp white frames. "It's nice to see you today," the caseworker glances to my file, "Tracey."

She clicks her keyboard several times. "I love the digital tools of today. Makes things so much easier." She laughs. "But what a trial it was inputting everything."

I make a noise of acknowledgement, caring only for what that digital tool has to tell me.

"Here we go."

Does my mother still care? Is the number on file the one I called last week—service disconnected—or…

"You're really lucky." The woman smiles broadly, displaying teeth that are straight but most likely exposed to too much coffee. "A lot of people, when they come looking for their birth parents, find addresses in the Adoption Disclosure Register ten, fifteen years out of date. This was updated three years ago. Obviously, your mother is proactive."

Proactive. Proactive would be contacting me. Proactive would be showing up at my door, not waiting for me to show up at hers. I smile at the woman with her frizzy hair and un-pressed suit, surprised at how ungenerous I feel. What's it like, holding the secrets of so many souls? Does she revel in her job? Realize the information she passes over so casually has the power to rewrite people's entire histories?

I thank her and stand—the information grasped firmly in my hand.

"Try not to have expectations."

"Expectations?" I sit back down.

"Yes. Try not to have expectations of what your mother will be like, of what the meeting will be like, of what you'll learn, of whether you'll establish a relationship."

"I don't want to establish a relationship."

She pushes out her lips then tilts her head back and forth like one of those dashboard bobble heads. "Still, sometimes we can create scenarios in our minds, good or bad. Try not to do this. Your mother could be a senator, she could be a crack addict. Be prepared for anything and expect nothing."

"Okay." I rise again, thank her, again. Her hair's not that frizzy, and who cares about wrinkles. I smile a genuine smile and close her office door behind me.

In the parking lot I stare at the sheet of paper in my hand. I've already been floored by expectations. I expected my mother would be an eight-hour drive away. Far, but manageable. Instead, we're separated by an ocean. The words on the page jump out at me: Charlbury, The Cotswolds, England.

My stomach clenches. I want to back away, to run, but there's nowhere to go that can get me away from what this paper is asking.

How will I find her? Rent a car, show up in a taxi, a bus? I've never travelled anywhere on my own. Never left the country. How could she do this, go so far away, make it so difficult? My hand shakes. What if I needed her, needed a kidney or a liver or—my breath catches—what if, one day, she needs one of those things from me? Old familiar anger bubbles within me. I stuff the paper in my purse and stride toward my car.

Autumn. Maybe Autumn can help. Give me a stopping place, anyway. The idea of getting off a plane in Heathrow and travelling directly to my mother's—my birth mother's— house is overwhelming. Ridiculous. But making a trip of it, visiting Autumn, touring England, and then, just because it's convenient, meeting my birth mother to request my medical history? Much more doable.

As I turn the key in the ignition, my phone rings. I turn the car back off again and look at the screen before answering.

"Hi!" Not a hint of the fear and nervousness racing through me makes its way into my voice. Years of practice.

"Hey, beautiful. How's your day going?"

"Oh, great." I add a smile to cement the facade. "Not too much going on. A relaxing day."

"That's good." I can hear Adrian's grin. "For a woman on vacation, you work far too much. Glad to hear you're taking it easy. So," he draws the word out: I can almost see the way his lip curls up as he does it, "my interview fell through for tonight. You want to catch a movie, maybe get some food on the waterfront?"

"Oh…" Tomorrow is Autumn's last full day in town. A bunch of us are supposed to get together to say our farewells, but the conversation I need to have with her is not one to have in the company of a dozen other people. I need to see if she can squeeze me in tonight, which means I need to keep myself open. "Sorry," I say, hating the lie, the second one in less than a minute. "I have plans with Autumn."

"Aren't you seeing her tomorrow night?"

"Yeah, but tonight's plans are more intimate."

"Oh, okay." The sound of a car rushing by travels through the line. "Have fun then. The day after tomorrow, can I get dibs on you?"

"Absolutely."

Rather than setting the phone down, I call Autumn. She's busy, but as expected, will squeeze me in. After a dinner with her family, she and Eloise are meeting to go over marketing ideas to promote Autumn's personal training business. "Why don't you come over an hour into it," she says, "we should be winding up by then."

"Uh…" Do I want to let Eloise know? Admit to her, too, the years of lying?

"Is it something you don't want Eloise to know about?"

"No." I've kept this secret long enough. "I'll see you then."

CHAPTER TEN

Walking up the stairs to Autumn's old room is like walking back in time. I haven't passed through her door since the month's after the accident when Autumn was recovering from not only her own injuries but the loss of her husband. During those few visits, walking up these stairs was like walking into a dark tunnel. Each time she seemed worse. The scar along her face was healing, improving, but the friend I knew grew further and further away. Nothing I did or said helped. I walked this hall scared I'd say or do something to make her pain worse. Today, terror runs through me for another reason. I'm about to reveal to my two best friends that, essentially, I've been lying to them for over a decade.

I tap on the door. Autumn, mid-laugh, tells me to come in. They're both on her bed, Autumn's legs curled up, one arm leaning against her thigh, her body folded over like a closed lawn chair. Eloise rests against the headboard, one leg crossed casually over the other.

"Perfect timing." Autumn props herself up. "We're pretty much finished with the marketing talk."

"Yeah, you've got a solid plan to start with." Eloise's smile lessens as she looks at me. "What's going on?"

I make my way into the room and pull out the desk chair. "I have some news."

Autumn sits up. "Is it the period thing? Did you learn—"

"No, no." I cut her off. "Nothing like that. Or at least, no new news. It's connected." Their gazes focus on me, waiting. "Where to start?" I laugh. Neither of them do. They don't know the joke, not that there actually is one. "I think I'm going to take a trip."

Eloise's eyebrow raises. Autumn shifts closer on the bed.

"To England, actually."

Autumn's face brightens. "That's wonderful. When?"

"Soon. Sometime before school starts. It's perfect timing, really. A trip like this during the school year would have been next to impossible. To go during Christmas break would, well, that's a lot of pressure and March break is so far away—"

Eloise cuts me off. "What are you talking about? Pressure. What's—"

I turn to Autumn. "I hope it's a time that will work out with your schedule. I don't want to impose too much."

Autumn pulls herself closer. "This will be great. You've never been to Europe, have you? We should see if we can plan some other side trips—maybe to France, or Scotland. London's amazing. I may have a bit of a hectic schedule when I get back, setting up some things, but toward the end of summer, when it's a bit more muggy, people aren't too keen to work out and they'll be taking the last of their holidays away." Autumn grins. "I could definitely carve out some long weekends. How long are you going for? Give it at least two weeks. Any less than that and—"

"Wait." Eloise moves forward and settles in beside Autumn. "How is this connected to your missing period?"

"Yes, well, it's complicated." I hear my mother's tone, her words, slipping through my lips.

"It'd be less complicated if you just spit it out." Eloise offers a smile—concern floats behind it.

"Well..." I pause, as if for dramatic effect, though really it's because it's so weird, after all of these years, to be speaking the words. "I'm adopted."

Both of their expressions are blank until confusion settles over their faces.

"You're adopted?" says Autumn. "So, Henry and Joanna, they're your—"

"Adopted parents."

Eloise's mouth hangs open slightly. Autumn's expression is unreadable. "Why didn't you tell us?"

"Why are you telling us now?"

I start to speak, then stop, not sure I have a good enough answer. These are the women I'm supposed to share everything with. For more than a decade, as far as I know, they've shared everything with me.

Eloise reaches forward, her hand on my knee. "I'm sorry. That wasn't a fair question. I'm sure you have your reasons. It's just…surprising. That's all."

"Yeah." Autumn looks between us. "Of course you have your reasons. I just…"

"Feel like you don't really know me?" I ask.

"No." She shakes her head. "Well, maybe a little. But as Eloise says, I'm sure you have your reasons. It's kind of a big thing, so…"

I sigh, then proceed to explain the constant questioning throughout my public school years, how people looked at me like I was different somehow, how even in my family I didn't feel like I belonged and was tired of feeling like that out in the world as well.

Autumn inhales. "That must be rough."

Eloise glances from Autumn to me. "So you didn't just learn you were adopted?"

"No, I've always known." I pick up a pen from Autumn's desk and twirl it through my fingers. "I remember being adopted." Next I tell them about the group home, the years there, how, when I was four, I went to live with my new family. I gloss over the years of sickness, of being scared, alone, and confused.

"My family never talked about it much. When we did talk about it my mother, my adoptive mother, presented it to me as a story of love—that my birth mother loved me so much but knew she couldn't give me the home I deserved so she gave me to a family who would love me forever and take care of me always."

But there had been no family waiting, at least as far as I knew. "She wanted me to think how lucky I was to have two mommies who loved me. She wanted me to believe those years at the group home," defined by fear and loneliness and feeling out of place, "were worth it because I was with them now, because I'd found my perfect family."

A moment of silence. "And Jojo?" asks Eloise.

"She's their real daughter."

"Tracey." Autumn leans toward me.

"She's their biological daughter. Mom always stressed we were both real." It wasn't true, though, wasn't possible. We had come into her life in such different ways.

I twist the chair back and forth on its wheels. "After Jojo was born Mom made it clear that me being adopted was no different than me being her biological daughter, or if it was different, both ways were equally special."

"That makes sense," says Autumn.

Inwardly, I roll my eyes. Outwardly, I might as well have. "She said they chose me and God chose Jojo. And both choices resulted in the best things that had ever happened to them. From how much she insisted we weren't different, it seemed pretty clear we were." A stifled laugh escapes. "You know, 'the lady doth protest too much' thing."

Autumn and Eloise glance to each other, then back to me.

"I knew I was loved. I never doubted my mother and father loved me. I just felt like an outsider. I still do."

Autumn swallows. "That's a lot."

"You and Jojo, you're not too close, are you? I've wondered about that," says Eloise.

"At first, to my sister I was just her sister. She'd never known our family as any different. As we got older that changed. I don't know if it was more because of me or her, or our mom. We love each other." I pause. "We also resent each other. If anything, if I'm honest, Mom probably doted on me more, made more of an effort to make me feel loved, special."

"So," Eloise sounds hesitant, "you've never met your birth mother. And I'm guessing she lives in England."

"Yep," my words come out tired, "she lives in England and no, I never wanted to meet her. If she loved me so much, wanted me with the perfect family, like my mother said, she would have made sure I ended up there. She wouldn't have just dropped me in some group home…or not even—" I hesitate. "I was somewhere else first. I'm not sure where. Some transition place I guess." My father's words float back again: a transition place, that's exactly where I would have been. A transition place and then the group home? Or was it a different group home, one that didn't have the space to keep me?

"You must have been angry," says Eloise.

I look to her, incredulous. Nobody has ever jumped to that conclusion. "Yes." I touch my hand to my throat. "Furious. She didn't leave any answers. She spent two years of her life with me. More than two years, over three if you count the pregnancy, and then left. Just left." My flesh warms as my voice raises. "Was she dead? Laid up with a horrible disease? Was she some druggie, and I hadn't been given away at all but taken by social services?" I speak through clenched teeth. "How could she have taken care of me all that time and then let me go?" Tension builds in my face, my chest. "That wasn't love. That could not have been love. No way." I choke. "She didn't want me." Unless she was dead. That was the simple answer. The only answer. But she wasn't. She isn't. And I knew it all along. The teddy bear. She left me the teddy bear and walked away. "She just didn't want me."

Autumn steps from the bed and drapes an arm over my shoulder. She crouches beside me somewhat awkwardly.

"Like you said, maybe she had to give you up, maybe her life was—"

"That still represents a choice, though, right? She chose whatever it was that meant I couldn't be with her. Chose it over me."

Autumn squeezes me against her as the fight drains out of me.

"I'm sorry, I—"

"Don't be sorry." Eloise looks away. "It's true you don't know your mother's reasoning, but it's also true she was your mother, and she left you. No matter the reason behind that choice, she still made it."

I stare at Eloise, shocked that in all of this I'd never drawn the parallel between her and her mother. In a different way, Eloise's Mom deserted Eloise just as much as my mother deserted me. More so.

Eloise's gaze locks onto mine. "It makes sense to be angry. Don't apologize for being angry."

I nod slowly. "I was mad at my mom for a long time too, for lying to me, for telling me my birth mother loved me when clearly she didn't. I didn't show it, I tried not to at least. I couldn't show it." I look to my hands. "I was too scared she wouldn't want me anymore either, especially when she had her own daughter, but the anger was there, brimming beneath the surface." I pause. "It still is. Somewhat."

"Tracey." Autumn's voice is soft.

"It's what I thought. It's what," my voice catches, "anyway." I shrug off the emotion and bring a smile back to my face. "I don't know why I'm talking about all of this right now. My birth mother decided she didn't want me, so I decided I didn't want her, but also that I'd never be like her. I wanted a real family. A blood family. I decided I'd make my own."

Eloise nods. "And now you've found out it's possible you can't."

"Yes."

Eloise lets out a long sigh. "And your constant pursuit of the perfect man all these years, an effort to start this perfect family?"

I pull back. "I wouldn't call it constant."

"Sorry. I didn't mean it like that. I just meant you have this goal, this image of what you want your life to be." She pauses. "Or at least you did, in the way you pursued men, in your hope of finding the one. That's changed in the last year, after …and the change is good. It just …it makes sense now. It was all about creating what you viewed as a real family."

"Well, yeah."

"That would be hard for anyone." Autumn moves back to the edge of the bed but keeps her gaze on me. "And now it's not just losing your hope of a baby, it's losing…Wow."

"She hasn't lost anything," says Eloise. "You still don't know anything for sure, right? You could be fine?"

"I could be fine."

"So your birth mother is in England and you're deciding to meet her…" Autumn's voice trails off, and Eloise's finishes the thought.

"To get your medical history."

I nod.

"That's really brave," says Autumn.

"Brave?"

"Yeah, brave. Exciting too."

A laugh trickles out of me. "Excitement isn't exactly one of the emotions I've experienced. Fear, nervousness, uncertainty, but not excitement."

We spend a few minutes chatting about what I want to learn from my birth mother, and I clarify that I'm not interested in anything but information. Both of them seem uncertain about this point—as if they don't believe me or don't think it's the best idea, but neither says a word.

"Have you called her?" asks Eloise.

"No."

"Do you plan to?"

"No."

Autumn perks up. "So you'll go right to her door. Make sure she has no chance to turn away or—"

"What if she's not home?"

I look to Eloise. "I hadn't thought of that, but I guess I try again."

"And if you try again and still no answer? It's the summer. She could be travelling or—"

"I don't know." My gaze settles on the carpeted floor as my stomach twists. Eloise has a point, a valid point. I could travel all the way to England and not even see her. I could waste my time, my money.

"You don't want to call," says Autumn.

"No."

"Then I guess you just hope."

I look up.

"Hope it works out, hope you get the answers you're looking for…if you don't, at least you'll know you tried. Then you can call. And you'll have seen a new place, travelled. I'll make sure your time is well spent. England is beautiful: all the history."

"It really is." Eloise smiles. "You'll love it."

They both stare at me, hopeful, expectant, supportive. I must seem crazy, holding this information from them all these years, always careful to never slip up, focused on hiding such a massive part of what makes me me. Eloise seems to read my thoughts. "So your adoption, it's a big part of who you are, isn't it?"

"It is."

"What you were talking about with your Mom, hiding away your symptoms when you were sick, that fear that she'd send you back, is that part of…I don't know how to say this…but your fear of failing people or not being like this perfect version of yourself or—"

So Adrian wasn't the only one to see it. All I thought was hidden seems broadcasted around me. Exposed. "Yes."

She's quiet as we sit and take it all in, as I realize all these years they've known me better than I ever thought. "It's a really good thing," says Eloise, "you going to meet your mother. No matter what happens, it will be one of the best things you've ever done for yourself." Silence falls over us again as I look from Autumn to Eloise. Terror still pulses through me, but strength too. These women believe I have what it takes. It kind of makes me believe it too.

CHAPTER ELEVEN

Autumn, Eloise, and I spend the next several hours searching flights and trip-planning. When Autumn learns my mother—my birth mother—lives in The Cotswolds, she squeals with delight. Jakob's sister, Emily, and she have been planning to take a trip there as it's Emily's favourite part of the country, and Jakob and Amalia will probably want to tag along too.

I almost tell her I don't exactly want this to be a group trip but decide against it. The more people, the more distraction, and I have a strong feeling I'll desire a lot of distraction. Besides, I've heard so much about the Andrevs, it will be nice to get to know them in person. Autumn even offers to have Jakob call before I come, posing as a telemarketer or some such thing, to ensure my birth mother actually is currently in Charlbury. Although this idea has some appeal, it's too weird.

Instead, I book a one-way ticket in case she is away and I need to extend my trip. To account for this possibility, we decide that even though it's not quite as convenient for Autumn, I'll leave in early August—about two-and-a-half weeks from now. Leaving so soon means I'll miss some key Aspire meetings, but Eloise assures me with the guest speakers we're bringing in, she has it covered. "That's what I get the big bucks for." She grins.

When Eloise and I get up to leave, it's almost two-thirty in the morning. "Thank you both," I whisper. My voice cracks as I pull them into a group hug and, for the first time since I sat in the doctor's office, let the tears spill down my face. "I don't know how I would have figured all of this out without you."

"You would have done fine," says Eloise. "But I'm glad you didn't need to."

"I'm sorry for not telling you, for—"

Autumn squeezes my arm. "You told us when you were able, which makes the timing perfect."

"About tomorrow night…" My words trail off.

Eloise places a finger to her lips. "Not a word."

"I'm just not sure if I'm ready to 'come out' yet." I make little air quotes with my hands.

"Whenever you're ready," says Autumn.

I laugh. "I guess when people find out I'm travelling to England to visit my birth mother, it may give it away."

"Say you're going to England to tour, to explore." Eloise waves her hand. "It's nobody's business."

We tiptoe down the hall so as not to disturb Autumn's sleeping parents. In the driveway, Eloise reaches for my arm before I can step toward my car. "Just…"

"What?"

"I don't know."

"Eloise at a loss for words?"

She smiles. "Don't expect too much. Your mom, your birth mom, she could be really disappointing."

The caseworker's words pass through my mind: a breeze of nervousness passes with them. "I'll do my best. No expectations." I back step toward my car. "This is about my medical history anyway, for now and in the future. That's what matters. Whoever she is, the person she is, is irrelevant." Eloise purses her lips. I know that look, it's not one she wears often, but it's the look that says she's holding back. I let her. "See you tomorrow?"

"Tomorrow. Drive safe." She flips her keys in her hand. "Hey, Trace?"

"Yeah?"

"If I don't say it enough, I love you. You're family. Know that, okay? Family is more than blood."

I blow her a kiss and slip into the car. My chest is heavy, my breath shallow. I swipe my fingers across my cheeks, obliterating any stray tears.

THE NIGHT AFTER AUTUMN'S farewell, Adrian and I walk along the boardwalk while the harbour glistens in the waning light. Tall ships line the harbour, their sails rippling in the breeze. A busker plays a peaceful tune on his guitar. Couples stroll and children laugh. Adrian draws me toward a bench where we watch a small sailboat come into port. "Have I mentioned that you look beautiful?"

I stifle a blush. "Only two, three times maybe."

"Ahh," he leans back, "two or three more times may be sufficient then, to really get the point across."

"You don't look so bad yourself."

He stretches his arm around my shoulders and draws me close. "So that conversation about moving in together, did we ever really finish it?"

I snuggle in. "I think we decided it's happening."

He turns to me. "When?"

"My lease isn't up until the end of November."

"Weird time of year."

"I suppose."

"Think you could get a sub-letter?"

I pause, considering. "It's possible."

"For a smooth transition I was thinking the start of September."

I tense. "Less than two months away?"

"Or," he tilts his head, "if that's too soon, maybe after the holidays? You month to month after your lease is up?"

"I can be." I speak slowly. "After the holidays may be more doable."

"Not quite ready to see this mug every day?"

"It's not that."

"It's fast, I know." He's silent and seems to consider something. "Your place is too small for the both of us. Would you want to move into my place or get a new place together? I'm month to month so I could go either way."

"I'm not sure." I shift my body so I can look at him without craning my neck. The past couple of weeks my own thoughts and life have so thoroughly consumed me I've hardly thought about the logistics of this request. "Your place is nice, and in a good location for me. I could walk to school."

"Yeah." His eyes gleam as his words tumble out. "That's what I was thinking, and I know it may seem kind of weird, the idea of you coming into my space, but the rent is so good for the location, it'd be a shame to lose it. And I'd want you to make the place yours, or ours…we could mix and match our furniture, pictures—I'd get rid of anything you didn't want and make space for whatever you need. I already talked to the landlord, and he said it's fine to paint—so if you want it to be fresh, like a new place for the two of us, we can make that happen."

My eyes widen. "You already talked to the landlord?"

He leans back. "Well, yeah. I wanted to know…I don't know, that you could make it the way you want." His hands wave as he talks, his gaze in the direction of the harbour. "See, I've got a plan. I mean what I think could be a plan if you think so too. Assuming everything goes splendidly and we end up," he glances at me, a shy, half-grin on his face, "falling madly for each other."

"Harder than we've already fallen?"

"Harder." He darts in to kiss me then sits back again. "I figure with us splitting the rent and…well, I don't know what your finances are like, but I know I've already got enough that after a year or so we could have a twenty percent deposit on a house. It'd have to be a little out of the downtown core, but if that were a big issue we could rent a few more years, maybe save enough to live near the school." He stops, shifting toward me again. "Or not. I mean these are only ideas and we have no idea what the future will hold, of course."

What to say? I'm amazed. Touched. He's the first man whose plans for the future have been more detailed and gone further than mine. I nudge closer, pressing my body up against his. He wraps his arm around me. With my head nuzzled against his chest, I want to say the words pounding within me. Instead, I tilt my head back further, and, as if reading my mind, he kisses me, long and deep.

"Get a room!"

We look up to see a group of tween-age boys walking by. They laugh among themselves and one, the one I imagine shouted the words, flushes red as I catch his gaze.

"That may not be such a bad idea," Adrian whispers.

"It may not." I tilt my head toward him. "But I also want to talk to you about something else."

"Yeah?"

I sit up. "I decided to meet my birth mom."

"Wow, Tracey, that's amazing. It's so good, it's—"

"Just to get my medical history. It won't be some human-interest story type reunion. I want to meet her, ask the questions I need to ask. That's it."

He nods. "Okay. That's still good. When, where?" He laughs. "This is big."

"In two weeks. In England."

"England?"

He's quiet and rubs his bottom lip. "It might be rough with some stories I have coming up, but I could come with you if you want me there. For support, and as a travel buddy." He grins.

"No."

His smile wavers.

I explain my plan, how I'll stay with Autumn, how I'll show up at my birth mother's door, how it's all worked out.

"So it's planned."

"Mostly, yeah."

He pulls away from me.

"What?"

"It's just…I don't know. We're together. We're thinking of moving in together and it's like you're filling me in as an afterthought."

"No, I…" I hesitate. Is he right? Should I have come to him first? "It just makes sense. Autumn lives in England. I don't know that I could afford staying at hotels right now, or that I would want to—"

"Yeah," he rubs his jaw, "it does makes sense."

"I need to do this alone, too. I mean, not alone, I'll have Autumn and her friends but…Thank you, though. Really."

"It's okay. I get it. Just know you can come to me with these things too. With anything. I want you to feel that way."

I look at him, looking back at me so serious, so genuine. "I've been going to these friends for the last decade. It'll be a little hard to get out of the habit." I smile. "But I'll work on it."

His grin grows. "This trip will be amazing. No matter what happens. It'll be transformative."

Transformative. I inhale and push out a smile. This is about medical history, and the news may not be good. He's excited, but I'm close to tremors. We sit, not speaking, the strains of the guitar drifting toward us, the gentle lap of the water against the boardwalk adding to the music.

As much as I want to deny it, this trip will be about more than medical history. What everyone says is true: the questions won't be asked in a vortex. I'll meet my mother. And, if I really didn't want to, all I would have to do is call. But I'm not. I'm not even calling to let her know I'm coming. The honesty of the realization fills me with a rush of panic, and fear, and eagerness. I want to meet her. I want to look into her eyes as she first sees me and learn the truth.

∽

SEVERAL DAYS LATER, I'M stepping through my door, energized after an amazing Aspire meeting, when my phone rings.

"Tracey?"

"Yes?"

Jojo's voice is breathless. "Thank God you're home. I need you to come over. Now."

"I'm just getting in." I balance the phone between my ear and shoulder as I lock the door behind me and pull off my shoes. "Is everything okay?"

"My sitter cancelled. *Lulu, put it down.* And Damien won't leave the store. *Lulu, I said put it down!*" Jojo lets out a groan of frustration. "He's leading a meditation session and cannot possibly think of cancelling." Her voice drips with sarcasm, which, five years ago, would have been normal. "I have my seminar presentation tonight and if I don't leave in thirty-five minutes, I'll be late. I can't be late. I'll fail and—*Lulu, if I have to ask you one more time.*" A crash reverberates through the phone. "Damn." Lulu's wails reach my ear.

"Is everything okay? And your seminar? What—"

"Tracey, please. You're thirty minutes away. This is tight here."

"Okay, okay. I'm coming." I hang up the phone, slip back into my shoes and make my way to the elevator. When I arrive at Jojo and Damien's little shop, I glance through the large glass windows to see Damien smiling peacefully, chatting with several young women in yoga pants. I bypass the entrance and make my way around the side then follow the stairs up to the apartment door. Jojo must have been watching because the door draws open the moment I reach the top step. She thrusts Neveah into my hands, says she'll be back in two-and-a-half hours and frozen pizza is in the deep freeze, then flees down the stairs before I even get a word out.

CHAPTER TWELVE

With Jojo gone, I make my way into the apartment. Neveah gurgles happily in my arms. I tickle her belly and she squirms with a small laugh. Is she hungry? When's the last time she ate? As far as I know Jojo is still breastfeeding. I walk through the living room, perturbed at the quiet. In Jojo and Damien's bedroom I hear a noise from the closet. I pry open the doors to find the twins curled on the floor with blankets around them and an iPad propped on Lulu's lap.

I lay Neveah in her crib and crouch to their level. "Hi, there."

Reggie looks up. "Hi." Lulu's gaze stays glued to the screen. From the sound of it, they're watching a musical. I glance down. A blue parrot dances and twirls.

"How are you two?"

"Lulu's sad."

I touch Lulu's shoulder. "What's wrong, honey?"

She shifts closer to Reggie but doesn't answer. "Lulu got in trouble. She made Mommy mad." Ah, the crash during Jojo's phone call.

"Mommy yelled at me." Lulu's lips pucker. She looks up, her eyes moist.

"Oh." I reach my arms out and she crawls into them. "Mommy had a really hard day. I'm sure she's not really that mad at you."

"She is." Lulu's voice is so soft I have to curl my head

down to hear her. "I broke her ballerina."

"Her? Ohh…" Jojo's ballerina. The one she got after seeing The Nutcracker on a family trip to New York almost twenty years ago: A ballerina en pointe in a snow globe fairy-world. When you wound the globe, the ballerina twirled to the tune of Tchaikovsky's *The Nutcracker*. Jojo loved it. She listened to that thing, seemingly transfixed by the twirling figure, over and over and over again.

"Mommy was probably sad." I smooth the girl's hair out of her face. "But she'll get over it. Mommy loves you much more than the ballerina."

Reggie crawls out of the closet and squats beside us, his elbows rest on his knees, his head in a hand. "Mommy be mad a lot lately. She yells all the time."

"But not when Daddy's home," says Lulu.

"Not *soooo* much when Daddy's home." Reggie scoots closer, so his elbows rest on my thigh. "But Daddy's not home too much anymore."

"He's not?"

"Not so much." Lulu reaches for one of the blankets and scrunches it up in her arms like a teddy bear. My stomach growls. "You're hungry." Lulu laughs. She pokes my belly. "I'm hungry too."

"Your mom said we could make a frozen pizza."

Reggie's eyes widen. "Pizza?"

I nod.

"Yes." He pulls his arm down in an exaggerated fist pump and Lulu scrambles out of my grasp. "We almost never get pizza, unless we make it ourselves. Daddy says boxed food is consoom-a-ist."

"And full of nasties." Reggie screws up his face.

I stand and reach for Neveah. "Consumerist?"

"That's what I said." Lulu leads the way to the kitchen. After the oven heats and we put the pizza in, Neveah whimpers, which quickly turns into screams. "Is she on formula?" I ask the twins.

"No." Reggie gives me an exaggerated eye roll, as if I'm clueless. "Formula is full of nasties too."

"Uh…" I jostle Neveah, "well, then—"

Lulu pulls open the fridge. "Mommy's milk!" she announces.

"Okay." I reach for a bottle. It needs to be warmed. I glance around the kitchen. "A microwave?" The twins look at me as if I'm speaking another language. "No, of course." I laugh. "You probably don't even have a microwave. Does Mommy warm it?"

"What's a—"

"Never mind. How does mommy warm the milk?"

"Hmm." Reggie rubs his chin. "I think it's warm out of Mommy."

"The bowl." Lulu points to the cupboard. "When Suzie comes, she puts the bottle in a bowl of hot water and then she tests it like this." Lulu mimes picking up the bottle and touching it to the underside of her wrist.

By the time the bottle is ready, the oven timer goes off. I serve the twins first then settle Neveah into my arms, the old familiar motion making me realize this is the first time I've babysat since Neveah was born. She's almost six months old. I need to get over more often. Shared blood or not, Jojo's the only sister I have…unless she isn't. My breath ceases for a moment. In meeting my mother, I may be meeting a whole new family. This thought had occurred to me in the past, that I could have other siblings, but not in years. And those siblings, unlike my mother, who gave me away, I may actually want to know.

"Auntie Tracey?"

"Yes?" I turn my gaze to the girl.

"You not going to eat? Your stomach was growling." She makes a face like a hungry bear.

"Oh, I'll eat." I smile at her, then look down to Neveah, sucking away with a happy, almost dopey look on her face. "Once Neveah's done."

"Oooo-kay!" Lulu picks up her pizza and makes 'nummy, nummy' noises.

Neveah's head rests perfectly in my arms. I want this. So much. I hope for this. As I revel in her gurgles, I think about the other nieces and nephews I may have. This trip could alter my life, changing the people who matter to me and the people I matter to, forever.

No expectations. The caseworker and Eloise are right. It's best to have no expectations. But I can't help it. I want a brother or sister, out there somewhere, waiting for me.

THE TWINS GO TO BED easily, well, mostly easily. When I ask about their bedtime Lulu tells me Mommy always lets them stay up until she gets home, a sly grin on her small face, but Reggie sets me straight. They start to get ready at seven, then read stories, and lights out is no later than eight-fifteen, even if the story is really good. Only if the story is really good, Lulu adds, deciding to get her share of truth in as well, otherwise lights out is eight. Reggie nods in agreement.

I've settled onto the couch and am only a chapter into my ebook when Jojo comes through the door.

"Did Damien come home at all?" she asks before I even have a chance to say hello.

I put my phone aside. "No."

She nods and lays her bag on the coffee table. Her shoulders slump and she sinks into the adjacent couch. "Thanks for coming like that." A tired smile covers her face. "I rocked my presentation."

"Presentation for what?"

"Oh." She raises her hands as if in wonderment. "I haven't told you about my business course. It's nothing special. A diploma course at the college, not a degree or anything. But I like it."

"That's great, Jojo!" I scooch to the end of the couch so I'm leaning on the arm, able to see her more clearly. "Really exciting. What's the focus and when did you start?"

"A couple of months ago." She looks shy, an expression I'm not used to seeing on my sister. "In May."

"What's the focus?"

"Business Management. I thought if I had more skills I could contribute more, to the store or," she pauses, "anything else. Just something good to have."

"Absolutely." I pursue the pause. "How have things been going with you? Life okay?"

"Life is life." She grabs a toy soldier from between the seat cushions and tosses it into a bin on the other side of the room.

"Good shot."

"I get practice."

"So…"

"We all have problems, right?" Her body language shifts, as if she's drawing inward. "I know you may think you've got the major share in this family, but you're not the only one."

"I never said—"

"Oh no?" She scoffs. "Sorry." She licks her lips then hugs herself. "It's just…"

"What's wrong?"

"What isn't wrong?" Jojo spits the words.

"Is it Damien?"

She laughs. It's not a pleasant sound.

"Well, is it? Is everything okay with him?"

"Oh, of course." Jojo kicks her feet onto the coffee table. "Everything is perfect with Damien. He's happy and in bliss, loving the way he drops in on his three lovely children several times a week. Loving his life of 'free love,' the openness and joy it provides."

"Several times a week?" I pause. "He moved out?"

"Oh no, he still lives with us. Our house is his primary

residence. He just lives other places too."

I sit straighter. "What are you talking about?"

She grabs a pillow and twists it between her hands, speaking as if she's talking to herself. "I thought it was so inspired, so enlightened when he talked to me about free love, about openness and how people were not meant to be forced into monogamy, how true love could only blossom when it was untethered, when people knew they were together solely because they wanted to be, not because they were legally or societally bound to be."

I consider her words. "So, he doesn't love you anymore?"

"Oh, he loves me." Her eyes squeeze tight. "He says he loves me more and more every day, every hour." She opens her eyes, shrugs. "He just loves another woman too and has slowly transitioned into splitting the physical representation of his love between the two of us."

"Splitting the?" I take in her words. She seemed so happy with her little brood of kids and with her 'one-loving' life, always smiling, always seeming at peace. "How long has this been going on?"

"It started when I was pregnant with Neveah and not in the mood for sex. I suspected, but thought, even if it were true, as soon as I was open for business again he'd choose me."

"I'm sorry."

She lets out a little laugh. "Me too. Pretty pathetic, huh? This situation I've found myself in."

"When are you going to leave?"

"Leave?" She laughs again. "I'm not leaving."

"But—"

"Tracey. I'm a twenty-four-year-old first-year college drop-out with three children and no source of income."

"Well, you're back in school now."

"For a diploma course."

"You can't stay with him."

"I can. What I need to figure out is how to stay with him without being pissed off all the time, without bitching out all over him."

"Jo."

"He loves me. He loves the kids. He'll keep providing for us."

I hesitate, not wanting to overstep but also not ready to see my sister succumb to this life. "You can't accept this. You deserve better than this. And Damien is obligated to provide for the children whether you're with him or not."

"We live in the shop. He couldn't even provide enough for us to live elsewhere."

"People figure it out. You'll figure it out. You'll get a job."

"And leave the children all day?"

"Women do it all the time."

"I'm not letting strangers raise my kids," she snaps. "Never seeing them because I'm working multiple jobs just to pay for the babysitters and some crummy apartment somewhere." Neveah hollers from the adjacent room. Jojo pushes off the couch and stomps away: no graceful, one-with-the-earth walk tonight. She returns, Neveah in her arms.

"Mom and Dad will help. You could even move in with them."

Jojo yanks down her shirt, then, as if realizing her forcefulness, slows, and gently guides the baby to latch on. She keeps her voice even and calm. "Oh yes, fess up to yet another way in which I'm a failure? No thanks."

"You're not a failure."

"You just don't get it." Jojo grits her teeth. "I'm not you, okay? I can't just adhere to everything they want and expect from me. I have to live my own life. I always thought it was nature's cruel joke: You should have been their real child. I'm the outcast."

Her words hit like a punch. "You're not. And I'm…If

Mom knew she'd have you she never would have bothered with me."

Jojo stares at me and I stare right back. Neither of us saying a word. At last Jojo sits back on the couch. "Bother with you?"

"Well, yeah." I ease back from the armrest, creating more distance between us. "You're the daughter she wanted, the child she tried for all of those years. Getting me? Well, I was just the consolation prize."

"That's shit."

"What?"

"It's shit, Tracey. You're just as much their kid. You're the one they're always bragging about, the one they're proud of. Mom was always doing things to show you how special you were."

"Yeah, to *show* me, because she didn't want me to see how unspecial I was compared to you."

"This is stupid." Jojo looks away from me. "It's like we're children again."

I hold my breath before speaking. "When I was eight or nine Mom had some girlfriends over, talking, laughing. One of them must have asked something about the adoption or having you or, well," I look away from her, "Mom said it was cliché, really, all those years everyone said stop trying, relax, it'll happen, and it infuriated her. But then at last they found me, they relaxed, I was their child, I made them parents. And then," I pause, "her voice changed, she sounded so elated, so satisfied. 'And then,' she said, 'it happened. Our little miracle.'" I look at Jojo and shrug. "You were their little miracle. I enabled them to relax enough so that their miracle could happen."

Jojo looks to the floor, her lips pressed together and her brow furrowed. "She shouldn't have said that. I'm sure she didn't mean it like that."

"Well, that's what she said. It's something you don't forget."

Jojo adjusts Neveah then returns her gaze to me. "That conversation at the birthday party, about you remembering…you mentioned it once when we were younger, but you never really talked about it much beyond that. Did you think about your birth family a lot?"

I nod.

"And you were older so…She, your birth mom, she raised you, started to raise you anyway."

I nod again. "Shit." Jojo shakes her head. "I couldn't imagine giving away one of mine, especially after holding them. After feeding them and changing them and seeing them smile." She gazes at Neveah, sucking away. "They make me crazy, but to let any of them go?" She raises her gaze. "That's messed up."

An understatement. "It is what it is. Something I have to live with."

"No. If I were you, I'd find your mother, just to yell in her face, to tell her what a crap move that was and demand an answer as to why she did it."

I hesitate, but then the words burst out of me. "I'm going to find her."

Jojo's eyebrows raise.

"Not to yell in her face. I want to learn about my medical history."

"Is something wrong?"

"Maybe." I take a breath. Of all my family, Jojo is the last one I thought I'd tell first. "I'm not sure. It would just be good to know about it."

Jojo waits as if she's expecting me to continue, but I'm not ready, especially not to her with all her unplanned children. "Do Mom and Dad know?"

"That I'm going to meet her? No. Don't tell them either. Maybe I'll tell them when I get back or," a sliver of fear weaves through me, "I'm not sure."

"You should tell them. They'd want to know."

"Dad would want to know. Mom would be frightened

she'd never see me again, that I'd make this woman and whomever she's connected to my new family."

"That's probably true." Jojo grins. "Proof she loves and wants you."

I let out a small chuckle. "I know she loves me. That's not the issue, it's just..." A puff of air escapes my lips. "Never mind. Don't mention it, all right?"

"Yeah, for sure." Jojo adjusts Neveah. "Wait. When you get back from where?"

"England."

"England!"

We chat for almost an hour more. It may be the longest conversation I've had with my sister since I moved out. It may be the longest ever. She's coarse at times, more like the Jojo I grew up with, who spoke what she thought and anyone else's opinion be damned, the Jojo I've hardly seen since Damien entered her life. As I'm at the door, I question this. "So, the language, the...you know...non-Zen-ness? What's that about? I thought you were this new peaceful, positive spirited woman."

She laughs, a loud guffaw, that makes Neveah whimper. "It's all an act. It wasn't an act at first, of course," she jostles Neveah back into slumber, "and yeah, meditation can be good, when I'm calm the children are calm, but really," she leans against the wall as I put on my sweater, "sometimes it feels good to cuss, to express what you feel instead of holding it in, to let your anger live rather than seeing it as...as unenlightened or something. And living with Damien..." Her voice trails off.

I hug her, Neveah sheltered between us. "I understand."

"Will I see you again before your trip?"

"Probably not."

She hugs me once more. "Go give 'er hell."

CHAPTER THIRTEEN

The morning of my trip I stretch in bed, the realization of it sinking into me: I'm going to England. I'm going to meet my birth mother. Adrian, who stayed the night, stirs under the covers. I roll over to make my way out of bed, but his hand captures me. He draws me toward him and cradles me, spoon style.

"Not yet."

"I need to get ready. We have to be at the airport in a few hours."

He groans, "Then especially not yet," and holds me tighter. I settle into his arms, enjoying the warmth and feeling of safety. The security. I close my eyes and let the sensation wash over me. At this moment, I need all the security I can get. I drift back to sleep and am awakened by the alarm a short time later.

I squirm in his arms until I'm completely turned and gazing at his face—squished into the pillow and streaked with sleep lines. "Now may I leave?"

One eye squints open and his lips upturn. "I suppose. But wasn't that extra few minutes worth it?"

"Completely." I lean in for a closed-mouthed kiss then push myself out of bed. I stretch my arms high above my head, my torso side to side, and reach for my toes.

"Do it again."

I turn to see Adrian propped up in the bed, grinning at me.

"The whole thing?"

He nods. I do. As I rise from touching my toes, his hands grasp my hips. He draws me back to the bed. "Morning breath," I squeak, only letting the corner of my mouth open. He holds me tighter. "I'll let you go, only if you promise it's for us both to brush our teeth and get back into that bed."

"But the flight."

"We have two hours before we have to leave. You're packed. Shower quick. We'll pick up breakfast."

"Well…"

"And I don't even know when you'll be back." He pulls me tighter to him and I nod my agreement. "To the bathroom."

We hustle to the bathroom and brush our teeth beside each other, grinning into our reflections with white, frothy smiles, then gargle. He ushers me back into the bedroom and pushes me onto the bed. He crawls above me, slowly, his movements reminding me of a tiger, then leans in. He stops an inch above my face and lifts his fingers to caress the hair falling along my cheek. "I'll miss you."

"I'll miss you too."

He kisses my nose. "I wish I could be there with you. This trip will be monumental."

"No expectations, remember?"

"Right. Either way," he smiles, "promise me you won't fall in love with a handsome Brit like Autumn did."

I want to tell him. I should tell him. Falling in love with anyone else would be impossible. I've already fallen, hard. Instead, I simply grin as our lips meet.

AS THE PLANE TAXIS OFF I grip the armrest and close my eyes.

"It's all right, honey." The woman beside me taps my arm. "You've never flown before?"

I release my grip. "Not often. But it's not the flying I'm worried about."

She tilts her head, seeming to indicate I continue.

"I'm travelling to meet my mother. My birth mother."

"Oh!" She makes a tut-tut noise. "Well, that is something to be nervous about. She know you're coming?"

I shake my head, surprised and pleased that I blurted this out to a stranger.

"Well, that is something indeed." She pauses, then laughs. "Clutch away!"

I laugh as well, but let my hands rest in my lap. My mind travels back to the conversation I had with my parents a few days ago. They seemed eager and excited that I'd asked to talk to them via Skype rather than on the phone. I didn't know whether I'd reveal the truth of my trip or not. When I mentioned England, that I'd be visiting Autumn, travelling with her, my father's face expressed excitement, approval. My mother's was less supportive, especially when she found out I hadn't booked a return ticket. 'But you're coming back,' she said, concern leaking into her voice. 'You won't stay there indefinitely like Autumn did.'

I assured her I would be back in time for the Fall term at school.

'And Adrian,' she clasped her hands, 'he's not going with you? Isn't that a little odd? The relationship's so new. Do you think it's wise to be travelling without him?'

I did not mention my birth mother. I might not ever. But Dad should know. He'll want to know.

WHEN I ARRIVE AT HEATHROW airport, with it' high ceiling, glass walls, and mass of people, a sense of overwhelm floods me. Everyone seems to know exactly where they're going, exactly why they're here. They speed by me. I press forward, my gaze checking and rechecking the signs until I catch a glimpse of Autumn's smiling face, her arm waving excitedly.

I clutch on to her then step back, laughing off my eagerness. Jakob greets me with a hug.

"How are you feeling?" Autumn rubs her hand along my shoulder.

"Good. Great." I grab my suitcase handle. "What a fabulous place."

"Isn't it?"

In the car Autumn chats about what's outside the window and what I've yet to see. I learn I'll be staying with Jakob's family, the Andrevs, as both Autumn and Jakob's flats are too tiny for comfort.

"That will change in the fall." Autumn grins back at me. "We're moving in together. We found a great place a short walk from the restaurant. I wish I could show you it, but we can't get in until September."

"That's amazing. So great. Congratulations."

Autumn beams. It is amazing. I try to calm my fears with this thought: A couple of years ago Autumn never thought her life could hold joy again, never thought she'd love again, and out of something so unbelievably horrible, joy has arrived. Maybe something good can come out of my pain. Maybe.

"So," I lean forward, "are you sure the Andrevs will be okay with me staying there? They don't even know me. You must have a couch, Autumn. I'd be happy to—"

"No, no." Jakob interrupts. "They're perfectly happy."

"Besides," Autumn laughs, "I'll be staying there with you. Poor Stefan will be positively flooded with estrogen."

"My father's pretty used to estrogen." Jakob laughs. "He won't mind."

The house reminds me of a book I used to read as a child—an old lady lives with two little girls, who are actually dolls. The house is gabled and surrounded by trees. Ivy runs up its outer walls and the garden is full and well maintained, though slightly wild, as if the gardener is letting nature take its course. As we walk up the path to the door, the scent reminds me of fireflies and dreams. Odd.

The house is equally as quaint inside as out, and it's clear a family lives here. Pictures and paintings line the wall, a backpack hangs on a coat hook, and an array of shoes are stacked neatly on a rack.

A young girl somewhere between the ages of fifteen and seventeen appears before us. Her smile is shy but welcoming. She seems willowy, as if a strong gust of wind could carry her away, yet an inner strength resonates from her frame. She hugs Autumn, kisses Jakob, then turns to me.

"Amalia." I extend my hand.

She grins and hugs me. "It's nice to meet you, Tracey. Welcome to our home."

"I'll take your bag up to your room." Jakob pauses. "Want to see it?"

"I'll give her a tour." Amalia turns to me. "Do you want to see the house?"

"Sure."

She leads me through the living room and kitchen, then toward the glass doors leading to the backyard. I ask a question here and there, comment on the grandfather clock, the plethora of books scattered about, and a family portrait.

"Wasn't my mother beautiful?" Amalia gazes at the painting, her voice wistful.

"You look like her."

She blushes. "She was more beautiful." We head up the stairs. "So you're a teacher? What do you teach?"

"English and Art History."

She pauses her step to look back at me. "You're in the right place."

I go to speak then close my mouth, shocked. Somehow in all the planning and concern around this trip I missed that fact. Even when planning the things I would do and see with Autumn and Eloise, their focus was on sights, the nightlife, the concerts, while my focus was on my birth mother. But Amalia is right. In University I dreamt of visiting England, seeing the sights that inspired the poets and authors I love, seeing first and the works of art I'd studied. "You're right." I laugh. "I'm exactly in the right place." Mentally, I rearrange some of the events and sightseeing Autumn plans for me.

"Who's your favourite poet?"

"My favourite?" We reach the landing and I hesitate, searching for an answer. "I don't know. I've had different favourites at different times. It depends. Whoever speaks to me at a certain point in life I suppose."

Amalia nods. "I get that." She shows me her father's room, Emily's, and Jakob's old room, where Autumn will be staying. "Right now, I'm a little in love with Wordsworth."

"He's a good love to have."

"Therefore let the moon/ Shine on thee in thy solitary walk;/ And let the misty mountain winds be free/ To blow against thee." Amalia takes a step away from me, as if embarrassed.

"Tintern Abbey."

Her face erupts in a smile. "My farfar and I used to memorize poetry…well, he already had most of it memorized, but I'd memorize it and then quote it, he almost always knew what it was."

"He passed a couple of years ago, didn't he? I'm sorry for your loss."

She smiles this weak, sad little smile, "My dear, dear friend," then waves me on, seemingly waving off her grief at the same time. We head up the steps. "My class went to Tintern Abbey a couple of years ago. It was a little disappointing: not like the painting. All of the vines were gone. It's for preservation." She glances back. "The vines were destroying the rocks. But it was still beautiful, haunted almost. A couple of the girls in choir sang these Gregorian chants. It wasn't arranged, they just did it. It was," she pauses, "a rare moment."

"Sounds wonderful."

"This is my room." Amalia pushes open the door. I step into a space I can't imagine many of my students would have. It's pristine. Prints of paintings and poetry line the walls. A large print of *The Lady of Shallot*, with Tennyson's poem printed on it, hangs above her bed.

"She left the web, she left the loom./ She made three paces through the room,/ She saw the water-lily bloom,/ She saw the helmet and the plume,/ She look'd down to Camelot." Amalia looks to me. "Isn't it beautiful?"

"It is."

"I can hardly get through it without tearing up. So tragic."

I nod, then gesture to the walls. "Who needs wallpaper."

She stands against a wall, her hand trailing over one of the papers. "I started it when I was memorizing to impress Farfar. It made it easier. Now it's a habit and," she purses her lips, "a comfort."

"It must be amazing to have all of these words surround you."

She looks at me, an odd but approving expression on her face. "It is." She steps toward me. "I lied to you, you know. Earlier."

"You lied?"

"Well," her head tilts back and forth in a fluid little bob, "sort of. I knew what you taught. I didn't need to ask. I had already asked Autumn."

"Oh." I laugh. "Okay."

"Come. Your room is next." The room is dark, with a slanted ceiling and wood panelling against the walls. Well, most of the walls. One is taken up with a floor to ceiling bookshelf, stocked full. "This is officially the reading room. But also the guest room." She motions to the shelf. "Feel free to read anything you like." Amalia sits gently on the trunk at the foot of the bed. "So, you're here to find your birth mother?"

I nod.

"And you've never met her?"

"I have." The reading chair in the corner looks inviting. I settle into it. "She took care of me until I was a little over two. I don't remember her, though. Just images. Flashes. A feeling."

"I hardly remember my mom." Amalia stands. "We should get back down to the others. It's exciting that you're getting to meet her. Are you scared?"

My gaze falls to the dark, curlicued carpeting then back up to Amalia. "Yes, I am."

"It's wonderful what you're doing." She pauses before heading down the stairs and glances back at me. "I bet she'll love you."

Love me? It's a thought I've not let myself consider.

Downstairs, Jakob and Autumn sit in the living room with who I imagine is Jakob's sister, Emily. She rises, a broad, gap-toothed smile on her face. She's beautiful. An aura of energy seems to shimmer around her. Her hair and eyes are dark brown, like Jakob and Amalia's, but where Amalia's and Jakob's fall in waves, Emily's is tightly curled. Her hand shakes as she reaches out to me. I grasp it, and she pulls me in for a hug. "It's so nice to meet you. Autumn told us why you're here. It's amazing."

"Thank you for letting me stay." I sweep my gaze to reach all the Andrevs. "It means a lot. It will make all of this so much easier."

"Our pleasure." Emily's smile is warm. "Autumn is family, and she says you're her family, so while you're here, you're ours too."

CHAPTER FOURTEEN

Over the next several days, I see the sights of London. At Amalia's request, she takes on the role of my official tour guide, which works out well as Emily is busy with her studies, Jakob has the restaurant and, although Autumn insists she would fit me in, she's clearly busy with her new business. It works out well for me too, as I doubt Autumn would get the kind of joy and excitement Amalia gets from showing me the sights. We spend an entire day at the National Gallery and almost as long at the British Museum, as well as an assortment of other galleries and sights Amalia insists I see.

On the evening before our trip, we settle in the backyard with tea and biscuits, a quintessentially British experience for me, and chat around the cast iron fire pit. Autumn, Emily, and Jakob tell me all about their trip visiting the Andrev's relatives, the Lombardi's, in Italy. Autumn has told me much of it before, but Jakob's impression of his grandfather and the tales he tells of living there as a boy are brand new. When I ask what cut the trip short their animation fades, which transitions the conversation toward Farfar's, and then Emily's, Parkinson's disease.

"That's part of why I'm here," I say. "To know if something like that is waiting for me."

Emily reaches forward to stoke the fire. Her hand shakes as she brings it back to pick up her cup of tea. She turns to me. "It can be good to know the time bombs that may be ticking away in your DNA, but it can also be somewhat debilitating," she glances to Jakob and Amalia, "not knowing when or if your life may change forever, but always, under the surface, expecting it to."

"Is that how you feel?" I direct my gaze toward Jakob and Amalia. "Like you have a time bomb ticking inside of you."

Jakob shrugs. "Sometimes. Emily's and Farfar's—it's the LRRK2 gene."

I squint my nose at him, indicating I'm not familiar.

He smiles. "I won't get into details, save to say mutations in this gene are a lot more likely to cause Parkinson's that seems to have a stronger genetic link than the disease being environmental or simply from unknown causes."

"Okay."

He stretches his legs out and drapes his arm over the side of his chair, letting his fingers interlace with Autumn's. "So, it means we already know we might get the disease. We could get tested, find out if we have the gene mutation, which would mean the chance was greater, but it still wouldn't mean we'd ever actually get Parkinson's. And years could be wasted in fear."

"So, you're saying…"

"I don't know." He chuckles. "I guess I'm saying, yeah, I might have a time bomb ticking inside me, or I might not. I try to think of it as little as possible. If it goes off, it goes off. If it doesn't and I spend my life worrying about it, trying to mentally prepare for it, instead of living, that could be the bigger tragedy."

"It would not be the bigger tragedy," says Emily.

Jakob looks to her, his eyebrows gather, a pained expression across his face. "No, you're right. That's not what I meant. But it would be a tragedy too."

Emily looks to the fire.

"But," says Amalia, her voice barely audible, "knowing the possibility is good too. It means we know the signs, what to look for. If it weren't for Farfar, it could have been years before the doctors suspected what Emily's initial symptoms meant, years she would have been getting progressively worse, rather than getting treatment."

"True as well," says Jakob.

"So you know what you know," I look to Jakob, "but you're not going to learn more."

"I'm not."

"I might." Both Emily and Jakob's heads turn toward Amalia.

"Really?" Emily leans toward her sister.

"I think so." Amalia looks between her siblings. "When I'm eighteen. Then I can get the test, without approval, if I want to."

Jakob sits up out of his reclined position. "You would want that hanging over you?"

"It's already hanging over me." Amalia's voice is stronger now. "And I've looked into it. If I'm tested and they know I have the mutation, this stronger possibility, then they can start testing and researching me sooner. Learn from me…if I do end up getting it. They'll maybe know even earlier signs or something and—"

Jakob cuts her off. "And you want to live a life of tests and evaluations and—"

"I want to live a life that may help prevent other families from living through this. That may let our future children not live through this."

Jakob grins. "You're pretty impressive you know, little sister. A stronger person than me."

Amalia lets out a similar but smaller grin. "Maybe."

"It's a lot to think about." My head reels with the news that may be awaiting me, the time bombs I haven't even yet considered.

"You may learn you come from the healthiest stock of people in existence," says Autumn, the only one here who knows the specific medical history I'm looking for. "You may learn you have nothing to worry about."

"Here's hoping," I say.

"Absolutely." Jakob places another log in the fire. It crackles and spits. Moments later the flames roar up around it.

AS WE DRIVE TOWARD The Cotswolds, the city melts away into rolling green hills and rock fences. Sheep graze in the fields and massive lone trees mark the landscape. The Andrevs' house seemed picturesque, as out of a storybook, but the houses here transport me to another time and life. They're built with a tan brick stone. Cotswold stone, Jakob tells me, a local limestone. Many have thatched roofs that remind me of a Jane Austen movie.

"Are you sure you want to go today?" asks Jakob as we get closer. "We could settle into our rooms, maybe do a little driving tour. We could even visit Oxford, then tom—"

"Don't try to dissuade her." Autumn swats his shoulder. "We'll have plenty of time to tour Oxford."

"I wasn't." Jakob glances into the rearview mirror, his gaze connecting with mine. "Really, I just didn't want you to feel rushed."

"Thank you." The scene out my window calms me. Anyone who lives here can't be too awful. "We'll settle into the hotel and then I'll go."

"All right." Jakob follows the signs for Charlbury. We pass a pond full of swans and make our way up a hill. The GPS tells me we're less than two minutes away. Here, the houses aren't quite as picturesque. Most are row houses, but still nicer than any back home. We're moments from the Inn, which means we're minutes from the house where I'll find my mother. I take a deep breath then release it shakily. Autumn grasps my hand and squeezes. Jakob pulls past the

Bull Inn and into a parking lot around back. The car gives a little sputter and groan.

"We'll go in, find our rooms, then everything is at your pace."

I nod at Autumn's words. Everything is at my pace. I'm in control. Until I knock on her door, and then my control vanishes.

The woman at the Inn's front desk reminds me of a hobbit. She's short and stocky, kind and smiling. She shows us to our rooms. I've opted to share with Emily and Amalia. Autumn offered to share with me, for moral support, but she's already doing enough. Stealing her away from her boyfriend for the weekend would be a bit much. The thought brings Adrian to mind. If he were here, he could walk with me to my mother's house. Hold my hand. Stand up the street or hide behind a corner while I walked to her door, so I'd know he was there, rooting for me, believing I can do this. "Food would be good."

Amalia and Emily look over from hanging up their clothing. "Are you hungry?" asks Emily. We just stopped for snacks about an hour ago.

"Not at all." I laugh. "But it would probably be good to do this on a full stomach."

"The Rose and Crown is across the street." Emily lays the sweater she's holding back in her baggage. "Let's go there."

"Great." A thought jumps at me: It's a Friday night. It's a small town. My mother could be out for dinner. I could see her. Would I know her?

Amalia and Emily both stare at me. Emily's voice is cautious. Has she guessed my thoughts? I shake the stricken expression off of my face. "There's a dining room here, perhaps that would be better? They may have room service."

"No, no." I smile—confident, assured, or at least that's what I hope I portray. "The Rose and Crown sounds great."

The pub could be any British pub back home. If only I could tune out the accented voices surrounding me, I could pretend I'm a few blocks from my apartment, instead of a continent away, out for a night with friends, instead of out as an effort to delay the act of potentially altering my life forever. I scan the room. No one seems like they could be my mother, but my mother could be just about anyone. I glance at my skin, the tan hue so much darker than that of my family's. Is it her I get this colour from? My father?

A woman walks from the back of the room. Her hair is similar in colour to mine, as is her build. But she's too old. In the caseworker office just weeks ago I learned something new. My mother was eighteen when she had me.

Chat floats through the air, both from Autumn and the Andrevs, and the pub at large. It's not until about half way through the meal that I realize my fish and chips is delicious. The realization fades away almost as fast as it came and I eat the rest of the food without tasting it. I nod and answer direct questions, but that's it. Every new woman's voice filtering in and out of the pub makes my head snap to attention.

"What now?" Autumn asks once we've paid the bill.

I reign my focus in from a group of women who've just stepped through the door. Young women. Young enough, anyway. Now is not the moment to imagine my mother's face in every face I see. Now is the moment to be present, focused. "I meet her."

"You want me to—"

"Stay at the hotel. So when I come back, if…just stay at the hotel."

"Will do."

THE STREET HAS NO sidewalks, but the cars travel at an easy pace. Still, the brick wall to the right of me feels claustrophobic. When it disappears my breath comes easier. This is the street my mother lives on, the street she walks on.

Rosewood Cottage. I expect one of those thatched roof houses, set back from the road, flooded with flowers and vines, but the house isn't like that at all. Not even a cottage. What stands before me is an unimposing, semi-detached house, and though not the least charming place I've seen, it isn't quite postcard material. The front door looks new and doesn't quite suit the building. The lawn is well maintained. I walk past the property, in the hopes of getting a better view and to delay the inevitable. Chickens roam the backyard. My mother has chickens…my birth mother.

A car sits in the driveway, which means there's a good chance she's home or, at least, someone is. My mind flashes again to the other potential this trip holds: family. Will my sister open the door, my brother, my father? Her name hasn't changed in all these years so either she's not married, she's gotten married but hasn't changed her name, or she's been married this whole time. The final scenario is one I'd rather not entertain. Somehow, it's far worse to imagine my mother and father gave me away together. Not likely. Father unknown, said the caseworker. Or unreported. Same difference.

I stand in front of the house so long it must look suspicious. Yet, I can't move. My brain tells my legs to step forward. They don't. They won't. Then at last they do, as if of their own accord. I watch, shocked, as my hand knocks on the door.

Shuffles sound, the call of 'I'll get it,' in a woman's voice. If it's her, if she's home, she's not alone. The door opens.

My held breath whooshes out in a long burst. The woman could be me in twenty years. Her hair is lighter, her skin paler, but beyond that…

"Oh." Her face goes slack, then her eyes widen the way mine would. A little of my father—my birth father—exists in me. This much is clear. His melanin. That's what I have. The rest of me is pure her.

"Lydia, is it the Thai? I'm ravenous." Lydia turns at the sound of the male voice, a look of panic and uncertainty crosses her face. "No. It's, uh…" She turns back to me with a look of apology. "It's just…someone asking about a lost cat." Her expression falls, as if she's disappointed herself.

A lost cat?

She steps outside then closes the door behind her. I back away, needing to maintain my distance, feeling, if I touched her, if I got too close to her in any way, I may explode. This could have been my home. This could have been the walk I ran up and down countless times as a young girl. But no, she wasn't living here when I was eighteen. This couldn't have been my home, but her home could have been mine.

The male voice. The man, hungry for Thai. My father?

Lydia doesn't line up with the frazzled, hapless teenager I'd imagined. All these years I saw her as someone weak and frail, someone incapable of caring for a child, incapable of creating a solid home, a solid life.

Lies. This is a good neighbourhood, a beautiful, quaint looking house. I Googled her last night—for the first time. She has the epitome of a solid life, a plethora of letters after her name, all listed below the title: Associate Professor at Oxford. History of Art.

She stares at me as I stare at her, her face unreadable. At last a veneer of composure settles, almost bordering on disdain. "I thought you weren't going to come."

"What?"

"It's been twelve years. I thought if you wanted to find me you would have."

So she thought she was home free? Thought she could safely tuck that part of her life away? What do I say to that? How do I even—? "I didn't come for you." The words tumble from my mouth, and all of a sudden she's the one looking flabbergasted. "I came for your history. To learn about your genetics."

She takes a step closer to me, her hand raised. "Are you sick?"

"Maybe." I shuffle back, almost tripping over the stoop. "I'm not sure."

The hand rests on her heart, and in that motion, in the look that passes through her eyes, I see some part of her loves me or did at one point in time.

"Are *you* sick?" I ask. "Or, I mean. Do you have any diseases? Conditions."

"Diseases? No."

I lick my lips and debate turning and running to the Inn as fast as my legs will carry me. This is not the way I meant to do this. Diseases. She thinks cancer. She thinks multiple sclerosis. Not something as silent and visibly unobtrusive as PCOS or endometriosis.

"Lydia." The male voice yells. "You can't save the cat."

Again, that slightly terrified expression covers her face. "I'm healthy. I…I don't understand what you want."

"I just want to know—"

"Lydia." Noises from within.

"Listen." She steps forward, looks like she's about to grasp my arm, then pulls hers back. "He doesn't know. I never told him." She glances back as the door opens, then returns her gaze to me. "Play along. Please. It's his birthday."

A man's face and body appears. He's tall. Probably over six feet with bright reddish-brown hair, a strong, masculine face, and friendly eyes. My guess is he's several years older than my mother. My mother.

"You lost your cat?"

I nod.

"We were just chatting. She's uh…"

"Tracey."

My mother gasps—a small noise. "Tracey is new to the area. Tracey, this is Westin."

"Well, welcome to our little part of the world." Westin reaches out his hand. I hesitate a moment too long and then take it. His grasp is warm and strong. He doesn't know, and he's even fairer than Lydia. He is not my father. "I hope you find your cat."

"Thank you."

"I'll be in in a moment, darling."

Westin looks from Lydia to me, a question on his face, but it passes almost instantly. He waves and gives me a grin as he steps away.

"I don't know exactly what you want, but whatever it is, just, not tonight. Are you here? I mean, are you staying here, how long are you—"

"For the weekend at least."

"Good. And—"

"The Bull Inn."

"Okay." Her face, again, is unreadable. Is she happy, scared, excited, put off? "Tomorrow morning. Ten a.m. I'll be in the dining room. Can you, will you?" Stress. That I can read. She is most certainly stressed.

I make a sound that's an assent.

"Okay. Good. Great. Tomorrow then." She turns to the door, her hand on the knob as she looks back. "I'm sorry." And then she's gone.

Sorry? Sorry for what? For having me? For closing the door in my face? For giving me away? For it all? Again, I stand in front of the house longer than seems acceptable. Of all the scenarios I'd gone over in my mind of how this meeting would be, reality fulfils none of them. This is it. I can never go back to my life before this moment. No more wondering if my mother is a crack-whore, a senator, or any of the million other possibilities that existed before today. My mother is real. She's a woman in her late forties who lives with a man named Westin in a house called Rosewood Cottage. She's a woman who has gone back inside that house to wait for Thai, with the child she gave birth to standing in the street. My arms and legs feel wobbly, disjointed, but somehow they move, and I find myself back at the Inn several minutes later.

Autumn, Jakob, Emily, and Amalia say encouraging words as I rehash the brief encounter. They provide excuses: she was shocked, she didn't know what to say, it'll be better tomorrow, it was his birthday, and since he didn't know...

Adrian expects my call, but I can't talk to him. I want to talk to him, but if I hear his voice I'll turn into a sopping pile of tears and snot—not a state I can handle right now.

We have two hours left of sunlight so Jakob suggests we tour the countryside then settle in at the pub. Karaoke, he says, should give us all a laugh. I beg tiredness but to no avail. I'm ushered into the car.

At first I feel trapped. I want to break free, open the door and run, but the car's not my cage. My mind is. I try to focus on the world passing by, to let the rolling hills soothe my scattered thoughts. The soft colours of the world outside my window deepen as the sun sets lower into the horizon. The buildings, cast in silhouette, calm me. We pass structures that have existed since the 12th century. They remind me that in the scheme of things, in the history of mankind, what just happened with my mother is inconsequential. How many people have lived and loved and laughed and lost? Millions. Billions. How many people have felt what I'm feeling? Probably more than I realize. And they've gotten through it.

We slow for a family of ducks as they waddle across the road. Amalia oohs and ahhs at the ducklings. I try to have perspective; this first encounter with my mother could have gone worse. She didn't slam the door in my face. She didn't deny who she was. She seems like a decent woman. Decent enough anyway, but then why?

"Still up for Karaoke?" Jakob asks as we make our way back toward Charlbury.

"If everyone else is," says Autumn.

"Will they let me in?" Amalia.

"They should. They won't let you drink." Emily.

"If they don't, we can get some snacks, watch a movie." Jakob.

"Not on my account." Amalia.

Decent.

"Tracey."

She seems like a decent woman. She is an intelligent woman. Oxford. She has to be.

"Tracey."

She must be a woman of means. Woman of means —he means to raise a child, care for her. Has she always lived this life?

"Trac—"

"Yes, hmm?" Me.

"Karaoke?" Autumn.

"Sure." Me.

THE ROSE AND CROWN isn't crowded at quarter to ten the next morning. Lydia sits at a table against the far wall, her presence ruining my attempt to get there first, to have a chance to feel composed. She stands. "You're early."

"I didn't want to be late." I approach the table.

"It's a thirty-second walk."

I stare at her.

"Sorry, that sounded rude. I didn't mean to be rude." She pauses. "I'm flustered."

"You're—"

"Flustered. Yes. This is, this is unprecedented."

I laugh—a little laugh. "For me too."

She gestures to the table. "So I'm the first biological mother you've met?"

I laugh again.

"Is this okay?" She gestures to the table. "We could—"

"It's fine."

She sits. I sit.

"Are you here alone?"

I hesitate.

"In Charlbury, I mean."

"No. I'm here with some friends from London."

"London." She leans forward. "Do you live in England?"

I shake my head.

"What brings you here?"

I open my mouth, close it, open again. "You."

"Oh." She places her hands on the table, her lap, and back on the table. "Oh, okay."

Neither of us says a word. She adjusts the collar on her shirt. I reach for the menu. The waiter comes and we both order. He leaves.

"So, uh." She reaches for her fork, picks it up, then puts it back down. "You want your medical history or, uh, I mean my medical history?"

"Yes."

"What exactly? I mean I can't get records or anything. Not right now. I could call the doctor's on Monday. Do you have specific questions? You said you might have a disease." She holds my gaze. "Is it serious?"

"Not for me. Not…not likely anyway. I may be infertile."

"Oh."

"And…"

"And?"

It's stupid being here, doing this. So what if she has

endometriosis or PCOS or anything else? That doesn't change a thing for me. I have it or I don't and there's nothing knowing her history will change. I lower my head, wishing the floor would swallow me up. If she has one of these diseases, it raises my chances, but I'll still have to wait for an ultrasound. Most likely, I'll still have to try a year to conceive…I should have asked my doctor about that. Why am I here? What am I doing? I look up. Lydia tilts her head. Her expression curious, patient, terrified.

I'm here to meet my mother. I'm here to learn about possible diseases, not just fertility related, but really—I take a deep breath—I'm here to meet her. I'm here to ask her why…but not yet. "I, uh, my doctor thought if I knew your history, your mother's history, that may give us some answers, direct us in the right direction."

"Are you trying to conceive?"

"I'd like to, one day."

She wants to say something. Her face looks full of things unsaid. Does mine? It must. Part of me wants to curl up in her arms, the other part wants to throw the coffee the waiter brings me straight into her face. "So what would you like to know?"

"Do you have any fertility issues or reproductive problems?"

She twirls her spoon in her coffee, looking at it, and not me. "You came with no problems."

"And then?"

She looks up. "I had my tubes tied."

"You what?" I inhale sharply, the coffee I was about to sip scalds my throat as it sails down too fast. I cough and sputter. That's how much she despised me. That's how much she didn't want me. Having me made her swear off children forever.

"I had my tubes tied. I had painful periods. Quite painful sometimes. I assumed it was from the procedure. My gynecologist said it could be from the procedure, that I could have developed endometriosis, maybe even because of the procedure, that sometimes that happens. Eventually, years later, when the pain was affecting me too much, I had surgery to have the procedure reversed, and they did find endometriosis." She speaks calmly, almost as if she's talking about someone else's experience. "They also said with the scarring and damage it wasn't likely I would ever have children, anyway. I haven't. Not that I've tried. So, I'm not sure. I mean…" She taps her spoon on the rim of her cup. "I'm not preventing. There didn't seem a point and, well…I had or have endometriosis, but I don't know if it's because of genetics or the tubal ligation."

"Why did you—"

Her eyes crinkle. Her voice is even, but rawness lurks behind it. "It was so awful. I was so awful—a horrible mother, a horrible woman." She stops, her jaw trembles, but her voice stays even. "I gave my baby away…to strangers. I didn't believe I had a right to ever have a child again. I didn't believe I was capable. Deserving—"

"But why—"

"I was young. I felt so guilty. I couldn't imagine ever meeting you, sitting across from you and telling you I gave you up; I gave you up and then I went on to have a whole new family."

She doesn't understand. I rephrase the question, making sure I get it out in full. "No." My voice is less than even. Anger rages behind it. "Why did you give me up?"

CHAPTER FIFTEEN

"Oh." My mother, sitting across from me in this little pub in a part of the world I didn't know existed just weeks ago, bites her lip, and it's like looking in a mirror. "Why did I give you up? I was young." She looks young as she says the words. I can almost see the twenty-year-old she would have been, deciding to let me go. "I was alone. I didn't want to give you up."

Words. Just words. "Did someone force you?"

"No, no. It wasn't like that." Her back is rigid, her body posture expressing someone who is self-assured, in control, and yet it seems like inwardly she has collapsed. I wait for her to go on. "I didn't know what else to do."

"Keep your child? Not throw her away?"

"I didn't." She stops.

It doesn't matter the scenario, whether she had something arranged. She still got rid of me. I stare at her, waiting.

"Did you have a bad life? The family...were they?"

"I didn't go with the family you picked."

Now her body follows that inner collapse I had sensed. She slumps in her chair, her arms slack at her sides. "What?"

I explain to her the information I recently learned myself, tell her about my years in and out of doctor's offices and hospitals, the group home, the foster homes, the fear, the confusion, the wondering where my mommy was and why didn't she want me. She doesn't interrupt. She sits, seeming to absorb the information. I start angry, my words clipped and fast, but as I continue they slow, the bite to my voice lessens. "So no," I finish, "I didn't have a bad life or a bad family. They were good people. But they weren't my family. They weren't you."

"Were good—?"

"Are. They are good people."

She rubs her hands along her upper arms. "I've wondered every day. I've hoped you were okay. I've hoped you were happy."

I consider going into the years of teenage angst; the years of always trying to please, scared if I wasn't perfect people wouldn't want me; the years of lying to my closest friends. But what's the point? "I've had good times and bad times." The fight drains out of me. "I'm not unhappy."

She nods and averts her gaze. Her eyes look distant, empty.

"Are you happy?"

She draws her gaze back to me. "Same."

"Okay." The waiter returns with our food. I stare at it, amazed I'm expected to eat at a time like this.

She picks up her fork then sets it back down. "I'll try to explain. Do you want to know? Stop me if…" I keep silent. "I was seventeen when I got pregnant. It was terrifying. The father, he wasn't, he…it was inappropriate." She looks away. "That's an understatement. He was one of my father's work associates. A man with a wife and three children of his own. The oldest was in my class. My mother had died, and I was going through a hard time…it just…happened." She looks to her plate, pushes her scrambled eggs back and forth. "Of course when I got pregnant he denied it. He wanted nothing to do with me. Claimed it…uh, you weren't his. DNA testing wasn't a common thing back then, and I didn't know how to tell my father. Dad was so distraught over Mom." She takes a sip of orange juice, plays with the eggs again.

"I was almost finished high school and here I was,

pregnant. I had plans. Dreams. I wanted to go to University. I had all these plans." Her hand holding the fork freezes. "I tried. I really tried. I went to school part time. My father, he was so angry. So disappointed. Then he died. I'd been living with him. He'd been helping financially and watched you while I was at my night courses sometimes. But then he died, and I had no one, no one but you."

She gazes at me as if waiting for something—what, I don't know. Her gaze trails back to her eggs. "I was nineteen and all alone except for a baby who constantly needed me, and I was never enough, could never make her happy, and everything I wanted in my life, everything I'd worked for was vanishing before me. Even the possibility of one day fulfilling my dreams seemed to sink away into nothingness, like it could never resurface again." She makes a little choking sound then meets my gaze. "I loved you. I didn't blame you. I've always loved you. But you were sick all the time. You cried. You needed me every moment. I couldn't handle it. I couldn't do my studies." Her voice raises. "I failed out of two of my courses. I'd never failed anything. I started getting angry. Angry and tense. Angry at you. Angry at everything. I thought I might hurt you one day. It was terrifying, that thought. Some days I let you cry because I thought if I touched you, I'd smother you." A hand flies to her mouth. "I can't believe…I shouldn't be saying this. I never would have. I absolutely never would have. I was young and confused and—"

"Go on."

She gives me a sad smile, her shoulders popping up then falling. "I hated the person I was becoming, and I thought if I hate me, you'll hate me too." Her smile crinkles. "You probably do. But I just…I wanted better. Better for both of us and I had no idea how to give that. I didn't think I was capable of that and so," she holds the words before releasing them, "I gave you away."

"That's it?" I take my first bite of pancake, chew, then

continue. "You were young and alone and I cried a lot."

"Well—"

"No, no." I speak with detachment, like a reporter trying to get to the bottom of a story that doesn't affect her life. Part of me understands, part of me sees how rough it would have been. I can imagine myself talking to one of my students, to Jayden maybe—rambunctious, talented, an amazing future ahead of her—telling her adoption may be the best choice. But after the child was two years old? After the child had come to love her, after she'd become the child's whole world? It's different. So different. To send your baby away because she is sick, because she cried too much. I take another bite and chew fully to let the moments pass. "I expected something more dramatic. I expected you to be a drug addict, or to be raped, or…I don't know, on your deathbed and physically unable to take care of me."

"I'm sorry you thought those things. I'm sorry—"

"Anyway." I put on my professional, happy to please face. "I guess it is what it is. I might as well get your contact information and what medical history I can now." I pull a notebook from my purse. "I suppose I have no siblings." The words sting coming out…all those years of wondering, hoping—the nieces and nephews I'd almost started to love.

Her voice is soft. "Not through me. There's, well, the three your father had."

I stare at her a moment, shocked that piece of information didn't register earlier. I mentally shrug it off: too much to process for this moment. "So," I glance at the pad with my pen poised, "you said both of your parents died young. Causes?"

"Oh." Lydia looks as if I've slapped her. "My mother died of cancer. She was a smoker."

A shiver runs through me. I enjoyed that look, the modicum of pain I could deliver after the years of hurt she bestowed on me. But hearing the words about her mother, any enjoyment disappears into regret. That is not an easy death. "So. Cancer." My voice is softer now. "But not likely because of any genetic disposition?"

"No. Not likely. I was fifteen when we knew for sure, sixteen when...She'd been sick for a few years but as far as I know it was lung cancer from smoking."

"How old was she?"

Lydia hesitates. "Fifty. She had me late. Still, I guess she was young, wasn't she?"

I swallow. "So you didn't have your mother around for most of your life either."

"No." Lydia finally takes a bite of food. "I didn't."

"Any brothers and sisters?"

"No."

So no cousins. No kindly aunts and uncles for me to meet. No family for Lydia. She was almost as alone as I am...more, I suppose. "Do you know why your parents only had you, and later in life?"

"I do not."

"They never mentioned any kind of struggle with conception?"

"No."

"And your father," I'm careful to keep my voice sensitive this time, "you mentioned he passed as well."

"Yes."

"The cause?"

She sighs, starts to say something, then stops. "A heart attack."

"I'm sorry."

Her eyes look glassy, dull. Her chin trembles. "It was a long time ago. We weren't exceptionally close."

"And he was?"

"Forty-seven."

"Wow." I set down my pen. "He was what, seven years younger than your mom. That's unusual."

"I guess it is." She rubs her arm.

"Do you know—"

"I think stress was the main cause."

I was going to ask if she knew how they met, what their story was, but I shouldn't be surprised at her answer. I'm the one who established a business mentality here. I almost re-ask the question, but I can't. "Okay. So, his weight, diet, general lifestyle?"

"Pretty good. Well, he maybe could have eaten better, but he ran regularly, lifted weights. He didn't smoke."

"So it could have been genetic factors too then."

"It could have." She sucks in and then releases a long breath.

"And…my father…do you know?"

"I haven't kept in touch with him, at all. I never even discussed the adoption with him. His name isn't on your birth certificate."

"Is he alive?"

"I don't know." She hesitates. "I could find out."

"You never told him? You never…what if he would have taken me?"

"He wouldn't have, Tracey. He denied you were even his. No support, no nothing. I'm sorry, I don't—"

"Your grandparents?" I ask, my voice clipped.

"I really don't know much about my grandparents, but I'm sure I could find some records somewhere or something if you really want."

Do I? Does it matter? "Okay." My voice is barely audible, but she hears me, or lipreads, or something. We stare at each other. I stand. The table shakes and my glass tilts, tumbles, the liquid spreads out. I right the glass and wipe the juice, glad only a sip or two was left. "Thank you so much. I really appreciate it." I place my sopping napkin on my barely eaten meal. "I'll, umm," I grab one of Autumn's business cards, flip it over, and scribble on the back. "Here's my email address. Please get in touch if you manage to get any more information for me. That would be wonderful. Even…even maybe, I don't know, family history stuff?" A yearning pulses through me, a desire to know these nameless people I came from. "I'd really appreciate it."

"Where are you going?" Still seated, she looks up at me.

"My friends. They wanted to go to Oxford, tour, you know. I've probably kept them waiting long enough."

She stands. "I'll go with you. I teach there. I can give you a great tour, get you into places you wouldn't get into otherwise."

"Oh." I step away from the table, surprised at her eagerness. I want to stay, I want to walk away never to see or talk to her again, I want to turn back the clock. "There's five of us."

"That's no problem."

"They may already have their own plans."

Lydia steps toward me. "I get that and I get, well…I won't try to be your mom or anything, I promise. I just thought since you're here, since…" She smiles. "Maybe we could spend some time together."

"What about the guy—the redhead?"

"What about him?"

"Won't he wonder?"

She shrugs, her head tilted to the side. It's a motion I've seen myself do in pictures, in home videos. "We talked about it. We had a long talk about it. I'm sorry about yesterday."

"I really need to go."

"I acted so badly. It's just Westin and I had some troubles early on. He wanted more children. I was young enough back then but refused to try. Eventually I told him about my tubes, about the damage it caused, but I never told him the real reason. I never told him about you."

My body tenses. I know what it is to tell the man you care about that you're broken…or at least you may be. I tug my purse against my shoulder. "I really have to go."

"Take my card." She sticks her arm out, her hand

floating in mid-air until I pull the card from her fingers. "Ask your friends, okay? See if they'd want me to take them around. If they don't, that's fine. Just promise me you'll ask."

I drop the card in my purse, promising nothing. I motion to the waiter for my bill.

"No." She laughs this little, somewhat self-deprecating laugh. "That's the least I can do."

I start to shrug, feel my head tilt, then stop and straighten. "Thank you." Again, I give my best smile. She smiles back. Does mine look as fake?

※

MY HANDS SHAKE AS I try to slide my key into the hotel room door. It opens before I've managed to undo the lock. Autumn draws me in and sets me down on the bed. All four of them are here. All four pairs of eyes focus on me.

"How was it?" asks Amalia.

"I got some information, some...she'll try to get me more."

"No, I mean how was meeting her, really meeting her. How is she? What's she—"

"Amalia," says Emily. "Let her breathe."

"She's nice, I guess. Water? Is there any—" Autumn hands me a bottle from the mini-fridge and I gulp half of it before speaking again. "She wants to go to Oxford with us, give us a tour. She works there."

"Really?" Jakob leans forward. "That'd be great."

Now Emily chastises Jakob.

"I didn't say yes. I didn't..." The room blurs and Autumn's arms surround me as I find myself sobbing into her shoulder. Ugly, nasty sobs that must make my eyes red and my skin blotchy. My chest heaves and shakes. I try to push away but she holds me tight. "I'm sorry," I choke.

"Really, I — Autumn shushes me and I give into the tears. When I've settled down, I survey the four of them—three practically strangers—and have no idea what I'm supposed to say or do next.

"So," Jakob's voice is tentative, "what do you want to do now?"

My mouth hangs open a little. I close it, then speak. "I don't know."

"Do you still want to tour? We don't have to, of course."

"No, no." I shake my head. "That's what we should do. I can't let you all sit here in this room the whole day."

"That's not even an issue." Autumn waves her hand. "We'll do whatever you want to do. Or I can stay here with you while the others go."

Old habits die hard. I want to stay in this room, huddled under a blanket and feeling sorry for myself, but that's not what Tracey Sampson does. Not at all. Tracey Sampson is pleasant. She smiles while, inside, parts of her are dying. She pleases, knowing that if she does people won't leave her. And I do not want these people to leave me. I put on a grin and wipe the tear-oaked strands of hair from my cheeks. "Touring Oxford sounds perfect. The perfect way to take my mind off of…of…well, everything."

Emily shifts, crossing one leg over the opposite one. "Are you sure this morning is something you want to take your mind off of?"

"Absolutely."

Autumn squeezes my shoulder and rises. Emily, Jakob, and I do the same. Amalia remains seated, her face focused across the room, her shoulders tensed. We all look at her. Her head snaps up. "This is ridiculous."

"What?"

"I don't know why you all are pussyfooting around—"

"Amalia." Emily hushes.

"No, seriously." Her gaze travels over all of us then lands on me. "This is a balls-up situation, I know. But deal with it.

She is your mother. Your *mother*. And she wants to spend time with you. You're here, you may never be here again, and all you want to do is get information about people who are already dead?"

"Amalia!"

"Stop it." Amalia looks to her sister, then back to me. "You're a teacher, right? You're supposed to be smart. So be smart. And if you can't think of it that way think of the story, the story of your life. Because that's what this is. What kind of character are you going to be? Someone who gives up, who turns away right at the point she has a chance to make a grand choice? The protagonist of a novel no one would ever read because the heroine's a scared-shitless coward?"

"Amalia!"

"No." Her gaze stays hard on mine, unwavering. Unnerving. Embarrassing. "Your mom messed up, royally, and I'm not saying be her best friend, I'm not saying erase the past, but spend the afternoon with her. Do that. Be the person you'd want to read about."

All the heroes and heroines I've loved and admired race through my mind. It's somewhat ludicrous to think of this situation in those terms, but then again, maybe not. Maybe Amalia has a point. I'm here. The room seems to breathe with my breath. Lydia's here. My chest tightens. She wants me. Or, at least, she wants to spend a few hours with me. Anger bubbles amidst the pain, the confusion. I want to say no. I want to hurt her the way she hurt me. I want to make her think I couldn't care less whether she's alive or dead. But what kind of heroine would that make me? A petty one? Maybe. A lying one? Definitely. Because I'm not disinterested. I care. I want to walk with her, listen to her tell stories, soak her in. That one gesture, her offering to show us around, made me feel less like an orphan than I ever have. "Okay."

"What?" Autumn steps toward me.

"Okay. Let's call her. If she's still available, let's let her show us Oxford."

CHAPTER SIXTEEN

With the hotel phone pressed to my ear, the line rings once, twice, three times. As I'm about to pull the receiver away, Lydia's voice stops me.
"Tracey?"
I hesitate. "How did you know it was me?"
"Call display. The Bull Inn."
"Right."
Silence.
"Are you okay, or? Is there—"
"I was wondering if the offer is still open to go to Oxford with my friends and me." I speak calmly, as if this is anyone on the line—a casual acquaintance, an old professor I've just bumped into. "I thought it would be nice to spend a bit more time with you, and Jakob, one of the people I'm with, would love an insider's view of the city."

The sound of her swallowing makes its way to my ear. "That would be great. Wonderful. What time?"

"We're ready to leave any time. The car only fits us, though. Can you bring your own?"

"Yes, absolutely." She's quiet again, and I'm not sure if I'm supposed to speak, what I should say. "Would it be all right if Westin came? He works there too, could show you some places I couldn't."

I switch the phone from one ear to the other. "Um, sure, I mean…It sounded like I was a sore spot or…"

"No, no. He just didn't know. It was his birthday, and I

didn't think it was quite the time to tell him, with you standing right there. Those troubles I mentioned, we're okay now. I'm not sure if he'd want to come, but he might. I could ask."

"Okay. Ask."

"Okay. Thirty minutes? Would that be good? I can be there in thirty minutes."

"Sure. Yes. Good. Great."

"Thank you, Tracey."

"Pardon?"

"For calling, for…thank you."

"Okay, bye," a part of me wants to say Mom, to know what it feels like when said to someone who truly is my mother, "Lydia."

THE FIVE OF US ARE outside the Inn in twenty-seven minutes. One minute later Lydia and Westin pull up. He hops out of the car, big and brawny. Somehow it didn't register yesterday: this is a gorgeous man. He could be the father of that red-headed heart-throb from the Scottish Highlander TV series. When he smiles, he's even more appealing. He shakes everyone's hand, coming to me last. Me, he hugs. "I guess all those hours I lay in bed worried about that poor lost cat were pointless, huh?"

"What?"

He rubs his hands on my shoulders. "I'm teasing, lass." He leans back as if assessing me. "But perhaps this isn't quite the time for teasing?"

"Umm, no. It's fine." I wave my hand in front of my face, dismissing my awkwardness. "As far as I know, all the cats in Charlbury are just fine."

He grins. In different circumstances, I would really like this man. Maybe I do. "I should have known." His voice has a laugh to it. "You're the spitting image of her." He knocks his fist to the side of his head. "It's this thick skull of mine, and that combined with a raging appetite…I was just dying for Thai." He laughs again.

I nod and scratch a non-existent itch on my arm.

"What do you teach?" asks Jakob.

Westin turns to him. "Medieval history."

Jakob wears a look of awe. "My undergrad was in History. My thesis was on the black plague and the consequence of trade."

"Ahh," Westin's eyes seem to twinkle, "that's a little vague. What specifically…"

The two chat until Jakob interrupts their conversation to ask if Autumn minds driving so he can hop in with Lydia and Westin. She doesn't.

"Would you like to join us as well?" Lydia turns to me.

"No, that's all right. I'll stick with Autumn."

Lydia smiles and steps into her car. On the drive into Oxford, Autumn, Amalia, and Emily talk about things unrelated to me and this odd situation we're in. Amalia, who will be seeing Oxford for the first time, chatters about C.S. Lewis and J.R.R. Tolkien and Lewis Carroll, expressing her excitement about walking the streets they walked and, hopefully, she nudges Emily, having a pint in the same pub the Inklings used to gather in.

"The Eagle and Child?" says Emily.

"Yes. The Eagle and Child." Amalia sighs. "Oh, to have gotten a glimpse of one of those conversations."

"See. I know something." Emily casts me a twitchy wink.

Amalia leans forward. "Do you think they planned out their stories together? Let each other know where they were in their world creation, gave advice or chastised certain ideas? Do you think maybe Lewis thought Gollum was entirely a too unlikeable character at first and encouraged Tolkien to make him more sympathetic?"

"Gollum?" Emily asks. "That's the little slimy one

obsessed with the ring, the precious or something?"

Amalia groans. "I still cannot believe you've never read the books."

Emily laughs. "Isn't watching the movies more than enough?"

"You can't compare them."

"Well, I read all the Tales of Narnia."

"Chronicles of Narnia. Chronicles." Amalia looks to me, seemingly wanting some support. I don't muster up more than a smile.

In Oxford, Autumn follows Westin's car into a private parking lot. Before we've even had a chance to get out, he jogs over with a parking permit for the car's dash.

"Are you sure it's—"

Westin cuts Autumn off. "It'll be fine. So where to first?" His hand drapes casually over Lydia's shoulder.

"The Eagle and Child." Amalia practically bounces.

"Maybe something a little more interesting," says Jakob. "Like a gallery or museum or—"

"The whole place is a museum." Amalia lets out a loud breath. "And you have already been here."

"Yeah." Jakob laughs. "But not with an insider."

Lydia steps forward. "We can follow a route that should have a bit for everyone and bring us to the pub right around lunch." She looks to Amalia. "Surely eating a full meal there would be more appealing than just a look around?"

Amalia agrees and we begin our walk. Her words, 'the whole place is a museum,' remind me to open my eyes. It's true. Walking through these streets is like walking in another world, or at least another time. It's unnerving to see people dressed the same as us, to see cars and modern bicycles share the streets with such history.

"It's beautiful, isn't it?" Lydia grasps my elbow. I look down to see I was about to miss a step. I nod. She grins. "Don't forget to keep an eye on the paths too. These streets can be a tad treacherous."

Our first stop is All Souls College. The building's magnitude is stifling. We enter through the halls and into the courtyard, signs indicating areas are "Private" apparently not applying to us. Amalia and Jakob are so full of questions, pumping both Lydia and Westin for answers, that no one else can get a word in, not that I'm trying to. I soak up the sights around me, equally awed at what I'm seeing as who I'm seeing it with—my birth mother.

After the college, we tour the Radcliffe Camera of the Bodleian Library, and here my awe increases: the massive ceiling, the rows and rows of books, the history, the smell. I take mental notes, imagining myself describing these sights to the crop of students I'll be getting this fall—the way you can spin and thousands of books surround you. They'll love it.

As we head down other streets, necessary pathways to the 'tourist' sights, it surprises me to see modern— compared to the buildings around them—shops and stores. Common places. A second-hand store, a record store, a grocery. This is a city, after all, not the movie set I seem to have perceived it to be. People live here, work here, construction happens. It's unnerving; in what I imagined a place standing still, time moves on. A man paints the facade of a building that could sit on the harbour front back home.

Something in my gut roils. This is a large part of what disturbs me so much about Lydia. All these years I pictured her a young girl. I pictured her wracked with guilt. I pictured her life paused at the exact moment she let me out of her arms. But her life continued, flourished. Sure, she suffered some guilt, maybe even regret, but she's moved on. She's okay without me.

My observation shifts to Lydia in her role of tour guide. I only hear half of what she's saying, but she speaks easily, with an aura of authority. She laughs, makes jokes, seems to pull seemingly disparate facts from the corners of her mind with ease: here answers a question about the Minoans, there provides an anecdote about Tony Blair, and then onto reciting a line from one of Auden's poems as we stand in the spot he's rumoured to have composed it.

In the Ashmolean Museum, where Jakob is enthralled and Amalia's found something to distract her, Lydia, free from their questions, turns to me. "So what do you do? Back home?"

"Oh." Should I withhold all aspects of my life from her? She doesn't deserve to know. But this seems childish. "I'm a teacher."

"Really?" Her smile widens. "What do you teach?"

I reply casually, as if I haven't yet drawn the connection. "English Lit and Art History."

Her whole body seems to smile now, a look of pride coats her face…which doesn't seem right. Something in my expression must tell her this because her smile lessens. "It's interesting isn't it?" I send her a questioning glance. "Genetics." She turns down a hall and I follow. "Or are either of your parents into the arts?"

"No." Genetics. I am made from her. Half of her at least. A yearning shoots out of me, the desire to know and be known. We share blood. The thing I've wanted my entire life is less than two feet from me. Blood family. And seeing as she's even more alone in the world genetically than I am, I may literally be the only blood family she has or will ever have. "It is interesting. Genetics."

"Are you close to your adoptive family?" Her voice wavers.

"They're good people. Loving people."

"That's good, really good." She glances at me then looks away. I didn't actually answer her question.

"I'm not very close to any of them. My father the most I suppose." I release these words cautiously, wary of betraying the people who raised me, the people who, despite all I've faulted them, were my salvation. "It's hard, knowing they're not my real family. Knowing…well," some things shouldn't be said, "knowing I don't quite belong."

She steps around an ancient urn. "You have siblings?"

"A sister." My mind travels to Jojo, her life crumbling around her and I haven't contacted her once since I arrived in England. "She's not adopted. She's six years younger than me. Their miracle baby."

"That happens a lot." Lydia steps around a corner and I follow her. "Families who can't conceive adopt and then a baby comes along." She slides her hand against the velvet rope blocking our entry to a hall. "That happened with a friend of mine. Is it what happened with your parents too?"

I notice she doesn't say adoptive parents and internally thank her for it. "Yeah. That's what happened." We walk silently for several minutes, pretending to observe the collections on display…or at least I'm pretending.

"Anyone special?" She stops, both her words and her body. "If this is too invasive—"

I smile, wanting her to know I have a life too, that just as her life didn't end when she left me, mine didn't either. "There is. There wasn't for a long time." I pause. "It was hard for me to trust people, to trust they wouldn't leave me." I don't say the words with an accusatory tone, but she still flinches. "But this guy," I can't help but smile, "he kind of worked his way in. We're moving in together."

"That's wonderful. What's his name?"

"Adrian."

"Adrian." She says the name as if she's savouring it or imprinting it into her memory. "And what does he do?"

Something jumps within me. I step back. She's asking too much. I rub my stomach. "Think I just felt a growl. You hungry? Perhaps we should make our way to the pub."

She grins, seemingly unfazed. Perhaps it's from Lydia, not my mother, that I get my ability to gloss over a situation, to seem calm and happy and pleasing, when inside I'm a mess. Genetics. I glance at some cutlery made out of stone, then back to Lydia. This conversation needs a new direction.

As we turn another corner I ask, "How did you end up here, so far from home?"

She smiles. "Determination, I guess." She takes several steps. "I knew I had to make something of my life, that I couldn't just sink into regret and misery. There were a few months there..." Her voice fades. "Anyway, being parentless had one benefit. I managed to find some pretty substantial scholarships for people in my situation. So I took advantage of those. I worked part-time jobs to cover the rest, and I graduated University with top marks. I secured scholarships for my master's and then a Commonwealth to do my postgraduate work in the UK." She smiles a soft, personal smile. "I fell in love with this country. My advisor had strong ties to Oxford, and I fell in love with it too. I did everything I could to secure a position here."

I look away. "That's really impressive."

"I worked really, really hard." Lydia's voice is low. "I knew after what I'd done, I had to make the life I'd chosen worth something." She stops and rests a hand on my shoulder. "Not that it erases...not that it makes it okay."

We leave the museum and as we walk along the broad street leading to the Eagle and Child, Amalia practically hums with excitement. She links her arm in mine and squeezes. "This is where it happened."

I squeeze back. "I know."

"They called it 'The Bird and Baby.'"

"I know."

"Sorry." She laughs. "I'm excited."

"Me too." We stand before the plain facade, absorbing the moment. "Let's go in." The pub is nothing special, though I can't deny imagining the conversations that went on here gives me a small thrill. Another tidbit to take back to my students. As we eat, Westin regales the group with stories of what he calls his 'swashbuckling' days. It all feels so normal. I almost forget what is really going on. I'm not just sitting here eating a meal, I'm sitting here eating a meal with my birth mother.

As we're getting ready to leave the pub, Lydia excuses herself. She returns a few minutes later, grinning and motioning us to follow her. Several minutes after that we arrive at a place for 'punting', which apparently means boat riding. We debate going for a tour but instead take a walk along the river. "A walk," Lydia starts to explain, "Lewis and Tolkien— used to"

"Addison's Walk." Amalia looks starry-eyed. "I know all about it." She scans her surroundings. "So that's Magdalen college."

"And what's so special about Magdalen college?" asks Emily, seeming only mildly interested.

"It's where Lewis studied and worked and—" Amalia pauses as if for dramatic effect, "reluctantly gave his life to God. And he loved to walk this walk." She twirls as we turn onto it. "Imagine the thoughts that were thought here. The concepts discussed, the—"

"Every place in Oxford is dripping with long ago thoughts," says Emily.

Westin, who's in the lead beside Amalia, glances back. "It drips with present day thoughts too. Some beautiful young lass *may* be amazed at the places I walked one day."

"Of course." Emily casts her lovely smile at Westin, but she grabs onto her left arm at the same time, holding it firm against her side. Her gait doesn't seem as smooth as when we started. For her, it's been a long day. I want to say something, suggest we turn back, but from what I've learned of Emily in the past week, if she wanted us to turn back she'd tell us.

We slip into silence as we travel around the lake. The evening is warm and balmy. At the end of the walk we find ourselves in front of Magdalen College. It's not nearly as impressive as some buildings we've seen, but still more impressive than just about any college back home. "And now," says Lydia, "my surprise. I made some calls earlier and you're in luck. Evensong is happening tonight. It's rare to find one this late in the summer but a dignitary is in town. Shall we?"

"Evensong?" asks Autumn, amid a number of nods.

"It's choral singing," says Amalia. "A college tradition, and beautiful."

"You've been to one before?" I ask.

"Not here." Amalia grins.

"Is it like church?" asks Autumn.

Jakob takes her arm. "Yes, and no. It's church, but you need no religious affiliation to be moved by it."

The chapel is modest. We're one of the first to arrive and the crowd fills after us. Moments before the choir enters, a man and his little troupe files in and takes the reserved seating across from us. Westin whispers a name that means nothing to me, but Autumn and the Andrevs seem impressed. When the music starts, I am transported. I've been to church. My mother's sister took me and Jojo a few times on Easter and Christmas Eve, but it was nothing like this. I don't understand a word being said, but I don't need to. The sound creates its own language. We're several minutes in before I realize there aren't even any instruments. All this sound, all this amazing sound, is coming from not more than two dozen voices. It fills me.

Lydia sits to my left, looking enraptured. A serene smile rests on her face. Autumn sits to the right. Tears glisten at the corners of her eyes. My gaze drifts back to Lydia. She meets it. "Thank you."

"What?" I shift in my seat.

"For giving me this day, even if it only ends up being one day. Thank you."

I give a slight nod and turn my gaze back to the choral singers. As their voices rise in an incredible crescendo, I'm tempted to reach my hand out to grasp Lydia's. I don't, but the fact that I want to…that's good enough.

CHAPTER SEVENTEEN

We part ways for the day, and somehow I agree to go to Lydia and Westin's for a BBQ before we head back to London tomorrow.

As we make our way to our hotel rooms, Autumn turns to me. "Was it a good day?"

"Oxford was great."

"Tracey."

"Yeah." I shrug. "She's not a drug addict. She didn't spit in my face or want nothing to do with me." I hesitate and wait for someone to say something. They don't. "She's great. She's fabulous. She could have been my mom."

My words seem to enter the hall with us and linger there like a heavy fog. Jakob lets out a gush of air and plops his hand on my shoulder. "I can't imagine, really, I can't. But maybe if she'd stayed, your mom she never would have become this fabulous woman."

"Oh, I know." I laugh somewhat caustically. "Getting rid of me was probably the best thing that ever happened to her."

"No." He shakes his head. "That's not what I meant. I mean for you. Maybe she wouldn't have been a fabulous mom for you. Maybe she would have been tired and bitter and resentful. Maybe *your* life would have been worse."

"Maybe."

Back in the room Emily crawls into bed almost immediately and Amalia heads for the shower. Not wanting to disturb Emily, I grab my tablet, a book, and leave for the hotel lobby.

Most of the emails in my account have to do with Aspire or school-related issues, but one is from my mother. My adoptive mother. As she's not the most technology savvy woman, only using the computer when she must, a fear jumps within me. I tap to open the email, expecting bad news.

Hello, my lovely girl!
Are you having a wonderful time in jolly old England? I hope so. If you see Prince Harry give him a kiss for me. We miss you and hope you come home soon. Your dad is making some progress on the basement. Just some. But I'm surviving. We all have our cross to bear! Make lots of memories to bring back with you. Take lots of pictures. Send your old 'mum' a note to let her know all is okay.
xoxo

It's just like my mother. Happy. Seeming simple. But I can read between the lines. She's nervous. She fears something bad will happen while I'm away. If I didn't know better, I'd think somehow she learned my real reason for taking this trip and is afraid I'll decide to stay with my birth mother. She misses me, she says. But it's not likely in this short a time she would have seen me, anyway.

The first few years after my adoption I never wanted to leave my family. Every time my parents left for more than a few hours I'd get anxious. I couldn't eat. Sometimes I'd break out in hives. They couldn't travel—even going out for dinner was difficult. The time they sent me to an overnight camp I had a panic attack. I didn't whine for my parents. I never complained about them being gone. I didn't talk at all. I threw up, without choice, any food that was put into me. I shook and sweat. And then it all changed. Somewhere between the last year of high school and the first of University I stopped caring so much. After I moved to attend University, it was my mother who got anxious, who worried I'd leave for good and be done with them. *My worries transitioned to fear my friends would leave if I wasn't just who they expected me to be.*

"Tracey?" Emily, wrapped in an over-sized sweater, stands above me.

"Oh, how are you?"

She smiles her sweet, deeply accepting smile. "I'm more concerned about you. A complex day I imagine."

"That's one way to describe it." I motion for her to sit. "It was long for you, though, wasn't it?"

She sits slowly, as if she has to concentrate on making her joints move the way she wants them to. "It was a long day." A sigh escapes as she sinks into the plush cushion. "But sometimes long days are good. They give me an idea of where I really am."

"And that's good?"

She shrugs. "It's motivating. My studies, my research. It's frustrating sometimes. Wondering if what I'm doing matters, if it's worth all the effort, all the constant disappointments. Perhaps I'd be happier following a different path. But then I have days like today when it's clear that, although my meds improve my life greatly, they're not enough. We need to find something that's enough. We need a cure. This could be Amalia one day. It could be Jakob. If I can be a part of preventing that in any small way, I have to be."

"Are you scared?" I ask. How could she not be?

"For me? Or for my family?"

"I don't know. Both."

"I'm scared for both. I nursed Farfar. It amazes me how strong he always was, how he kept his humour, his love of life." She laughs, a tinkling little thing, and I imagine in another life she could have been a royal. Something decidedly regal exists in Emily Andrev. "He never seemed angry. I spend most of my life angry."

"You don't seem it."

She grins. "Maybe I should have gone into acting. I can see it now, cast as Juliet, about to end it all with my happy dagger then, wupps, a shake and the dagger jabs into my arm instead. A bloody, un-deadly mess."

"See," I smile back at her, "you've got humour."

She looks to the corner of the room, the smile still on her face, her lips tight. "Well, maybe that's how Farfar was too. Angry-terrified inside—it's always there, even in those happy moments. The anger, the terror—but laughing on the outside."

"Do you ever talk about this? With your family?"

She shakes her head. "Not really. Not much." She pauses. "I wished I'd talked about it with him." She smiles again: it's so soft. "Jakob and Amalia have their own fears. For me. For them. I try to be strong. I'm the matriarch, after all."

"You've been the matriarch for a long time."

"Someone's got to do it." She flexes the fingers of her right hand open and closed. "I have a lot to be thankful for. When I was diagnosed, I thought by now I'd be a lot worse off than I am. Really, though, it's not that bad."

"Not that—"

"Considering." She stares at her hand as she flexes. "Considering what it could be. Already the improvements in medical care from when Farfar was diagnosed are significant."

"But you were so much younger, weren't you?"

"Yes. Which is why I thought I'd progress so much faster."

"Sorry." I lean into the chair's arm and pull my legs up. "I don't know a lot about the disease."

"Not a lot of people do. Thank goodness for Michael Fox." She laughs again. "Let's just say some of what I'm benefiting from may not have come to be if it weren't for the awareness his fame allowed. Even just people understanding, making that mental connection. A few weeks ago I was trying to balance eggs, some juice, in my hands at the grocer's. A bit of a fit came on, a huge jerk of my hand, and the eggs splattered all over. Of course my hands shook as I tried to collect what I could." She stops again, her gaze to the floor. "I think years ago—in fact Farfar even told similar stories—people would have assumed I was drunk, on drugs, something. But I could see that little bit of awareness in the eyes of the bag boy who bent to help me. Whether he guessed Parkinson's or not, who knows? But he was aware of something more." Again she's silent. "It makes it easier."

"You're really brave." This whole trip I've been so focused on me: My fear about *maybe* not being able to have a child. My fear of what it would mean to find my mother. Emily hasn't had a mother for years, and…can she be one? Will she want to, with what she knows? "Incredibly brave."

"It's not bravery." She reaches for a throw from a basket under the coffee table but seems to have trouble grasping it. It's so warm in here. Can she really be cold? I reach forward and offer the blanket. She lays it on her lap, tucks it around her. "I don't have a choice. Unless I actually reached for that dagger." She chuckles. I don't. "It's just living. Now you," her smile brightens, "that was bravery. You had a choice. You didn't have to meet your mother. But you did."

"It wasn't necessarily bravery."

"I know you had specific reasons, but it was bravery too. And touring today. Agreeing to meet up tomorrow. It's not easy."

"She's nice. Seems like a great woman. Of course I should take the opportunity to spend some time with her."

Emily's smile grows. "You're an actor too."

I finally chuckle. "It's complex."

Emily nods. She rubs her wrist, then her fingers. "Here." I cross to the chair beside her and reach for her arm.

She sighs as I massage each finger, her palm. "You'll be

glad you did."

"Hmm?"

"No matter what, you'll be glad you took that extra time with her. Even if she disappoints you, even if too much disappointment has already happened. She's your mother. Without her, you wouldn't exist. No amount of anger or confusion can change that."

※

WE SPEND THE NEXT MORNING touring more of the area, then in the afternoon I find myself back at that little house with the lovely landscaping.

"You ready?" asks Autumn as we stand outside the door. "Of course." I knock and moments later Westin appears with a large smile and flourish for us to come in. The house is full of interesting artifacts. Not cluttered, but full. Before we've even made it past the entryway Jakob is asking Westin a question about what looks to be some sort of tribal mask. Part of me thinks I should feel more comfortable, it's my mother's house, after all, but awkwardness lingers over me like a stench.

It's a home, a real home. As we make our way deeper into the house, Lydia's head pops around a corner. She steps out, wearing a polka dot apron, her arms spread wide. Autumn, who's several paces ahead of me, steps in for a quick hug. Emily follows suit. Amalia is eavesdropping on Westin and Jakob so I'm next in line.

I turn to a painting on the wall. "This is beautiful."

Lydia, thankfully, seems to understand my diversion. She steps beside me but makes no move to touch. "It's one of my favourites. So peaceful, isn't it?"

I nod. Ships sail in a night that seems straight out of a dream. "I've always liked Turner. I saw my first real ones last week."

"Really?" Lydia's smile is welcoming. "Well, this is just a copy. One day, though, if the price is right, I'd like to get my hands on an original."

Emily steps over. "And what would make the price right?"

Lydia laughs. "That, I do not know."

"It smells delicious." Autumn hovers near the kitchen. "Anything we can help with?"

Lydia turns. "I've got it under control. And Emily, you can eat everything but the cheesecake, so Westin picked up a dairy free, gluten-free cupcake for you. Hopefully it's good."

"Oh," Emily waves her hand, "that's too kind. It wasn't necessary."

"Nonsense."

The kitchen is laid out well, its utensils and appliances obviously chosen as much for practicality as for aesthetic appeal. Everything is bright, colourful, and pleasing—no standard whites, blacks, and stainless steels. The fridge is adorned with photos, one or two of Lydia and Westin but mostly of children.

Lydia steps to the counter and fluffs the makings of a quinoa salad. "Westin's family." She gestures toward the fridge. "There's a whole brood of them. They just keep procreating." She points to a photo with two red-headed kids who seem to claim the biggest proportion of fridge space. "These are Westin's children. Sasha and Cooper."

"Westin's children?" My voice catches. "And this is recent?"

"Fairly. About six months. Sasha," she pulls the photo from the door, "is thirteen and Cooper is ten. It's a shame this wasn't our week. Well, we usually have them the last two weeks of the month but for the summer we had them all of July and their mom has them all of August."

"So they live with you?" I take the picture from her hand, focusing on the faces of the children my mother is partially raising. "Part of the time, anyway?"

"Mm-hmm." Lydia opens the fridge. "They don't call me Mom or anything like that." She pulls out a pitcher of bright red liquid. "Who would like Sangria?"

In her own home, Lydia is even more at ease than yesterday, her demeanour more consistently natural. She places the cool drink in my hand. I should be happy for her. I am happy. She's getting the chance to raise…partially raise, what look to be beautiful children. From the way she said their names, she loves them. It's wonderful. It's great—I take a sip, the drink is strong and sweet. Delicious—but why don't I feel happy about this news?

What would I want if I could turn back the clock? Her not letting my sorry excuse for a father sleep with her, avoiding this whole mess, avoiding me? No, not that far back. I appreciate existing. To when, then? My conception was practically statutory rape, which means, mostly, the wrong was his. His wrong. So his wrong shouldn't have meant she had to go her whole life living with the guilt of giving away a child she couldn't handle then, as some twisted sort of retribution, not letting herself have another. What then? What do I want? Maybe that she just loved me more. Loved me enough. Maybe that her father hadn't died when he did, that she hadn't been so weak. Maybe if any of those things had happened, she'd deserve this happiness.

"Tracey."

"Hmm?" I look to see Autumn's hand on my forearm. "Earth to—"

"Let's move this party outside." Westin nods to the back door as he, Jakob, and Amalia enter the room. "The grill is hot and I am hungry."

We carry out what seems to be a copious amount of food and drink. The backyard is small compared to standards back home, but large enough for our purposes. The BBQ sits in one corner on a slab of bricks, and lawn chairs form a semi-circle around it. Flowers and bushes add a burst of colour and several trellises line the fence, each seeming to house a different plant—some for beauty, others for harvesting.

"Who's the gardener?" asks Autumn.

"Both of us, actually." Westin places the first steaks and breasts on the grill. He smiles at Lydia. "It's one of our things."

"One of your things?" Jakob settles into a lawn chair.

"Yeah. Couple things." Lydia sits across from Jakob. "That we do to strengthen our bond." A twinkle sparkles in her eye, as if this is a joke. But clearly it's not.

"Do you have things?" asks Amalia of Jakob and Autumn.

"Well," Jakob looks to Autumn, "I'm much more fit since this one got a hold of me. Running. Interval Training. What's that thing you made me do last week, the really weird one?" He winks and Autumn laughs.

"Squash?"

"Yeah. Some crazy form of torture that was."

"You loved it." Autumn perches on his lap, a fake threatening look on her face. "And don't you tell me any different."

"All right, all right." He wraps his arms around her. "I loved it."

The discussion reminds me I haven't heard Adrian's voice since I arrived in Charlbury. We've only texted. He knows I met Lydia that first night and planned to meet her at the pub for brunch, but he knows nothing of how brunch went, of the Oxford tour, of the fact that I'm here. I should be talking to him. I want to talk to him. But he'll be full of optimism and excitement; he'll probably think I should be too. I don't want to disappoint him.

I draw my attention back to the lunch. The steaks and chicken breasts burst with flavour, the quinoa salad's a perfect mix of sweet and savoury, the guacamole is fresh and tangy. Conversation fades as we focus on the tastes and textures. Once we've finished eating, we laze in the sun with mini food comas. It's a good excuse to be quiet. I almost always know what to say, how to present myself, but today I'm at a loss.

"When are you heading back across the water?" Westin's gaze is on me.

"Oh," I take a sip of my drink to delay my answer. "I haven't quite decided. I have to be home in a week and a half at the latest. I may stay in England another week."

"Brilliant." Westin glances from Lydia then back to me. "You know, if you're in no rush, you'd certainly be welcome to stay with us for a few days. We could drive you back to London almost any evening."

"Uh." I look to Lydia. Her expression is mildly hopeful but also reserved. "If I stay longer, we might actually do some other short trip. Maybe zoom over to France, even do a quick stop in Italy."

"We have family there," says Amalia, addressing Westin and Lydia. "On a beautiful vineyard. If they go there, I might go too."

"That'd be lovely." Lydia stands a little too quickly. "We need some time before dessert, would you all agree?"

We nod, all except Jakob who says he could fit it into him anytime.

"Well, I actually have sort of a present for you, Tracey," continues Lydia. "Something I think you should have."

"A present?" A constricting feeling takes over my chest. "What kind of present?"

"Well…" Lydia smiles. "You wait here. Westin, will you help me get it?"

CHAPTER EIGHTEEN

When Lydia and Westin return, they each have one hand on either end of a wooden trunk. It's not massive, but large enough to be awkward for one person. It looks pricey. Antique.

"A trunk?"

"Well." Lydia laughs. "No, not the trunk. Not exactly. I'll be keeping that for now."

They set it in front of me and Westin stretches his arm. "You may have to adjust your will."

Lydia looks to him. "She's in my will." She turns her gaze back to me. "The trunk was my mother's. It's what's inside the trunk I want you to have now."

I lean forward, perched on the edge of my chair. It could hold anything.

"Go ahead," she says, "open it."

I undo the latch and raise the lid. Inside lays an assortment of items. I swallow and look up at Lydia. She pulls a chair beside me. "This is everything I kept. Well, just about everything." She lifts out a onesie with pink stripes and green trim around the collar. "This is what you came home from the hospital in."

Autumn gasps. I take the item in my hands, my whole body tingling.

"This was mine." It's a statement, not a question.

"Yes."

My gaze flits across the other items in the trunk. More

clothes. Teeny, tiny shoes. An old-fashioned toy rotary telephone. Books. Lydia picks up a frilly white dress. "Your christening gown."

"You're Catholic?"

She smiles. "Anglican. By birth, not choice. I don't really practice anymore. Didn't then much either, obviously."

Her joke isn't funny. None of this is. Betrayal fills the space between us. "I was baptized." The words come out pinched. "Shouldn't that have been in my family history? Something I and my parents had a right to know?"

"Uhh," Lydia looks at the dress then back to me, "I don't remember a line for religion. I would have—"

"And isn't part of the ceremony a promise? To raise the child up in the way she should go or something? To raise her up with…with…to raise her!"

"Here." Lydia pulls out an album. "Obviously you can't take everything with you this trip, but I thought you might want to take this."

"Mind if we come look?" asks Autumn. My head shakes back and forth, my lips pressed so tight together it hurts. Autumn, Emily and Amalia crowd around us. Lydia opens the cover. A little baby swaddled tightly, her face squished and hardly visible, rests in the arms of a girl who looks at the camera with an expression that is equal parts exhaustion and conqueror. I lean closer.

"Oh, Tracey," Autumn's voice holds wonder, "that could be you first-year university. Well, almost."

My thoughts exactly. The worn out girl with a baby in her arms couldn't be my identical twin, but no one would ever question we're blood.

"Seven pounds, three ounces." The pride on the girl's face creeps into Lydia's voice. "And seventeen and a half hours of labour."

Who was taking the picture? My grandfather? A nurse? How alone was she? Lydia turns the page. The baby is older now. She's propped up on her elbows. She's laughing with a huge grin plastered across her face. She's looking scared over something. She's in her mother's arms, a shocked expression on each of their faces as a giraffe's head hovers inches from them, its tongue extended. In each picture the baby wears a different outfit, is slightly older. In Jojo's baby album every shot is accompanied by at least a handful of others taken minutes or hours apart. In her kids' online albums, several dozen. Here, each moment is unique.

"My father had the camera. He took most of the shots."

"But didn't like getting in front of the lens?" asks Amalia.

"No." Lydia sighs. She points to a picture, tells a story about what made the baby look scared. Something about a friend's dog. She turns the pages, tells more stories, but I can't exactly make sense of the words. They blur in my head the way the photos blur before my eyes. Where are the shots of me in the hospital? Where are the shots of a crying, sick, miserable baby? An exhausted, overwhelmed, terrified teenage mom? Wasn't that the reality? Wasn't that the reason I'm only seeing these photos now, thirty years late? What's the point of looking at this fabrication?

Lydia turns the page again. "This," she says, pointing to the first thing that's truly recognizable, "was Buncey Bear." The little girl that is supposed to be me has her arms wrapped around the toy; she squeezes it so tight that if it were animate she'd have squeezed the life right out of it. A party hat sets atop her head but no other children surround her. In this shot, she is in a hospital bed. She looks weak and frail. Her mother is beside her, smiling bravely, though you can see in her eyes no bravery exists.

"Was Tracey sick?" asks Amalia. It seems a weird question. I'm Tracey. I'm right here. This little girl's life might as well be the life of a stranger.

"Yes." Lydia's gaze stays on the photo.

"What—"

"Not sure exactly. They were never sure exactly." Lydia looks to me. "You seem well now. I always wondered…if it was some food allergy we weren't aware of back then. Celiac or...do you know?"

"No."

"You're good now, though?"

I push the words out, my eyes glued to the picture with the bear, to the moment, presumably, it entered my life. "It just...went away." If she'd waited longer, if she'd been patient...

"Good." Lydia's face is tender. "You can't imagine how many hours I spent wondering, hoping you were okay, hoping—"

I turn the page, feeling as if my blood literally boils within me. *How many hours she spent wondering?* Am I supposed to sympathize with her? She gave me away. You don't just give a child who knows you, who loves you, away. The page turns and the pictures return to the fake history of my life. Smiling. Laughing. Hugging. I notice for the first time the captions written beside each picture—little handwritten stories and snippets.

The album's pages are worn. It's been looked through. Often. She had the memories. She hoarded them. She shouldn't have kept this. She should have sent it with me. Why didn't she send it with me? She gets this—my life—and leaves me nothing but a dirty old stuffed animal? That's the memento she chose to give.

Her finger lands beside a photo: me dressed up in a frilly little dress, a sash around my neck; her sitting beside me, in a decidedly less frilly dress, but also with a sash; the bear beside us, complete with matching sash. We have plastic teacups in front of us. "This was at a library," she says, "in their play section." Her voice drips of wistful happiness. "It was taken two weeks before Tracey's grandfather died." Tracey's grandfather? My grandfather. As if I have some claim on him. As if I'm part of this fictional life she's describing! She laughs, looks at me. "You really tried to get him to wear that third sash and join us, but he insisted it looked better on Buncey." A tinkling, happy laugh. "At last you acquiesced." Her hair shakes with her laughter. She rubs her hand along the side of the album and turns her gaze to me. "Do you remember Buncey?"

The quiet boiling turns to a rampant rumble.

"Tracey."

"Stop it." I shoot up from my chair. "Stop. Just. Stop." The album, which rests between us, tumbles into the trunk. "You can't do this. You can't pretend everything's okay." I gesture to the others. "Pretend you're telling my friends stories of my childhood, telling me stories of my childhood, like everything is normal. Like this isn't the most…the most…fucked up thing ever. Like you loved me."

"I did love you. I do. I never—"

"Shut up, okay. Shut up with your wounded, woe is me victim act. You gave me away. You *gave* me away. Yes, I remember Buncey. Of course I remember Buncey. That's the *one* thing you left me with of my past. The one thing. A stupid, dirty old bear. No history. No reason why you got rid of me except what I could figure out myself. I was sick. I was too much work. I was a burden. And now you say you worried about my sickness? Worried if I was okay? If you were so worried you would have kept me."

"Tracey, I explained. I—"

"Screw this." I step away from her, from the trunk, from everything, almost tripping over a flowerpot as I pass. My feet rush me through the house, out the front door, and down the street. I stop several buildings away. I'm shaking. My arms, my legs, my mind. I have never in my life yelled at anyone like that. Not once. I never yelled at my mom, even when she was driving me mad. I never yelled at Jojo. Never at the many men who deserved to be yelled at. Never at my students. Spoke forcefully, yes. But never like this. Nothing like this.

I don't cry. I just shake, and shake, and shake. Realizing my fists are clenched, I unfurl them. They tingle. And I feel so pathetic, a little girl in the midst of a tantrum. I fall against the stone wall that just yesterday made me feel claustrophobic. Today, I sink against the rough, solid structure, all the rigidity my body held turning to mush.

I don't know how long I sit, but it can't be long. A figure settles beside me that I know is Autumn. She doesn't touch me, doesn't say anything. Just sits. After several minutes I raise my head, offer a weak smile.

"That was something." Her knees are pulled up to her chest, her arms rested atop them, her head nodding. "Really something. It's lucky you don't have any Carrie-esque powers."

"Carrie? Oh," I let out a little chuckle, "right."

"Could have been disastrous. A real massacre."

"Autumn." My mind drifts back to the night a bunch of us girls watched that movie in our dorm lounge, how we laughed over the carnage, joked over how nice it'd be to have that power. Under the laughter I ached for the times I'd felt like Carrie. Alone and misunderstood. Unlovable. "Was I that bad?"

"No. No." Autumn shakes her head. "Not that bad. Honestly, I'm surprised it didn't happen sooner." She squeezes my knee. "You hold things in too much. You were bound to burst."

A squeezed laugh escapes me. "Thirty years of 'holding in' erupted in one explosion. Perhaps not the best method."

"Perhaps. It's okay though."

I guffaw.

She grins. "I still love you."

"Well, that's good." I shift toward her. "How's ground zero? Is Lydia…?"

Autumn taps her fingers on her knee. "She's okay. I mean…obviously…" She bites her lip. "I think she gets it, though. I doubt you burnt any ties as far as she's concerned. Everything you said, it may be one-sided, but from your side, it's true."

I glance up and down the street: here and there a stranger. "Where are the others?"

"Still there, I suppose. I said I'd go find you."

"How awkward."

"And oh how you hate awkwardness." She wraps her arm around me. "Do you want to go back, or—"

"No. No. I can't…" I put my head in my hands, glance up at her through a slit in my fingers—such a child. "What's worse?"

"I'm not in a position to answer that one."

"To offer an opinion?"

"If you think you can speak…uh…calmly? Maybe go back, maybe talk it out—"

"I don't know what there is to talk out. Nothing she can say can change anything I said. I know already. I know she was young. I know she's felt some semblance of regret or at least uncertainty about whether she made the right decision. But it's not like that's enough. It's not like that can erase my whole life."

Autumn nods.

"I need to head back to the hotel. Will you get the others?"

We stand. "Of course." Autumn gives my hand a squeeze. "I'll be back soon."

ON THE DRIVE TO LONDON no one talks about my blowout. They don't talk about Lydia or Westin either. The conversation centres around the Andrev's restaurant, Autumn's first few clients, and whether or not I want to travel with Autumn, and potentially Amalia, before I leave. I just don't know.

Back at the Andrev's I decide it's time to talk to Adrian. I log into Skype on my tablet. He's on too. The moment his face lights up the screen, a wave of missing floods me.

"Hey, beautiful."

"You busy?"

"I'm always busy. The presses never stop." He makes an exaggerated motion of typing furiously. "But for you, they will pause." His eyes dart away. "One sec." He must be closing whatever article or link he's working on. His gaze lifts back to the screen. "I've been wondering about you. Missing your face."

"It's been busy."

"I figured."

"Yeah." We're both silent.

"So busy you couldn't make a quick little call?"

Don't pressure me. Just—

"You needed time, to figure things out. I get that."

"You get everything, don't you?" I manage a laugh.

"I try. You, Miss. Sampson, are a mystery I'm thoroughly enjoying the pleasure of unravelling."

I offer a smile.

His smile turns to a look of concern. "What's up? You're not looking yourself."

I sigh, wanting and not wanting to tell him everything. "I met my mom."

"Yeah. I know. The brunch went well? Or…"

"Well enough. She wanted to spend more time with me."

"That's great."

"She and her…partner took us, all of us on a tour of Oxford."

"Fun?"

"She's very smart. He is too."

"Uh huh. Did you enjoy it?"

"It's a beautiful city."

He sighs.

"We went to an Evensong. It was amazing." I describe the experience, mention the BBQ invite, how good the food was.

"A great summary of activities." I can almost see him tapping his foot, the way he does when trying to get to the bottom of a story. "Still not a word about how you're handling all of this, what you're feeling, why your face looks like the face of a person whose puppy just died?"

I don't want to be here, an ocean away, talking to him. I don't want to talk to him. I want to curl up in his arms and feel my head against his broad chest, to feel safe. Instead I have this, him looking at me, wanting me to open up, wanting more than I'm able to give. "Adrian."

"You just spent the last two days with your birth mother. What's going on? I can see from what's behind you that you're back at the Andrev's. Are you seeing your mother again?"

"Stop calling her that."

"Okay. Lydia. Did you make plans? What's—"

"I blew up."

"Huh?"

"Fully blew up." I recount the after dinner fiasco. The trunk. The christening gown. The album. My parting words.

"So that's how it was left? You haven't talked to her?"

"No."

"Will you? Can you get back there? Call, email, apologize?"

"Apologize?" My voice raises.

"Yeah."

"What am I supposed to apologize for?"

"You were a little harsh."

"Everything I said, every single word, was nothing but truth." That bubbling feeling in my blood starts again.

"Okay, okay…" He rubs a hand over his chin and leans back in his desk chair. "But maybe the way you said it wasn't the best."

"And maybe it's none of your business." My voice comes out even, but barely.

"Tracey, come on."

"No. Okay. This is my life. *My* life. Not some story. There's no specific way this is supposed to play out."

"That's not what I'm saying."

"Isn't it?" The evenness fades. "You were going on and on about how I needed to meet my mother, how it would be this transformative experience. Well, maybe me finally learning to express how I really feel was that experience. Here you go, transformation."

"I don't think you cussing out your mother in what sounds like a temper tantrum is exactly transformation."

"My birth mother." I'm nearly shouting now. "My birth mother. Not my mother. That woman is not my mother."

"Okay."

I try to breathe, to mentally count to ten, like I tell my students. *One*. I know it's not really Adrian I'm angry at, that he's not responsible for this fiery feeling inside of me. *Two. Three*. Not entirely at least. *Four*. But he should be supporting me, not…*Five*. Screw counting. "And besides," I spit the words, "weren't you saying how I needed to open up more, let people see the real me, not be so closed?" I spread my arms. "Well, this is me. Me not closed. So if you have a problem with it—"

"Tracey."

I turn my head from the screen. He's trying to be here for me, in a way I don't want, but still, trying, and this is how I treat him? He'll leave. This is it. He'll leave me and—

"It's okay, all right. It's okay to be angry."

"Of course it's okay. Of course it is." Tears mix with that boiling feeling. Why do I think like this? Why did such surety fill me that he'll leave? He said he loved me. *But so did Lydia*. Stop it! This is just a fight. Only a fight. And I have a right to be angry. "I have a right to be angry," I snap into the tablet. "She *left* me. She was my mother. She took pictures. She kept mementos. And then she *left* me. She went on to lead her own life. Her own wonderful life. And now she's raising kids. Two kids. But she couldn't raise me."

"It was a different situation, and maybe if—"

"No. Screw defending her. Defend me, okay? Defend—"

"I think maybe once you calm down—"

"I don't need to calm down."

"You'll realize you don't want to leave things like this, realize—"

"I don't need to realize a thing and I don't need you telling me how to think and feel." I end the call then stare at the screen in disbelief, feeling like a fifteen-year-old. Would my fifteen-year-old students even act this childish? I stare at the screen and will him to call me back. *Ring.* Nothing happens. *Ring.* I debate calling him, but what if he doesn't answer?

Minutes pass and the screen remains blank. This is stupid, thinking he won't want me anymore, that he's done. Normal people don't give up on each other so easily. He won't give up on me. He won't. I stare at the screen, clutch it so tight my knuckles whiten. I'm just about to call him when at last a notification pops up. *This conversation isn't over. Got a message on a lead. I'll call you tomorrow.*

A lead over me? He has to be angry. A torrent of thoughts flood through my head, the most forefront one being, *what if I've ruined everything?*

CHAPTER NINETEEN

The next day I'm taking my first bite of a maple soaked pancake when my phone lights up. Adrian. Not now. This is a conversation to have in private. I return my gaze to Autumn.

"If you want to go back to Charlbury, we can make that happen."

I shake my head.

"Any thought then, on what's next?"

"Paris." I smile. "Paris for a couple of days." I look to Amalia. "The Louvre, the Musee d'Orsays." She nods enthusiastically. "And then onto the Lombardi's?"

"Absolutely." She practically squeaks. "Yes. Yes. Yes!"

"About a week. That will give me a couple of days to get ready and settled back home for the Fall term."

Autumn's voice sounds cautious. "Sounds like a plan. I'm sorry I can't go with you. This new client—"

"I know." I smile at her. "It's no problem. None at all. Amalia and I will have a grand time."

"It'll be so nice," says Emily, "knowing Amalia's travelling with someone."

"I'm not a child." Amalia takes a dainty sip of her tea. "I would have been fine."

"I know." Emily smiles a mother's smile. "And now you get to visit Paris again too. It'll be great."

❦

THE NEXT TIME ADRIAN tries to call I'm in the shower. Not just that notification, but a text message awaits me when I get out: *Sorry I missed you, but we definitely need to talk.* He won't leave me over this, I know it, but there's an inkling feeling that isn't so sure, that thinks: if this is the end, I don't want to know yet. *Can it wait until I get home? I'd rather just see you.*

All right. He replies. *Make the best of your final days.*

Will do! I put my phone aside.

In the airport lounge I send a newsy message to my parents, letting them know my final plans and the date I'll be back. I include all the sights I've seen and all the ones I plan to, but nothing about Lydia.

Paris hums with energy. At our first major stop, the Musee D'Orsay, both Amalia and I flit through the halls like kids in a candy store, overwhelmed by the wonder that surrounds us—all these amazing paintings I've studied, some prints I have on my wall back home, here, in front of me. Although I knew the originals were bigger than the prints and photos in textbooks, seeing how massive they are delights and shocks. Some that I've loved in images smaller than the palm of my hand now tower above me. They live. They breathe. I imagine it's something like living your life glimpsing the world through nothing but a TV screen then stepping outside and realizing your whole life you've seen nothing.

My heart palpitates with excitement. And then the thought hits: Lydia has been here. She's probably walked these halls so many times that to another person they'd be commonplace. Not to her, though. While touring Oxford Amalia had asked if Lydia was still amazed at the history around her. Lydia said some things will always be amazing, and if they're not, you know there's something within you that needs adjusting. A beautiful way to look at the world...a way I'm not sure I see it. But I'd like to.

I push thoughts of Lydia away as Amalia draws me through a room, laughing. Paintings that feel like old friends line the walls. My heart expands. It's the most present I've been in years. My potentially screwed up uterus seems unimportant. Fixing the situation with my boyfriend whom I've angered and isolated seems like the trial of another woman. My mother who is and isn't my mother and my mother who isn't and is my mother both seem like problems that can and will be solved.

"Isn't it wonderful?" gushes Amalia, her face reflecting the same dream I'm living.

"It is."

When we leave, our next step is the Sacre-Coeur. It glows in the light, seeming pure and appropriate. We trail through the Montmartre, stopping to look at this painting, to listen to that song. Our feet aching, we make our way to the Eiffel Tower and all the joy slivers out of me. I don't know what expectations I had, but the view before me shatters them. Rather than the striking, iconic image I imagined, a tourist trap stands before me, its tacky twinkling lights making the whole massive structure seem little more than an item in a chintzy tourist shop.

"What is it?" asks Amalia, apparently noticing my expression. "It's kind of cheesy, huh?"

"Yeah." I wrap my arm around her. "Really cheesy."

I wanted that iconic image: A statue of what Paris would mean to me. And the reality, despite the fact that so much else of today has either met or exceeded my expectations, deflates me. We walk around. We take the required photos. I smile fetchingly in them. I expected something of Lydia too. And she wasn't it. In many ways she far exceeded my expectations, but not in the ways I wanted. I wanted things to play out a certain way. I wanted justification for all my years of anger, for feeling abandoned. I wanted a screw up who would have made my life miserable if she'd kept me. I wanted someone who truly, for whatever reason, didn't have the capacity to care for me, someone who either would not have loved me and so did the best thing ever by giving me up, or someone who loved me so much she knew the best thing for me was to give me away, because she was incapable of providing the life she wanted for me.

But the Lydia I met could have managed it. It may have been hard, but she could have made it work. Maybe she wouldn't have the wonderful life she has now, the career, but she would have had me, and *we* would have had a life. We would have been okay. I walk beside Amalia, nodding at something she says without hearing the words. My mind can't seem to leave Lydia, Lydia, who—plain and simple—chose her dreams over me. That's the way it played out and of all the possibilities, this is one of the worst. Some things may be ever amazing. Others are just pathetic.

"You hungry?" Amalia looks over at me. "Should we head back to the hostel?"

"Sure." As we leave the throng of tourists, Adrian filters through my mind. I don't know if I was fair. I was truthful. That matters more. I may have had a tantrum, but she missed out on years of potential tantrums, of childhood dramas, of teenage angst. She's getting her dues.

But I'm not a child. And she owes no dues: she gave up the role of being my mother. She's just an individual now. One who perhaps deserves an apology. It's this point I get stuck on. The humiliation. I'm not going back there to stand on her step and ask for forgiveness. But can I pick up a phone? Say it in an email? Both options seem weak. I'm so tired of being weak. I could just never see or talk to her again. So what if I don't get those records? Genetics are only one small part of my life's equation, anyway. But ignoring what happened, not offering an apology. That'd be weak too.

The time in Paris speeds by. In Italy, at the Lombardi's, a

welcome party goes on behind me as I stand on the edge of their vineyard. It's easy to see how this place soaked into Autumn's soul. The strains of a fiddle flow over the fields as the sun sets in a blaze of orange and purple. A cool breeze pushes through the vines. The smell of roasting fat tantalizes. Here in all this beauty, I find myself wondering what Lydia is doing right now, if she's looking over that album, and how many times she has before. I shouldn't care, but I do.

THE DAY OF MY RETURN I manage to get on an earlier flight at a transfer point and arrive home four hours early. I expect my apartment to look different, but everything is exactly as it was. I've been half a world away and nothing but me has changed. Toulouse's presence is the only thing missing. I'll need to go to Adrian's to pick the cat up, which means I can't delay the talk we need to have.

Trying to delay the inevitable anyway, I take a shower. Before leaving, a message appears from Jojo.

I've left him! Or, well, told him I'm leaving. The kids and I are still in the apartment. I'm kinda freaking out here. I know you just got back…or maybe you're not even back yet? I can't remember. I know you could be freaking out for your own reasons. Just…I need my sister.

I look at the clock. Toulouse. Talk with Adrian. Drive to Jojo's. It should work. I'll be at her place before I'm even supposed to be getting off the plane. And if the talk with Adrian is drawing uncomfortably on, the need to see Jojo will be my legitimate escape. I text Jojo to say I'll be over in a few hours.

The key Adrian gave me a few days before my trip sits in my purse. Still, I knock. He opens the door while rubbing a towel to his hair. His hand falls.

"You're back."

"You forgot?"

"No. No." He ushers me in, tosses the towel, and wraps his arms around me. "I was about to head to the airport to meet you."

"But," I push away from him, my defences ready, "I told you I would handle it."

"So what?" He grins. "*I* wanted to handle it." He kisses me and I melt a little, both with relief and confusion. "If you can't tell, I've kinda been missing you."

"You aren't mad at me?"

"Mad at you?" He sits on the edge of the couch, looking adorable with his damp, tousled hair. "Worried about you. Frustrated that our last conversation ended like it did and we didn't connect again properly." He grins again—that carefree grin. It's never looked so good. "But no, not mad."

"I yelled and hung up on you."

He laughs and draws me toward him so my pelvis settles against the couch, just between his knees. "You think you're the first woman to ever hang up on me? I'm surprised we've lasted this long without it happening."

"Seriously?"

"Seriously."

"I don't think I've ever hung up on anyone."

"Well," he kisses my nose, "I guess you care enough to let me get under your skin. "So," he tilts his head, "you were worried I'd be mad at you, and here I've spent the past week thinking you were fuming mad at me. Guess if you'd made some time to actually talk to me, each of us could have done a lot less worrying."

"I guess." I hesitate. "That was our first real fight."

He laughs again. "I'd hardly call it a fight. Trust me. More of a spat. And I'm sure if we last till we're old and grey, which I'm kinda hoping will happen, we'll have several more of those." He rubs my waist with a glint in his eye.

"It's true what they say. Absence does make the heart grow fonder. You sure I can't convince you of that September move in?"

"That's in less than two weeks."

"Precisely."

"I thought you said we needed to have a serious talk, that the conversation wasn't over."

"Right down to business." He flips his legs over the end of the couch and settles down on the seat, patting the spot beside him. "If you wish. I thought perhaps that seriousness could wait a bit."

"Well…"

"No. No." He smiles and angles himself toward me. "If there's anything we need to get off our chests or say, you're right, we should say it first. Then have some fun."

"I, uh, I have to go to Jojo's in a bit."

"Ack." He grasps his chest. "You're killing me here. Okay. Talk fast."

"What?"

He smiles and gestures his head to the bedroom.

I can't help but smile. "I don't know where to start."

"Okay. I'll start." His expression turns contrite. "I'm sorry for trying to pressure you into apologizing. You were right. It's your life. It's your choice. I shouldn't have judged…I think that's kind of what I was doing. But I don't know. I can't know what you were going through. And although I think I'm entitled to an opinion, that doesn't mean I should try to push that opinion on you."

"Adrian."

"Really, Trace. I'm sorry about that. You were clearly upset, clearly hurting, and I didn't help. Next time anything like that happens, I'll try to do a better job of listening."

I'm silent.

"I'm sorry. Will you forgive me?"

Never has an apology sounded so genuine. I'm flabbergasted. So much so, it's hard to speak. He hopes I forgive him? At last the words come out. "Of course I forgive you." A grin erupts. "Where did you learn that?"

"What?"

"You're so, I don't know. Did you rehearse that?"

He laughs. "A bit. Doesn't mean it's any less true. I just thought about what I wanted to say. Don't you rehearse things?"

"All the time. It's just—"

"And I've been to counselling. Money well spent on how to express myself."

"Oh…"

"With my wife."

"Right."

"But we're not here to talk about me. How are you doing? How were your last few days? Where's your head at?"

Toulouse slides into the room and rubs her head along my ankles. I lift her to my lap. Her little body rumbles. "I'm sorry as well. It was childish and just…not right to yell at you like I did. To hang up on you. To not call you back. I was scared."

"Scared?"

"Scared you wouldn't want me anymore, now that you've seen how awful I can be."

"Tracey." He leans forward. His hands cup my face. "You need to find a way to let go of this. Okay? This fear that people won't love you if you're not perfect. Trust. It would take a lot more than a little blow-up to push me away."

I swallow, phrasing my words as a joke. "Oh yeah? What exactly?"

He takes a breath, not joining in the joke. "A lot. An amount I'm sure you're not even capable of."

"It's hard for me to believe that."

"You'll get there." He leans back. "So your last few days?"

"They were great." I snuggle into him. "A little dampened by…everything. But overall really great. I had some amazing moments. Some wonderful experiences."

"I'm sorry they were dampened but glad they weren't fully ruined."

"No, not ruined." I edge over on the couch and he lays his arm around me. That safety I was yearning for enfolds me. "You can ask."

"Did you contact her again?"

"Nope."

"Will you?"

"I don't know. For now, no. She still may send me those records. We'll see."

"Okay."

He rubs my arm. This feels like home. More, perhaps, than anything ever has. I look up at him. "We've been focused so much on me lately, what's been going on with you?"

"We've been focused on you 'cause you have some monumental stuff going on."

"So what? What have your last couple of weeks been like?"

He smiles. "Besides missing you, really good actually. The weather's been great and my brothers and some friends from Uni met a few times to play soccer."

"Did you dominate?"

He laughs. "Of course."

"What else?"

"The sex trafficking story's going really well. A few of my other pieces have gotten good reader feedback. My niece Chrissy had her tenth birthday. It was a ball of a time." He chuckles. "She was quite perturbed that you missed it though. Oh, and my piece unearthing the political misspending pretty much went viral on social media."

"Did I know about that?"

"Yeah, you might have missed it. Anyway," he stretches

out on the couch, "if we don't have time for a trip to the bedroom just let me hold you a bit, soak you in."

I cuddle against him. He pulls me closer and kisses the top of my head. Until it's time for me to go, the only sound is our breath and Toulouse's purrs.

CHAPTER TWENTY

The door opens at Jojo's. "Toulouse!" Lulu and Reggie jump up and down at the sight of the cat in my arms. I let Toulouse down. He darts through the apartment as the twins race after him. Jojo's gaze follows the commotion. Her hair seems frazzled. She's wearing jeans and a t-shirt, not her usual flowing garb. Her smile is tired but relieved.

"Hiya, world traveller!" She hugs me tighter than she ever has before.

"Hi." When she finally releases me, we make our way to the living room where Neveah sits in a bouncy device with a swivelling table of activities around her. At a second glance, I realize it's her that's swivelling, not the table. "Have you told Mom and Dad?"

Jojo lets out a sharp laugh. "Have you?"

"No."

"No."

"This is totally different, though." I settle into the couch. "Your situation isn't a betrayal of them."

"And neither is yours." Jojo sinks against the cushions. "Though you think it is. If anything, not telling them is probably the bigger betrayal." She chuckles. "You know, Mom probably would have wanted to send her something. A pound cake or...I don't know. Some offering to show she raised you up right."

"That's ridiculous."

"But not out of the question."

I hold back a grin as Toulouse and then the twins dart through the living room. "No. Not completely out of the question."

"So," she slaps a hand on the armrest, "how was your trip? Is your mom, sorry, your birth mom, a crack whore?"

"Aren't we here to talk about you?"

"No," she leans back, "to take my mind off of me. I've had nothing but 'me' for days now, and the little hellions that came out of me. Talk about you."

"I could say the same. Minus the hellions."

"Crack whore or no?"

"No." I rub my hand along my arm. "Not at all. She's an Oxford Professor."

"*The* Oxford?"

"The Oxford."

"Huh." Jojo glances up as if something toward the ceiling attracts her attention. "I guess that explains where you got all of your book smarts."

"Teaches History of Art."

"You're kidding."

"I am not."

"That's crazy."

"Yeah."

"So, what else?"

I go over the whole trip with Jojo. She interjects here and there, but, for the most part, doesn't have a lot to say. Amazingly, the twins and Neveah interrupt less than a handful of times. When I tell her of Lydia and my final interaction, she gets quiet. "Did it feel good?"

"Telling her off?"

"Yeah."

"I don't know."

She smiles. "I would have paid to see that. Tracey blowing up. Losing her cool. I would have paid a lot."

"Thanks."

"Seriously, though. What'd it feel like?"

"Intimidating."

"Intimidating?"

"Yeah. It was like my mind went for a hike. Like my body, my blood, was doing the thinking, the reacting."

Jojo laughs heartily.

"What?"

"You never had your teenage rebellion. My body was doing the thinking for probably three straight years. Right through until I met Damien and found 'peace.'" She air-quotes the final word.

"So was the breakup, ending it, peaceful?"

"Oh, here we go."

"What initiated it?"

"Umm…The past year and then, more specifically, Reggie."

"Reggie?"

"Yeah. The other day he started puking and puking. He looked so pathetic. All pale and weak and limp. You can't imagine what it's like, seeing that, knowing there's so little you can do to help." She shudders. "And of course there's still Lulu and Neveah to take care of. So I go down to Damien, getting some stuff from the shop that's supposed to help him. You know Damien would be all against the amazing symptomatic powers of something like a Tylenol PM. Anyway, I ask him if he can come up to give Lulu her bath and he says, 'Oh no, Babe. I've got to head over to Crystal's.'"

"Crystal?"

"Yep. The other woman. Appropriate name, eh? Apparently she's all into crystals too. Came in the shop looking for them."

"Okay."

"And I just stare at him, you know? Kind of flabbergasted. And he says, 'What? It's her night.'" Jojo laughs. "'It's her night,' like this is completely reasonable.

Like I shouldn't be upset by this, like I should maybe even be apologetic for forgetting that it's this other woman's night."

"That's crazy."

"I know. So I tell him this is your child's night and fuck the other woman. He laughs, he actually laughs, 'Well, darling. That's what I'm on my way to go do.'"

I inhale sharply, about to interject, but Jojo's on a roll.

"That was it." She smiles, looking satisfied. "I snapped. But this cold snap. I'm done, I said. Done. He stared at me like I was joking. Leave tonight, I said, and never come back."

"And he?"

"He laughed again, 'Baby, come on.' You know, that kind of thing. But I stayed cold, this resolve just beaming through me. Then he got angry. Started yelling about how this was his house, his property, so I needed to make sure I was thinking clearly. That if he left what would I do? Where would I go? This went on for a while as I stood there. Cold."

Jojo grins. "He got calm again. Asked if I'd been connecting to 'my one' lately. Had I been meditating, could I see clearly what would happen if I left him. Still, I'm standing. Cold. He gets angry again. Like, 'You going to drag your babies out onto the street? Gonna send your babies into the dark?' And I said I'm not sending my babies anywhere. That this was *their* house. My house. And if he didn't want to be part of this family, he could find somewhere else to live. Go move in with Crystal, if she'll take you."

"And what'd he say?"

"A flurry of things. Nonsensical things, you know, mumbling to himself as he grabbed his shit together."

"And when was this?"

"Last night."

"And have you talked to him since?"

"No."

"Did he open the store today?"

"Oh yeah. I assume he's down there now, which is why I'm kinda freaking out. Will he come back in? Will he try to smooth things over? Will he get violent?"

"Has he ever been violent before?"

"No. Oh, no."

"Okay. Good." Toulouse, who must have escaped the children, leaps onto my lap. I shift to accommodate him and a stab of pain runs through my lower abdomen, right around my left pelvic bone: it throbs and wrenches. Neveah gurgles in her playpen. We both glance at her. She smiles and shakes a sock in the air. I massage the spot, breathe slowly, and feel the pain subside. "So what will you do if he comes by again?"

"Tell him to get lost. Give him what stuff he wants. I don't know."

"But it's over? Over, over?"

Her shoulders slump, as does her expression. "Yeah. I'm done with this. I deserve more than this."

"Of course you do."

I glance at Neveah. "But the kids…have you thought about how that will work? Will he have any claim or—"

"He's their father, and he's not an awful father when he's actually around. I won't cut them off from him or anything."

"This might mean lawyers, social services…"

"I hope not. That freaks me out."

"I know."

"He talks big, but my guess is if I let him see them a couple of times a week, even for a couple of hours, he'll be fine. Pretty much the only time he's ever even alone with them is when I go to class. And that's only about half of the time. Most of the time I have to get a babysitter."

Neveah burps then giggles. I glance from her to my sister. "I'm sorry, Jojo."

She shrugs.

"I am. I'm really sorry you're going through this. But I'm proud of you. This takes guts."

She keeps her gaze on Neveah. "It's the money I'm worried about. What will I do if I have to get a job? What if he uses that? He won't keep paying for food, for utilities, for this place. The building's in his name. Can he force his own children out?"

"I don't know."

"That would probably mean involving the law."

"Have you considered moving back in with Mom and Dad? Getting their help."

"Tracey."

"Okay. You're not there yet. Just remember it's an option."

"Sure." She sighs and pulls a pillow to her chest. "So you're moving in with Adrian, right?"

"That's the plan."

"Make sure you get your name on the lease."

My heart wrenches for her. "Okay."

THE FOLLOWING DAYS PASS in a blur, full of the final summer Aspire meeting, prep for the Fall semester, and time with Adrian, Jojo, and the kids. Before I know it, I'm getting dressed for the first day back at school. When I log onto my computer to double check my lesson plan, an email from Lydia awaits. My mouse hovers over the name but I 'x' out the screen and navigate to the lesson plan. Whatever she has to say, it can wait.

The first day of school is always an exciting one. It sets the tone for the year. I push aside any stress or wondering about that email and stand in front of my class with confidence. I've been transferred to a grade twelve homeroom this year, which means I already know the majority of the students, some of whom were in the Aspire program. A low pressure start to the day. My next two classes are grade ten English—full of new students. They go well, though one better than the other. A reasonably good morning. I walk into the teacher's lounge for lunch, feeling satisfied.

"Tracey, darling!" Charlise, a teacher who is more a friend than a colleague and who spent the last school year off on maternity, waves to me.

"You look great." We embrace. "You ready to take this on?"

Charlise laughs, her body shaking and her afro jiggling. "I'm trying to survive. I started sending little Zola to the daycare early so I could know what it's like to be away, but let me tell you, it's hard."

"She must be so big. I haven't seen her since...what? Last June at the BBQ?"

"She's grown." Charlise pulls out her phone and navigates to a recent picture.

"Gorgeous."

"If I do say so myself." She tucks her phone away. "It's hard to imagine what life was like without her. How was your summer?"

We spend the next few minutes filling each other in on our lives. As we sit down to lunch a stab of pain, like at Jojo's but worse, shoots through my torso. I gasp and Charlise raises an eyebrow. "Nothing." I smile. "Indigestion."

"I feel that." She shakes her head.

Only this is nothing like indigestion and it doesn't go away. The strong stabs are off and on, but a dull pain remains, constant. They're somewhat like period cramps, but sharper, more concentrated to one spot—down low on my left side. Though my cycle is still fairly irregular, I have to be at least two weeks away from my period. At least. The only thing that gets me through the day is the ibuprofen I swallow down and massaging the area whenever I have a moment alone, which isn't often.

By the time I reach home, the pain isn't so bad. I open up my laptop—a different pain still waits for me. The email is further down the list, hovering with possibilities. Lydia is friendly but to the point. She makes no mention of our final moments but says how great it was to meet me, how thankful she is that I let her spend time with me, and if I want to send her my mailing address ,she'll send me the album and anything else from that trunk I'd like to have.

She attaches some documents with what medical history she could find on her extended family, which isn't much, and apologizes for the lack. At the end of the email she lists the name, work number, and address of my birth father. She couldn't bring herself to contact him but knows the contact information is correct.

She warns me he may not be receptive, could even deny I am his. 'Don't let him bully you,' she writes. 'Insist on a DNA test if he won't help you. That's your right.' She doesn't know if he knows she put me up for adoption. Finally, she says if I find it too difficult to contact him, she will.

The pain in my pelvis intensifies, and I try to remember when I took the last ibuprofen. Too soon. I read the email a second time, making sure I haven't missed anything, rub my pelvis, and glance at the attachments. They don't tell me much: Cancer, presumably from smoking. A car accident. Old age. More heart disease.

My birth father's name and address seem to pulse on the screen. Sebastien Medina. He works several blocks from my apartment at a law office. I could walk there in fifteen minutes. I've walked by the building before. Many times. I've never been in the building—one of the tallest in the city with dozens of offices—but I've walked by it. A few keystrokes, a click of the mouse, and his image appears on the screen: swarthy, maybe Mediterranean, maybe Middle Eastern. He's handsome for a man who must be in his early seventies. Have I walked by him? *A man with a wife and three children of his own. One of those children was in my class.* Somehow I'd forgotten these words, let them slide by me. This name, this address, doesn't just connect me to my father, but to my siblings as well. One the same age as my mother. Are the others older? Younger? Could I know them? They'd all be older than me. But how much older? And what does that matter? In a city of only four-hundred thousand, it's possible, definitely possible we've been at the same concert, sat near each other in a restaurant, brushed shoulders, never knowing.

I flee to the kitchen, my hands on the counter, my shoulders hunched, my body raging. I pop two more pills, remembering only after I've swallowed that it's an hour too soon. I refill my water glass and return to the computer screen.

Who is this man, this man who had an affair with a seventeen-year-old, a girl young enough to be his child, and left her helpless and alone with a baby—denying his role in our lives? Do I even want to know?

Maybe I'm one of many. He could have dozens of illegitimate children running around. I gulp the water down so fast I choke, cough, and sputter. I could have dozens of siblings. A dribble runs down my chin and I wipe it away. Or Lydia was a one-time thing. I was a one-time thing; one he's regretted daily. Or forgotten entirely. Me pushing myself into his life could destroy him and his family. My eyes blur. The pain rages. I feel shaky and tense and woozy. The phone rings. "Hello?"

"Hey, Baby."

"Adrian?"

"Yeah. You okay?"

"Yes. I...I'm good."

"How was your first day?"

"My first—"

"Tracey, are you?"

The pain shoots through me, like a knife slashing.

"Tracey?"

The blurring turns to black.

※

WHEN I COME TO, I'm staring at the ceiling, one ankle dangling over my desk chair. My name is repeated, over and over. My head shifts. As sight returns more clearly, I see my phone resting at the tips of my fingers. The sound of my name grows louder as I draw the phone to me. "Adrian?"

"Tracey, what happened?"

"I don't know."

"I'm on my way over. I just got in the car."

I start shaking, suddenly terrified. Why am I down here? What happened? "Did I faint?"

"I don't know. Why do you—"

"I'm on the floor."

"I'll be there soon. Don't move, okay? Are you hurt?"

"I…" the pain in my pelvis has faded. It's there, but less. Is that what he means? I do a mental scan of my body. My elbow throbs. I must have hit it during the fall. Everything else seems okay. Pain-wise at least. I push up on my forearms, glance down at my skirt and the spreading moisture. I collapse back down. "I'm okay," I tell him. "I'm fine."

"I'm coming."

"Use your key."

I prop myself up again. My arms shake. The room blackens and spins. I take several deep breaths, then adjust so I'm fully sitting. Breathe. Push myself up to my knees. Breathe. Stand, bracing myself against the wall as I shuffle to the bathroom, strip off my skirt, my underwear—breathe—

wrap them in a plastic bag—breathe—wash myself down and pull on some sweats—breathe.

Feeling more steady, I grab a cloth, make my way back to the living room and wipe up the lingering dampness on the floor. The scent of urine remains. A squirt of air freshener…make that three, and I settle onto the couch as Adrian turns his key in the lock. He rushes toward me.

"You okay?" He puts his hands on my face, my arms, my hips, as if checking me for damage. He draws me to him. "You scared the shit out of me."

"Literally?"

He laughs. "No, not literally. What happened?"

"I don't know." I shrug. "I wasn't feeling well today. Cramps or something. Then I got an email."

"An email?"

"From Lydia."

"Oh."

I smooth my hands over my sweats.

"That bad?"

"No." I look up. "I don't know why…I don't think I've ever fainted before."

"So that's what happened?"

"I guess. How long was I out?"

"Thirty seconds? Forty? I'm not sure."

I squeeze my hands against my legs.

"What was in the email?"

"She gave me the name and address of my father. He lives here, works at a practice in the Tower downtown."

"Wow." Adrian puffs out his cheeks then grins. "Can this be the human interest piece?"

I swat him.

"I'm joking. That's intense, Tracey. So, you could have walked by him or seen him or…did you look up his picture?"

"Yeah." I point to the computer.

An array of pictures slides by. Adrian disables the screen

saver and there he is again: Sebastien Medina. My father. Adrian looks back at me. "This is him?"

"I think so."

"Guess that's where you get your tan."

I inhale deeply.

Adrian swivels. "I'm sorry. This may not be the time to make jokes, huh?"

I close my eyes, not sure what disturbs me more, my father's close proximity, the faint, or wondering whether the news or the pain caused it.

Adrian sits. "Are you going to meet him?"

I shake my head vigorously.

"But for medical purposes?"

"It's something that comes from the mother. That's what matters. The mother."

"But other things?"

"I don't know."

Silence surrounds us as he holds my hand.

"Is that why you fainted?"

"I don't know."

"Are you feeling better now?" I nod. "That's good. It's not like you have to make a decision this instant. You can think about it."

"I may have met him." I turn my head toward Adrian. "I may have stood in line with him somewhere, been in the same theatre."

"I guess…"

"Or my siblings. I may have—"

"Siblings?"

"He has three children…" Realization floods me. "He had three children when I was born. Who knows? He could have had more."

Adrian squeezes my hand. "This is intense, huh?"

I laugh. "Definitely." I look to my lap, to my hands sitting there, the one not held by Adrian still trembling slightly. Do I tell him about the pain? It could be anything.

It could be a one-off. I don't want to talk anymore, anyway. I don't want to think. I lean into his arms and kiss him. He responds eagerly. I lose myself.

In the bedroom, the pain comes back. Strong and fiery. I yelp at the shock of it. Adrian stops. "It's okay." I smile. "A muscle spasm." But it wasn't a spasm. Nothing like it. A knife slicing into me—over and over. I've had discomfort before but not this. Never like this. The pain rages on until he's finished. I smile and sigh. I lie. I wanted escape. Relaxation. An hour later the ghost of the pain remains as a stabbing discomfort. Something is wrong.

CHAPTER TWENTY-ONE

Over the next few weeks I do my best to ignore the pain. It lessens. At times I can almost forget it. I try to forget about my father too, how close he is, how easily I could walk to his building, get on the elevator, and be standing outside his office.

Feeling obligated, I write a thank you note to Lydia. I don't acknowledge my final words or ask about the album. I actually want it, to see the pages I didn't see, to try to understand something of the transition from Lydia being the woman who loved me, who took pictures and put them into an album, to the woman who decided her life would be better without me. I can't ask without apologizing, but I'm not sure I know how. I should forget about that too.

But forgetting is impossible. The album. Lydia. My father. I start an email to Lydia twice. I walk by the Tower multiple times. I make excuses, telling myself I need a certain perfume I can only get at a shop nearby, or pretend I have a craving for tea at the little café in the building's lobby. I sit at a table, scanning the faces that come in and out. Sebastien Medina. Sebastien Medina. Sebastien Medina. He never appears.

ON A THURSDAY EVENING, just as I'm getting ready to leave for a date with Adrian, my phone rings. "I need you to take the kids."

"Jojo?"

"The kids. I'm on my way over now."

"Jojo, I'm—"

"He locked us out."

Shoot.

"I took them to the clinic, Neveah's got an ear infection, and when I came back the locks were changed."

"What the—"

"I'll be there in a half hour. Maybe less."

"Don't—" the line goes dead, "speed." I swipe to Adrian's number. He picks up on the fifth ring. "Change of plans."

"Hmm?"

"Jojo's bringing the kids over. I can't come out."

"What happened?"

"Damien changed the locks."

"Whoa. Should I come over or—"

"If you want. It doesn't sound like Jojo's planning to stay."

"Be there soon."

Jojo bangs on my door, Neveah in one arm, a huge bag in the other, and the twins engaged in a tug-of-war over some toy. She thrusts Neveah into my arms, steps over the threshold, and drops the bag in the foyer. "She needs two drops every three hours."

"How long will you be gone?"

"I don't know."

"What are you even doing?"

"Confronting him. He can't do this, can he?"

"No, of course…" I jostle Neveah, who whimpers, her arms outstretched for Jojo. "I don't think so."

"It's probably just a play, like he thinks this will get me back."

"He hasn't lived with you this whole time?"

"No. Stop it!" She yanks the toy out of the twins' hands and stuffs it in her purse. Lulu howls. Reggie looks smug. "I let him come in to get his stuff," Jojo yells over Lulu. "That's about it. He took the kids out a few times."

"Okay." Neveah whimpers into my shoulder now, giving Jojo a look of betrayal. The twins dash off after Toulouse, who screeches as one of them grasps her tail.

"Stop it. I'm warning you!" Jojo shouts. She snaps her gaze back to me. "If things don't go well, we'll be staying here tonight."

"Sure. Yeah."

"I'm leaving!" The twins race back toward us. They clamour at Jojo for hugs and kisses. She slams the door behind her.

"Did you eat?" I ask the twins. They shake their heads. "Tuna fish sandwiches?" Reggie screws up his face. "Egg sandwiches?"

"Yuck!" Lulu.

"Pancakes?"

"For dinner?" Reggie.

"Sure."

"Yea!" They chorus then run off in search of Toulouse again. Thankfully, my apartment has plenty of places to hide.

I set up a makeshift playpen by putting the couch and a trunk in a 'V' against one wall and, despite half a dozen interruptions from the twins, somehow manage to have the pancake mix ready when Adrian announces his arrival. He looks dashing as he sweeps into the kitchen and wraps his arms around me for a kiss.

Lulu squeals. "Ewww!"

I laugh and an ache erupts within me. Will this ever be our lives? Another ache threatens to overpower it. This one is physical. Sharp. Awful. Today is a bad day.

The twins chat excitedly as we sit down to eat. I try to calculate…three hours since the last painkiller. I shouldn't take another. Not yet. But the pain is getting worse. Day by day it's getting worse. I'm sure it's worse. It's not just the fear that something's wrong that makes me think so. This is not normal.

I put on a brave face—smiling, laughing. I'm used to it. I do it all the time. But that doesn't make it easy. By the time all three kids are sleeping, I feel as if the life has been syphoned out of me.

"Tracey?" Adrian returns from the bathroom to find me sprawled on the couch. "What is it?"

"Hmm? Nothing." I smile at him, masking a wince.

He sits beside me. "Try again."

"Just cramps."

"You take anything?"

"Mm-hmm."

"And they're still this bad?"

"They're not—." I grasp my side as the pain rockets through me. "Okay, some of them are pretty bad."

"Is it always like this for you?"

"It's hard to say." I push out a grin. "Pain is so subjective."

"Does it have anything to do with what you were talking about before? The fertility issues?"

"It could."

He's silent. "Anything I can do?"

"I need a distraction. Maybe put on a movie or something? Comedy."

"Sure." He turns on the TV, navigates to the on-demand section, then hands me the remote. "You choose."

The movie starts and I get the impression he's watching me more than the film. He squeezes my foot. "Should you go back to the doctor?"

I press pause. "Maybe. I don't know what she could do."

"Well, you didn't have this kind of pain before. Maybe…maybe if you explain…"

"I'll think about it." I pat his hand, not wanting to talk,

not wanting to think. The pain is like a growth: spreading, pulsing, fostering a life of its own.

I send Adrian home after the movie, not wanting any questions when Jojo comes for the kids. Only, she doesn't come. I send her a text, then another. At midnight I call. No answer. Fifteen minutes later the phone rings. She's speaking too fast for me to understand. Something about an officer, something else about trying to work it out, and can I keep the kids through the night. She'll come in the morning.

"But Neveah," I ask, "when does she need to feed? Is there—"

"She'll let you know. There's enough milk."

"Before school, Jojo."

"Before school."

My body feels beaten from within. All I want is to sleep, but as I hang up with Jojo, Neveah's whimpers travel down the hall. I heat up a bottle and open the door to my room just as her whimpers turn to a howl. Amazingly, neither of the twins wake. Her yells calm the moment I pick her up. She grasps the milk. Settled in the crook of my arm, she suckles happily while running her fingers up and down the length of the bottle. Her eyes close. Her fingers' movements still. Her warm body relaxes into mine as she succumbs to sleep. It's wonderful. In this moment the pain that throbs through me hardly matters, except for the fear that because of it I may never hold a child of my own. I need to go back to the doctor.

WHEN JOJO ARRIVES THE next morning her eyes are bloodshot. Her hair's a mess. She reeks of alcohol and marijuana.

"Jojo?"

She pushes her way past me. "Don't."

"But—"

"Don't."

"Mommy!" Lulu runs from the kitchen and catapults herself into Jojo's arms. Jojo clings to her so long Lulu squirms to get out of her arms.

"You ready?" Jojo smiles and brushes a toast crumb from her daughter's cheek.

"Allll-most." Lulu skips to the kitchen.

I reach for Jojo's arm, halting her walk toward my kitchen. "Are you okay?"

She doesn't turn to me. "We're back in the apartment. For now, at least."

"Okay."

She kisses the top of Reggie's head then tousles it. He grins back.

"To drive, though, I mean…"

"Yes," she spits out the word. "Sorry." She looks at me directly for the first time since entering the apartment. "I'm fine. I'm good. It was a long night. A long morning. I went to a friend's place. Not the best environment but I'm fine." She gestures to her children. "Thank you. So much." Passing through the kitchen to where Neveah is back in her makeshift playpen, Jojo lifts the baby and undoes her shirt. "Whoo." She sighs as Neveah latches on. "That feels better." She rubs her breast and smiles at me, looking older, hardly my little sister at all. "They get so sore when they fill up."

I stare at her, unsure what to say, what my rights are. As the pain revs up again, I realize for the first time that my sister and I have something powerful in common. We're both broken.

I CALL MY DOCTOR'S OFFICE during my lunch hour and book an appointment. Amazingly, she has an opening the next day. At the appointment I explain the pain that's practically become a constant companion, sometimes barely noticeable, sometimes the only thing I can notice. When I tell her about fainting from it, losing control of my bladder, her demeanour changes. She doesn't say it, but as I look at her expression, as I answer her questions: whether I've ever fainted before; the pain on a scale from one to ten; to describe, in as best detail as I can, the types of pain; any known triggers, I know this is worse than she thought. The words she uses—growth, blockage—they don't tell me anything concrete, but they terrify.

I EXPECTED TO WAIT months more for an ultrasound, but Dr. Keer gets me into one two weeks later. As I sit in the waiting room, willing my bladder not to explode, words repeat like a broken record in my mind. *Don't let it be cancer.* The technician calls me in. *Don't let it be cancer.* The jelly smears over my body. *Don't let it be cancer.* I'm released to the bathroom, return, brace myself for the second ultrasound. For the invasion. *Don't let it be cancer.* "Everything look okay?"

The technician smiles awkwardly. With her forearm, she pushes her long brown hair off her shoulder. Her shiny lips upturn. The sheen reminds me of the Lip Smackers I used to buy almost two decades ago. "I'm sorry. I'm not qualified to read the results."

I stare at the screen, the black and grey shades and shapes meaning nothing. "Of course." I nod. "But you're used to seeing them. You must have some idea."

"Your doctor will contact you shortly."

"But you'd know if something was different than normal. You'd—"

She gives me a pleading look.

"Sorry."

"You can get dressed now." She slips out of the room.

Before starting my walk home, I reach for my phone to take it off silent. A text from Adrian awaits. *How'd it go?*

I pause, considering. *Kinda slimy and cold. But my bladder survived! :)* I put my phone on vibrate. He may have other questions, but I don't have answers.

The day is warm. I breathe in the rich fall scent and drink in the vibrant reds and bronzes with my gaze. Draping my coat over my arm, I contemplate the multiple routes I can take home. It's a perfect day to walk along the harbour. The Tower looms ahead of me. Three different streets will lead me back onto the road home; one will pass my father's office building.

In the past two months I've mostly let thoughts of him linger in the far corners of my mind, popping up from time to time but not making much impact. It's basically the way he's always existed for me: his existence technically a reality, but not a very real one. Him, even more than Lydia, I want nothing to do with…except I do want something to do with Lydia.

The wind picks up as I approach the harbour. It whips my hair across my face and into my mouth. Then, the moment my foot hits the boardwalk, it settles. Few ships line the docks, even fewer people walk along them. Last time I was here the boardwalk thrummed with people, music, laughter. Now, a lone man walks in the distance.

The words that replayed in my mind at the clinic start their cycle again. The answer exists inside me, just sitting there. Cancer? Something worse? Something better? I want to look inside, cut myself open, know. As if aware of my questioning, the pain gives me a little nudge. I walk until my only choice is to return to the street or turn around. I turn and follow the boardwalk back, passing all the little shops, closed for the season, sad in their vacancy. I hesitate at the street that leads up to The Tower, then walk one more block.

My buzzing phone startles me. "Hello?"

"Tracey Sampson?"

"Yes."

"This is Dr. Keer's receptionist."

"Oh."

"She'd like to make an appointment to see you next week. Would Tuesday at ten in the morning work?"

I hesitate. "Any evening slots available?"

"Not for two more weeks. She'd really like to see you."

And she's calling. So soon. Do they ever call this soon? "Tuesday at ten is great."

I hang up the phone and walk in a daze.

CHAPTER TWENTY-TWO

During Thanksgiving I take the opportunity to finally write Lydia. I make it casual, asking if she still celebrates in England, if there are any big differences from the way we do it here, and then wish her and Westin a good time together. I ask for the album and, at last, apologize for my behaviour. I write the apology four times, deleting each, until I simply put, with no further explanation: I'm sorry. I should not have behaved that way.

We split the long weekend between my family and Adrian's. His parents' house is full of his brothers and sisters, nieces and nephews, laughter, food, and excitement; my parents' house is full of tension over why Damien isn't with us, tension over Jojo's announcement she'll be moving in with Mom and Dad—just for the short term—her body language and tone making it clear their house is the last place she wants to be, and the secret tensions I hold: guilt over Mom and Dad still not knowing the true reason for my trip or that my birth father works just blocks from my apartment, and that other secret…something is wrong with my body. Very wrong. I keep silent about it all, even to Adrian. It's a weekend to be thankful, to share joy. I just want it to end. Like all things, at last it does.

❧

"Tracey. Hello." On the morning of my appointment Dr. Keer welcomes me into her office. "How has the pain been?"

"Off and on. I still haven't had my period. It's definitely worse just before and on my period."

"And that would make it…"

"Late again. Forty-eight days."

She takes a seat and makes a note. I settle into the chair across from her. Cross my legs. Uncross them. Set my hands on my lap.

"We have an answer."

I lick my lips.

"You have endometriosis."

My brows furrow. "I thought endometriosis could only be determined through, what was the exploratory surgery called…lapa…"

"Laparoscopy. Yes. Usually that's the case. The reason is the ultrasound can't definitively pick up any cysts larger than a grape or a marble. It's rare that cysts are larger than that, especially before a confirmed diagnosis. But if they are, that changes things. Technically, we can't unequivocally confirm it's endometriosis without sending in a sample, retrieved during surgery. But that's a technicality."

I breathe in, waiting.

"It's a little complicated but based on the way the cysts show up on the screen we can decipher what they're made of. We know."

"Okay." I look at my hands, just sitting there. Helpless. "So I have cysts. And they're bigger than a marble."

"Yes."

"But they're not, uh…cancer?"

"No, no."

"And this is better than cancer?"

"It's...yes, I'd say it's better. I was concerned so, really, this is almost good news."

Almost? "Okay. So multiple?"

"At least two." She leans back. "You could have more. Smaller ones. But we can't see them." She pauses for the briefest moment. "How much do you know about endometriosis?"

"I looked it up after we first talked about it. Researches aren't exactly sure why it happens, but it's some sort of blood or autoimmune disorder. The blood travels back up the fallopian tubes rather than...well, rather than out."

Dr. Keer looks pleased. "Yes. That's one of the theories. The one that makes most sense to me."

"And it can create fertility problems in women, can cause pain, but it doesn't always."

"You've done your homework." Dr. Keer smiles. It's not comforting. "Now," she grabs some files from her desk, "I believe in giving my patients a realistic idea of what is going on. Currently, we have no cure for endometriosis. The most successful treatment for pain management is to go inside and use lasers to remove the cysts and adhesions. This often will help significantly with pain and several studies, a Canadian one, in particular, have shown positive results for fertility."

"Okay." I look back at my hands, still helpless. "Let's do that then."

"It's a little more complicated than that. Based on previous conversations, I got the impression you're extremely interested in having children one day."

"Yes." I lean forward. "Very."

"Okay. So the unfortunate news is that the cysts have developed within your ovaries. And, as I mentioned, they're rather large." She lists dimensions and my face must look as blank as my mind feels. "Each one is about the size of a ping-pong ball. Large enough to show up on the ultrasound. Stage IV endometrioma cysts don't usually even show up on an ultrasound."

"How many stages are there?"

"Four."

A gasp escapes.

"Are you okay?"

I nod vigorously.

"Okay. So that means we can't actually remove the cysts. Not fully. If we did, we'd be removing your eggs."

"Removing my…"

"We won't do that. The cysts can be drained, cauterized. This isn't my field. Really, you should be talking to a surgeon, but I talked to a friend of mine who's a specialist. I wanted something to tell you."

I will my expression to stay poised. "Thank you. So—"

"So if you decided to have surgery they would go in, get those cysts as small as they can, clean up any other damage they can—scar tissue, adhesions, other smaller cysts—and hope for the best."

Her words swirl through my mind. I swallow again. "So let's do that. And that would raise my chances? Help with the pain too?" I speak in my teacher's voice. Even. Strong. In control.

"The thing is, Tracey, surgery always has its complications. Each time we go in, scar tissue develops, which can impede fertility as well. And I won't go into the details, but there's always a chance something could go wrong. Always a risk. The other thing is, unless the surgical team is able to get every growth of endometriosis, which they can't do in your case, the condition will continue. Each cycle following surgery your chances of conceiving could lessen again." She smiles once more, like a parent smiling at a confused and injured child. "If you can handle the pain, and if pregnancy is your end goal, I wouldn't recommend surgery until you're ready to conceive…"

The words swirl harder, faster. My spine loses some of its firmness.

"…maybe not even until after you've tried for a year…"

The blood drains from my face.

"…it's possible we could speed that process up since we know you have a high chance of infertility. Six months, perhaps, depending on the wait list." She offers yet another smile. "You're still young, so, unfortunately, you're not considered a priority in comparison to women who are older, even if they don't have your condition." The smile remains, tenderness behind it. As I focus on her words, it's as if rushing water swirls around me, as if I'm about to be sucked under, and all my dreams of a family pulled down with me. "It is possible that these cysts won't even impede your chances of conception. If your tubes are clear and you're ovulating, it's still perfectly possible you can conceive."

"If?"

"With the irregularity of your periods I'm concerned about ovulation. If you were able to get back to a consistent cycle again that would be a good thing. Sometimes birth control is prescribed to—"

"I'm not going on that again."

"Okay." Dr. Keer looks at her notes again, or perhaps just looks away from me. "The fact that you were on birth control for so long…My guess is it was slowing or even preventing the cyst growth. The fact that they're so large now, what, not even a year after you went off—"

"Over a year."

"Okay. Well, either way, if returning to birth control is not an option you're interested in, that's fine. There are life changes we can talk about. Diet changes. It's not exactly my area but I can give you some tips, recommend a nutritionist."

"And the tubes?"

"I'm sending you for another test, a dye test. With the position of the cysts, well, it may be inconclusive, but it may not."

"So…"

"So, think about it, Tracey. How long away are you from wanting to start a family?"

"I don't know." I rub my arms, tilt my head, want to be out of this office. "My boyfriend and I, it's still new."

"Okay, so, if the pain's too much, absolutely you can have surgery." She hands me some pamphlets—*Endometriosis and You. Laparoscopy. Living with Infertility*— "But if you can handle it and your long-term goal is to have your own children with as little medical intervention as possible, I would recommend that you hold off. Not everyone would, but my opinion is in cases like these the less invasion the better."

"Okay…Umm."

"Take some time to think. If you have any other questions, you can book another appointment with me. If you decide you seriously want to consider surgery now, I'll refer you to my friend. She's one of the best."

"And the nutritionist?"

"Of course." Dr. Keer writes a name on a prescription pad. "You can always find your own as well, but I know this woman has experience with hormonal and fertility related issues."

We spend the next few minutes talking about some basic causes of the condition and basic suggestions for regulating my cycle—a healthy diet, regular exercise, ample fibre—things I already focus on. My arms and legs feel like limp noodles as I say goodbye to Dr. Keer. I slide into the driver's seat of my car and hold the door open just enough to not feel trapped while letting it shield me from the biting wind. With my head on the dash, I breathe slowly, imagining the balls of what…old blood? …sitting inside of me. I push open the door fully; the wind rushes in and howls around me. My head over the pavement, I gag several times but don't vomit. Once the urge has faded, I lean back in the car, protected again. The clock blinks 11:00. I booked off the whole morning so technically I don't have to be back at school for another forty-five minutes, but I can't think of where else to go. I turn the ignition, put the car in drive, and make my way across town. In my usual parking spot I linger in the car then pull out my phone and text Eloise. I kept this appointment, the ultrasound, to myself. Adrian's the only one who knows, but I can't talk to him about this. Not yet. *Emergency meeting. My place. 5:30?* Minutes later she replies: *Just me or the whole team?* A group of students huddle as they cross the parking lot—five girls braced against each other as they push through the gusts. Autumn's in England. Allison and Sheila, as far as I'm aware, don't know about any of this: my pregnancy scare, my adoption, the real reason for my trip. But they should. *The whole team.*

"Wow." Allison shakes her head. "This is like…wow."

"It's a lot."

"A lot a lot."

All three women stare at me. Allison looks completely shocked. Eloise concerned. Sheila, as always, is hard to read.

"Sorry. Sorry." Allison lets out an uncomfortable chuckle. "It's a mammoth to wrap my head around. The adoption. Meeting your mother. Learning about your father. But the big thing are these cysts, right?"

"In my mind." I take a deep breath. For the first time in the fifteen minutes I've been laying out my story to them, my voice quivers. The tea I've set before them all has yet to be touched. "I don't know what to do."

"You don't need to know what to do yet." Sheila reaches for her cup of tea, adds a plop of honey, and gives it three quick stirs. "This isn't a decision you should make quickly."

"I know."

"What are your initial thoughts?" asks Eloise.

"Well...I'm not sure I've even taken the time to figure that out yet. The pain sucks. Really sucks. I passed out from it a couple of months ago."

"What?" Allison yelps.

"Yeah...I'm kind of scared of surgery, but they perform these surgeries every day, right?"

"Right." Allison brings her voice back to normal.

Sheila shifts and takes a sip of her drink. "But as your doctor said, each surgery brings with it new complications."

"Yes."

"And if you want to have your best shot once you are trying to get pregnant..." Sheila's voice trails off.

"I should probably wait." None of them respond. "Is that what you all think?"

"This is totally one of those got to be what *you* think scenarios, Trace." Allison grabs Toulouse as he slinks by and nuzzles him up against her cheek. "Right?"

"Yeah. Yeah." I nod, not looking at any of them. My body feels constricted.

"What is it?" Eloise puts her hand on my shoulder. "There's something more."

With my eyes closed, I answer. "Adrian."

"You think he'll...you think...what?" asks Allison.

"He wants kids. I think that's important to him. I don't know how important but..." I love him, and I've been too scared to tell him. Now I have to tell him this.

"You think he'll leave you?" Eloise gives my shoulder a squeeze. "I don't think so. He wants to move in with you. He wants to start a life with you. Didn't he tell you he wouldn't let fertility concerns be an issue?"

"It wasn't as real then."

"But it's not necessarily real now. Your doctor said you could still have a chance, right? So, try not to work out every scenario. Try to trust."

The breath leaks from me. "But I have to tell him. It'd be wrong not...but what if—"

"What about adoption or…is that too weird?" Allison reaches for one of the cookies I laid out. "It sounds like you didn't have the best time with it."

"My parents tried. They did their best, but I wouldn't want to have a child go through what I went through, wondering, uncertain, feeling abandoned." I stop. "Maybe it would be easier for a newborn, but newborns can take a decade."

"Take a decade?" Allison finally grabs her tea and gives it a long sip.

"There's a wait period." Sheila shakes her head. "Everyone wants a baby."

"But you try, right?" Allison licks her lips. "Tasty." She takes a breath. "I mean it's an option. It's a last resort type of thing."

A cold laugh escapes me. "Would you want to be someone's last resort?"

Allison gulps and stuffs another cookie in her mouth. Sheila looks away. Tension settles like a thick fog.

"It's just options. Possibilities." Sheila draws back her gaze. "Really, that's all you have. And you're right, you have to tell Adrian. I'm no superstar when it comes to relationships but something like that…It is big, Tracey. We all know that. As awful as it sounds, it's a potential deal-breaker. I've seen marriages dissolve for less than this. In ugly ways. It would be wretched if," she stops, as if considering her words. "This fertility issue isn't something you can control, but especially with not wanting adoption, you need to lay it out to him. And I'd advise doing it before you give your notice at the end of this month."

"Intense, Sheila." Allison scoffs. "A little less?"

Eloise looks to Allison then me. "No. Sheila's right. It's not that he has a right to influence or make your decision, but if this could be huge for him, for both of your sakes, you need to talk about it."

My voice quivers. "He could leave me."

Eloise nods. "He could."

A part of me wants to lash out at her, at Sheila. But they're right. Fear and sadness rise in me like a ball of hot liquid. I squeeze back the tears.

"Like a band-aid." Sheila snaps her fingers. "Tell him tonight. Rip it off."

※

WHEN THE GIRLS HAVE left and I'm alone in my apartment again, I text Adrian to ask if he's home and if I can come over. He replies in the affirmative to both and questions why. I don't give an answer for that one but grab my purse and head to my car.

"To what do I owe this surprise visit?" He grins when he opens the door, but upon sight of me his grin falls. "What's up?"

I walk into his house, which in less than a month is supposed to be mine. "I saw the doctor today. About the ultrasound."

"Oh." He leads me into the living room. We sit on the couch, angled toward each other. "I take it the news isn't great. I haven't been asking. I didn't want to push."

"I don't have cancer." I smile. "So that's good."

He nods. Then, for the second time today, I relay all the doctor told me. I look away from him as I talk. "But I'll try when the time comes…if it's with you, with someone else, I'll do what I can to make it possible to have a baby." I turn back to him. He's staring away from me. "Adrian?"

"Uh huh?"

"Are you, uh…"

"Yeah. Yeah. Sorry." His gaze darts from point to point around the room, but never at me.

"Adrian."

"I…uh." He rubs his hands across his face. "I guess I,

uh…I didn't think it was real or…I thought it would kind of be nothing, you know? Some weird, unexplainable thing. Women are always going through these weird unexplainable things."

"Okay." I shift away from him. A wave of rejection crests; I breathe lightly, willing it not to collapse.

"What are the chances, huh?" He looks at me. "That something so…I did some research." He lets out a choking laugh. "You know, the journalist in me. When you started talking about the pain, made that ultrasound appointment, I did all this research. And endometriosis, in a lot of women the cysts or gatherings or whatever, they're like, maybe pencil eraser size or something. That's enough to cause problems. That's enough to require surgery."

This isn't news. I've done the research too. "Yes."

"So what you have. That's uh…big. Really big. Does the size, does that make it exponentially worse?" He pushes out that odd laugh again. "Exponentially. Is that even the word I mean to use?"

"I'm not sure."

"Because I was reading, and it's not just the pain and the trouble getting pregnant ,it's uh…" He picks up his remote control then tosses it back down again, adjusts a seat cushion then another. "Maybe you don't want to know."

I probably already know. "What?"

"It uh, even when you or, uh, women get pregnant, which can be really hard, that's just hurdle one."

I close my eyes, knowing the word he's about to say.

"Miscarriage."

I've been trying not to think of it. It's the second hurdle. One I may never even get to.

"I can't remember the percentage. I could look it up again. It's really high, though." He pauses. "Really high. Maybe three out of four."

I could elaborate—three out of four for *any* woman who has endometriosis. And I have stage four—but I don't.

"Yeah." He taps the back of his fingers on his leg. "Three out of four confirmed pregnancies end in miscarriage."

A pressure seems to radiate through me, but I hold it in. "Yes."

"So, you're saying you'll try but getting pregnant, doing whatever you think you need to do—surgery, drugs, or that...implantation thing or", his words flow faster ,"whatever, and then you could be two months along, four months along, further and you or...we...if and still...we could see and hear the heartbeat, we could see the pictures and then lose it, again and again."

"Lose—"

"The baby. Miscarriage. I don't know."

The pulse in my throat throbs. My hands tremble. "You don't know what?"

"I..." He runs his hands across his face, through his hair, again. I've never seen him like this, so tight, so far away. His expression changes, slightly manic for a moment then back to the Adrian I'm used to seeing. "But it's okay." He laughs again, less alarmingly this time. "I just raced *way* ahead. If we...I mean...if this is our future we're talking about it doesn't need to be so complicated. There's nothing you would need or have to do. And it could be years away, right? We're not in a rush." He taps his fingers again. "Yeah. We're not in a rush and when we're ready, if we're ready, maybe we could try for a bit, but if it's rough, if it's not working or if...well, maybe we should focus on adoption right from the get go."

I grit my teeth and stare. He looks so casual now, as if every worry he held just moments ago has melted away.

"You're adopted. You're great. My cousin's friend is adopted. He loves his family and his family loves him. It's the best thing that ever happened to all of them. And you know, it's like, better chances than a lottery, right? With your own kid, own pregnancy, anything can happen. When you adopt you already know the kid is healthy and well—ten fingers, ten toes." He stops. "Not that…I mean I know you weren't healthy at first but…"

"No."

"What?"

"No." Even as I push the words out, I know this could be the end. "I'm not adopting."

"We could try for a bit, see if maybe you're one of the lucky ones and the endometriosis isn't—"

"I'm not adopting, Adrian."

"But—"

"I will not adopt."

He stares at me, his face a display of struggle. It rests. "Then where does that leave us?"

I sit back, my expression firm but my hands still trembling, my pulse throbbing away. A sliver of sweat works its way down my spine. "I guess that's up to you."

"You absolutely will not consider adoption?"

"No."

He holds both of my hands in his, speaks so softly I can hardly hear him. "I wanted something simple. Fun. Straightforward."

My mouth slips open.

"You seemed that. At the Aspire event. I looked over at you and there you were, gorgeous. Sweet. Caring. And you seemed to have it all together. You seemed like someone I could live this beautiful life with. Strong and loving and…" He looks up. "Maybe we could wipe children off the table altogether. Not even try. Decide it'll be me and you."

"You want to be a father."

"I do, but," he stops, "I want you too. I just…what do you think? Maybe if we end up sticking it out for the long haul, we can decide it'll just be me and you. That will be enough."

I pull my hands out of his grasp. It can't be the end. Not yet. Not like this. "Children are still possible. Natural children, our children, if, like you said, if we're in it for the long haul. To make a decision like that now, it doesn't make—"

"All the trying, the potential loss. Tracey, it sounds like a nightmare."

"I'm sorry, I—"

"And you're the one who's cutting off the easy answer." His voice is sharp, distant. "You're the one who's saying no to adoption, this viable option."

But it's not viable. Not for me. I'll take the nightmare. "Adrian—"

"Maybe we both need some time to think."

"Adrian."

He stands and stuffs his hands in his pockets. "This is all really new, right? And it's big. It's a lot to take on. Just some time apart to think."

I stay on the couch. Frozen. "How much—"

"I don't know."

"I need to give my notice in a couple of weeks, to my landlord, should I—"

"I don't know."

At last I stand. He shifts several feet back. I make my way to the door. He follows and opens it, his hand on the lintel. Is this what it is to feel shell-shocked?

CHAPTER TWENTY-THREE

Two days go by, three, four, and still no word from Adrian. I'm just about to step into a bath when my phone rings. I race to it, not bothering to check the call display.

"Tracey, darling!"

"Hi, Mom." Disappointment drips from my voice but she doesn't seem to notice. Her voice is light and cheery.

"I'm calling to ask about Christmas plans. Will Adrian be joining us for dinner?" She pauses, her laugh like tinkle bells. "Oh my. Will you even be joining us? I imagine you'll have to choreograph events between the two families."

"I don't know, Mom. It's pretty early, isn't it?"

"These things take planning. I know it's been a long time since you've had someone serious, but you have to consider, it's not just dinner. It's present opening. It's the Christmas Eve's Eve annual get together. I'm hosting this year. There are ten other families in—"

"I know. But one person—"

"Two if you're both gone or both here."

"Fine."

She's silent. "You two are still…you haven't been having problems, have you?"

"It's really early to know, Mom. Not everyone plans so far ahead."

I can almost hear her pressing her lips together. "Well, let me know when you know then."

"I will."

"Tracey?"

"Yes."

"Why don't you come this weekend for a visit? Adrian's welcome to come too if he's available. Your father and I would love to see you. You're so distant lately."

I've always been distant. It's just my body that's not with her right now. How can she not see that?

"Your sister too. You should take her out. Go see a movie or get your hair done or—"

I can't help but laugh. "Jojo isn't exactly the 'go get your hair done' type of girl."

"Something else then. She's not seeing her friends. She's not doing well. She needs out of this house for a bit and away from those kids."

I let a few moments pass. "How are you doing?"

Mom's quiet longer than an honest answer would require. "Wonderful, just wonderful."

"Sure, Mom. I'll come."

AFTER WORK ON FRIDAY, I pack an overnight bag and check my phone again to see if Adrian has responded to the text I sent this morning—the first one all week—letting him know I'm heading to my parents'. Nine hours later, he has. *That's good. That's great. Tell them I say hello.* Nothing else. Nothing more.

The instant I step into my parents' home, the scent of fresh-baked banana muffins floating in the air, a weird mix of comfort and fear treads through me. Maybe it's the cysts, the knowledge that at some point in her life my mother went through something very similar to what I'm going through, and what I have ahead of me; maybe it's Adrian's withdrawal and the subsequent conversation with my girlfriends, in which they all unconvincingly assured me it's nothing, he just needs some time to think; maybe it's the guilt over withholding so much from the woman who, despite her faults, did her best to love me. Whatever it is, the feeling unnerves me while also making me want to curl up on a couch with my mother's arms around me. That probably won't happen, but I have a gift for mother, one I hope she's happy to receive. The album from Lydia arrived two days ago. I've yet to look at it, but I will tonight. We will.

"Tracey!" Mom steps from the kitchen wearing an apron and her beautiful smile. She hugs me tight against her, and in this moment I want her to be my mother, really and truly, in the way she probably wants, in the way I've never let her. I want to believe she loves me as much as she tries to make me think she does. "How are you, darling?" A frown forms on her face. "You look tired. How's your skin regime? Are you getting enough sleep?"

I step back from her embrace. "I've had a lot on my mind."

"Well," she grins, "we should have a girls' night. All four of us. Facials, aromatherapy. We can send your dad out with Reggie." She giggles, almost like a child. "We can even use all natural products so Jojo's in line with it...though I'm not sure how much she cares about that anymore."

I'm about to reject the idea but decide it may be what we all need. "Sounds great. I'd love to." I set down my bag. "Where is everyone?"

"Neveah's sleeping. The rest will be back soon. Your dad had to get some groceries in town so Jojo took the twins to the nearby park."

"Is the basement done?"

Her face lights up. "It is! I had my doubts, but it looks great. For a while I didn't think he'd ever get it done. It's different, you know, working on someone else's dream with a strict budget and timeline, compared to bringing into reality your own dream." She laughs. "Dreams and reality are not always the same thing. But he pulled it off!"

"That's great." I follow her into the kitchen. "You must be glad to get rid of that mess."

"You have no idea." She turns to me while beating some concoction with a whisk. "I'm proud of him, though."

"Did you tell him that?"

She pauses in her whisking. "You know what? I didn't." Bowl in hand, she turns her whole body toward me. "How are things, really? Is it Adrian or...what's going on? Trouble at school?"

"School's fine." Nervousness simmers. Do I tell Mom and Dad together? Show them the album together? The twins could disturb the moment. They could also ease it. Dad will be emotional yet happy, but Mom...Mom... "Mom?"

"Mm-hmm." Her back away from me again, she pulls over the tray and a spatula then starts expertly adorning each muffin with a creamy, delectable looking icing. "How long do you think before the others return? I have something I wanted to show you. To tell you."

"Is everything—"

"England. It...it wasn't just a vacation." She sets down the spatula. "I went...well...I went to meet my birth mother."

"Oh." She wipes her hands on her apron, her smile almost convincing. "That's exciting."

I shift from foot to foot. "I don't know that I'd call it exciting. It was," I pause, "interesting."

"I imagine." She takes off the apron and steps toward the kitchen table, pulls out a chair. "What's she like?"

"She was nice. Nothing like I expected."

"What did you expect?"

"I don't know." I sit down beside her, the bag that holds the album in my lap. "I don't know if I want to get into all that."

"Okay…what can I ask? Her profession? Any other children? And only your mother?"

"She's a professor at Oxford."

"Oxford University. The Oxford University?"

"Yes." I smile. "Jojo asked the same thing, in the same way."

"Jojo knows?"

I nod.

"Well," she smooths out a napkin that doesn't need smoothing, "that explains why you're so smart, doesn't it?"

"History of Art, too."

"Wow."

"No children. No natural children. She's a step-mother, by common-law. I met her partner too."

"That's great. So are you…are you close now or—"

"It didn't end so well."

"Oh, Tracey. Was she, did she not—"

"It was me. It was just too weird, too—I know you don't like talking about it or thinking about, anyway, I was angry and—"

"You can talk about it." She folds the napkin. "If you need to, that's fine."

"We're not close. I haven't talked to her since then, just email, just, mainly, to get this from her." I reach into my bag and set the album on the table between us. "It's my baby album."

"Oh," my mother's hand rises to her mouth. It shakes. "Your…she kept your baby album."

"Yeah. I've only looked through the first few pages while over there, then things sort of went downhill, but I thought it may be special for you to see it, for us to see it together."

She reaches her hand out and places it atop mine. "Thank you." She smiles and our eyes meet. "Let's open it up."

As we turn through the pages my mother cries freely. Seeing her, I can barely keep my own composure. "You were so beautiful." She runs her finger along a picture of me, probably about six months old, smiling broadly. "So beautiful." She reads each caption, progressing slowly. "It's amazing," she comments, "how alike you two look."

When we reach the photos I've yet to see, my focus increases. I remember none of it, but looking through it with my mother, who recognizes the face of the little girl she brought into her home, I'm able to connect the images of this little girl to the person I once was. At the final page of photos my mother stares at the blank one beside it. "I can not understand how any woman could have let you go. To have known you, to have held you..." Her voice cracks and she draws me to her side. "Thank you for showing me this. You have no idea what it is to have loved you so much, to know you were meant to be mine but have these first years lost."

My father coughs and we look up. He's standing in the entry to the kitchen, arms full of groceries. Jojo stands behind him.

"Tracey met her birth mother. In England."

"That's my cue." Jojo pivots 180 degrees and turns to the living room, where I can hear the twins laughing.

Dad sets down the groceries. "Your birth mother?"

"Yes." My mother waves him over, her tear-streaked smile beaming. "Come see."

ON THE DRIVE HOME Sunday night it feels as if one layer of fear and uncertainty has lifted away. My parents were curious, probably more curious than they showed, but they respected my privacy, not pushing when I was hesitant to answer a question. As expected, my father was clearly happy for me, made sure I knew if I wanted to pursue a relationship with Lydia they'd support it. My mother was happy about the pictures and, it seems, happy my interaction with Lydia went no further than it did.

As I enter the city limits, I can't shake the other layer of fear and uncertainty still covering me. My phone rings. Seeing the face that glows on the screen, I pull to the side of the road and answer the call.

"Is this an okay time?" Adrian's voice is heavy.

"Sure." I turn off the ignition and put the car in park. "I'm on the side of the road but—"

"Are you okay?"

"Yeah, I just…for the phone call."

"Right." He lets out a loud sigh. "I owe you an apology."

A truck zooms by, shaking my vehicle. "It was a lot to hear." Something within me trembles. "I understand if…"

"I was just really scared. I didn't handle it well."

"Okay…"

He makes a frustrated, moaning sound. "There are things I need to tell you. This isn't a conversation to have on the phone. Were you on your way somewhere or can you come over? Or I can go to your place, or—"

"I can come over. I can be there in fifteen minutes."

"Okay." Both of us are silent.

"Well, I'll see you then."

He's sorry. He didn't handle it well, but that means nothing. What if what he has to tell me is that he can't handle it all? And if Adrian doesn't want me, who would?

He stands at the door waiting as I walk toward his house, as he has so many times before. He smiles, hugs me, but the usual energy and excitement behind these actions is missing. He looks more tired than I've ever seen him. His shoulders slump. His body stoops.

"You have a good time with your family?"

"It was nice." I waver at the door, waver with what to say. "I told my parents about Lydia."

"Oh." He steps back, his wan looking face registering surprise. "Wow. Good for you. That's awesome. That's great. How'd they take it?"

"Better than I thought they would."

"I'm glad. That's…I'm glad. And Jojo?"

"This is not the best phase of her life."

He nods. "Dissolving a relationship is rough work."

I cringe and follow him into the living room. He sits on the armchair, not the couch, so my only option is to sit somewhat diagonally from him. He hunches forward, his elbows on his knees, his head in his hands. "I'm a bit of a wreck. It's been a hard few days for me…going back into things…emotional places I haven't visited for a long time."

"I didn't mean to…I…"

"You didn't do anything wrong, Tracey. You did everything right. This isn't about you. Or at least not in the way you think."

"Okay."

"I spent a lot of time with my brother this weekend, talking things out, trying to make sense of what I'm feeling and fearing, and of what I want."

"Alright." The ticking of his living room clock strikes louder than I've ever heard it.

"I haven't exactly figured it out yet but whatever happens, I think I owe it to you, to what we've built so far, to let you in on the process."

"Adrian…"

"Sorry." A raw laugh escapes. "I know I'm not making much sense. I want you, Tracey. That I know. That is clear. But I don't want you to have to give up any of your hopes and dreams to be with me and I don't know if I'm strong enough to…I don't know if…"

He's silent again, for so long. I want to press him, to pull the words he's struggling to say right out of him, but I let the silence linger.

"I had a daughter. A beautiful little girl. Christine."

Christine. Silence again, but this time I can't handle it. "Had?"

He nods.

"With your wife."

"Yeah. Yes. My ex-wife." His gaze darts around the room, then lands on a picture of his nephews and nieces on the wall. "She was so beautiful. This perfect little person. We hadn't planned to have a baby. I was still in school." He swallows, rubs a hand along his jaw. "And then there she was. I never knew I could love that much. I'd always thought, sure I'd have kids one day, more because it was the thing to do, you know? Propagate, ensure the future of the human race, but the moment I saw her heart eat, heard it, it was like my life took on this whole other dimension. And the moment I held her. Forget it. I was hers. Forever. Her life became more important than anything."

I stay on the edge of the seat, perched there, wanting to reach out, hold him, ease his pain. But I don't. I can't.

"We didn't know what happened. No one really did. At first we thought it was SIDS. You've heard—"

I nod.

"So one day she's there, happy, gurgling, so full of life, changing every moment. Then one day she's not." The ticking again. It's as if the hands of the clock crash with each second. "I found her. Cold. Stiff. I'd been working on a huge project the night before. I get in the zone sometimes. I thought, maybe she cried out, maybe if I'd—"

"Adrian."

"No, no." He looks back at me. "There was nothing I could have done. They assured me absolutely nothing would have made a difference. Julia assured me too. They ended up doing an autopsy at my request. It turns out it was actually a heart defect, something that had formed in the womb. Something that, maybe, could have been prevented. Maybe not.

"I had school, you know? Things still needed to be done and so I sucked myself into that. Julia wanted to get pregnant again. She said it would help. It made me so angry, like she thought Christine was replaceable."

I wince.

"She wasn't replaceable. I couldn't imagine loving another child the way I loved her. But if the love could even come close and the same thing happened again…apparently it was a genetic defect generally passed on through the mother. A few other babies over the generations died mysteriously. But no one knew why." He stands. "Do you want a drink or…are you thirsty?" I shake my head. "I'm thirsty." He strides to the kitchen and I follow him. He downs a glass of water in one motion then pours another one. Sips it. I lean against the counter. He stands against the far wall.

"I hardly touched her. For months. We had sex less than a handful of times, and I always insisted we use a condom. Eventually we stopped altogether. I didn't even really care, or I thought I didn't. I had my work. It was easier to not—" He looks to the floor, pauses his story, then draws his gaze back to me. "Then one day she came to me, her bags packed. Said she was pregnant. Said she'd found someone else, and they were starting a family. She'd been seeing him for five months. I didn't even suspect.

"I was pissed. Enraged. Here I thought I was so wronged. Here I thought…I blamed it on her, for leaving me, for not understanding my side of things, but the truth is I left her long before she left me."

That clock again, the sound travelling from the other room. The ticking resonating along to the beating of my heart. Each second of silence weighs heavier and heavier. "I'm not sure what to say." I take one step toward him, but no more. "Is this…so you don't want children?"

"No. No. I do. It scares me, but time you know, I don't know that it heals all wounds, but it certainly numbs the pain. I hurt over Christine every day. Just not as much. Still, to go through the trying, the strain, to hear the heartbeat of a new child knowing it's no guarantee…"

"It's never a guarantee."

Adrian sets down his glass. "That's true." He taps his finger on the counter. "I was almost relieved when you told me about your fertility issues in the beginning, or possible issues. I thought, well, this will give me some time to get used to the idea, figure it out. Less chance of an 'oops' I wasn't prepared for. That's horrible, it's—"

"It is what it is."

He crosses the room, puts his hands on my waist. "You made me want to try again. Try joining my life with someone new, maybe have a family someday. But I'd never want to do to you what I did to Julia, draw myself so far away, sink into my own pain while being blind to yours."

My brows furrow. "But you're aware now. Do you really think…"

He shrugs. "I don't know. It's not just that. I don't know if I could handle it. I don't know that I would even want to try, especially if it's hard, especially if we have to put all this effort into conceiving, knowing even that a positive test meant so little."

"But the surgery could give a stronger chance. That would—"

"I'm not there yet. I just…I want to be there. I'm trying to be honest." He holds me at arm's length. "I think I even said it to you once, that Julia wasn't the person I thought she was, that that's why we ended. In some ways that's true, but I think really it's more on me. I wasn't the person she thought I was, or that I even thought I was. I gave her nothing when Christine died. It was all about me and my pain, or rather my refusal to deal with my pain. All about what I could or couldn't handle. Julia wanted to look at pictures of Christine, to keep her room just as it was. I didn't. I hated her for trying to constantly make me remember. When she finally gave up trying, I was relieved. I didn't even realize she had also given up on me."

He hangs his head and I reach my hand up and draw it

through his thick strands. He holds his hand over mine, so I'm cupping the side of his head. I cannot lose this man.

"I'm aware now. I know what I did. But we sink into the ways of being that are natural to us. I could—" His voice breaks. He shakes his head and stands up tall, letting our hands fall. "Even if you could trust me, I don't know that I could trust myself."

I step back, my mouth gone dry, and wish I'd taken that water. "So where does this leave us?"

"I don't know. Yet. I just…this silent treatment I was giving you, it's basically like I said, old habits or ways of being. So I wanted you to know."

I scan his face, look for something more, but can't decipher what I find. "Thank you. I mean, for trusting me, for—"

"There's the other side too. Maybe you don't want to take the chance on me, knowing what you know."

I step toward him and gesture between us. "This. I want this." I stop, my hand resting on his chest. "I love you, Adrian."

He smiles, the most hesitant one I've ever seen him wear. "Yeah?"

"Yeah."

"I wondered."

We share a meal then lie in each other's arms while a movie plays across the screen in front of us. As I'm getting ready to leave, he pulls me against him, his arms wrapped around me so tight it's as if he's trying to absorb me into himself. We stand like that for a long time. Before I go, he squeezes my hand. "I don't know what I can or can't handle. But I know I want you. I know I want to make this work. If the uncertainty's not too much, give your landlord that notice." For the first time tonight, he gives me that boy-grin I love.

CHAPTER TWENTY-FOUR

At home, I lie in bed replaying the night. Adrian's loss makes me ache. How could I not have known? His little girl. The ache extends through me and for me—I hadn't seriously considered miscarriage. All that hope, all that potential effort…no wonder he's scared. It's terrifying. The memories flood back to me: four years old, palms sweaty, mouth dry, waiting to be told, yet again, that I'm not wanted, not good enough. Adrian says I'm worth it, worth the fear, the disappointment, but how can he know? He can't. I rub my eyes. I'm so drained even that movement seems an effort. I should be happy, elated. Adrian wants me despite the emotional torture my body may cause us, despite the fact that I may never give him a child. I should be joyful.

Over the next few weeks Adrian and my contact goes back to normal. We don't talk about my fertility issues or his fears. Which one of us is avoiding the topic, it's hard to tell. Perhaps both, perhaps neither. As far as I'm concerned, or at least as far as I convince myself, neither of us needs to make a decision about the future today. It's the present that's important. After a year or so of living together, we'll know whatever challenges lie ahead are worth it…or we'll know they're not. We can figure it out then.

We spend our time together going over final plans for the move: whose bed, whose couch, whose table, paintings, and dishware we'll keep or give away. We make Christmas plans. Christmas Eve's Eve with my family. Christmas Eve with his. Christmas morning with mine. And Christmas afternoon just the two of us. By mid-December we start moving my furniture and boxes a little at a time. The week before Christmas, once school is out, we enlist our friends (mostly his) to help with the big items, and on December twenty-second I walk through the empty halls of the apartment that held my life for the past six years. When I finish the walk-through, unnerved by these bare walls that will soon hold someone else's story, Toulouse paws at me. He looks up with his head cocked to the side. I scoop him into my arms and whisper a goodbye to the small space, part of me excited for the future, the other part terrified it will crumble around me, making me not just alone but homeless too. Adrian bounds up the stairs. "So that's the last of it?"

I draw strength from his smile. "That's it."

He wraps an arm around my shoulder. "Lucky the snow held off. This could have been much more difficult."

"Absolutely."

He grins and it's like my heart explodes. He loves me. I love him. We're moving in together. He tweaks my chin. "You excited?"

"Yeah." I smile up at him. "A new adventure."

He squeezes me tighter. "It will be."

After the last of my items are out of the truck and in Adrian's place, he holds up an envelope. "Your first item of mail in your new home."

"Who has my address?"

"Mail forwarding. Remember I set that up?"

"Right." I reach for the envelope. "It's…"

"From Lydia. Yeah."

Nervousness tingles through me. "What do you think it is?"

"From the size of the envelope I'd guess it's a Christmas card."

"Right." I slide open the seal.

"You want privacy?"

I glance toward him then back at the envelope. "No. It's fine."

The image is of a thatched roof house with a dusting of snow. A lit Christmas tree shines through the window. The inside is blank, except for Lydia's strong cursive.

Dear Tracey,

I debated weeks about whether to send this. So long, in fact, I can only hope it gets to you before Christmas. I hope I'm not being too forward but for the last twenty-eight years I've wanted the chance to wish you a Merry Christmas, to pass on joy for the season, so now that I can, I am. I could have before. I could have found you. Perhaps I should have found you. It's so hard sometimes to know the right thing.

Merry Christmas. May it be full of love and friendship and excitement. This is the first Christmas I won't devote a portion of it to wondering if you're okay, hoping you were placed with a good family, hoping you're healthy. So thank you for that. Even if those two days are the only two we ever see each other, I want you to know that they were the best gift anyone could have given me.

With much love and hope for your continued happiness,
Lydia.

It's only when I've reached the last word that I notice the streams of tears running down my cheeks. I wipe the moisture away then look to Adrian, who stood watching as I read. "It's nice. It's a nice card."

He offers a smile. "Good. I'm glad."

"So," I slip the card back in its envelope and set it on the counter, "where do we start first? Bedroom? Living room?"

He stares at me for several moments before responding, a look I'm learning means he's debating whether to push me to open up. "The bedroom," he finally says. "It'll be a challenge figuring out where to put all of those clothes."

"Oh," I grin as I walk past him then turn back with a

wink. "You'll have to get rid of most of yours."

※

THE DAYS FLY BY, FULL of family and laughter and squealing children, turkey and stuffing and desserts galore. At the end of it I'm tired and happy and ready for a relaxing Christmas afternoon—just Adrian and me. I stretch and step to the window. The snow falls gently. Two kids run through a field, throwing snowballs. Further out, a young woman glides across the Oval rink in the middle of the Commons, her blades barely seeming to touch the ice. She spins, her arms stretched above her like a ballerina. Life feels beautiful. I turn from the window, step around the boxes that litter the apartment, creating a virtual obstacle course in our living room, and plop down on the couch. "It's such a mess." Piles of books, paintings, and photos cover tables and chairs, waiting to be hung.

"It's our mess, though." Adrian wraps his arms around me from behind and leans his chin on my shoulder. "It's perfect."

I turn into his arms. "Only you could think this disaster zone is perfect."

"It's not the zone."

"My Mom would be freaking out."

He kisses my nose. "Good thing you're not your mother."

"Should we do some unpacking?"

"We should sit down and relax."

"After all of our hard work the past few days?"

"Yes, absolutely." He pulls me toward him on the couch. "It's hard work doing all that smiling and laughing and loving with family."

"You think so?" I tilt my head toward him. "I thought that all came easy for you."

"No." He shakes his head. "It's takes effort to be that delightful. It's like…uh…it's like…riding a bicycle on a tight-rope."

I laugh. "A bicycle on a tight-rope?"

"Yeah." He squeezes me. "I like this. Just the two of us."

I snuggle into him. "What do you want to do?"

There's a grin in his voice. "I have another Christmas present for you."

I pull away to see his face. "You already got me more than enough."

"It's our first Christmas together. You can't blame a guy for going overboard. You want it?"

I nod. Adrian leaves the room then comes back with a hand behind his back. "Close your eyes," he directs.

I do, then open them to see a little velvet box. I expect earrings or concert tickets. A solitaire diamond glimmers.

"Adrian?" He sinks to a knee, but I pull him back toward the couch. He rises, a crushed look on his face. "What are you doing?" I gasp.

"I thought it would be obvious."

"No, I mean—"

He stops me with a hand on my leg. "You're thinking it's fast, that I'm not thinking things through, but I am."

"How can you be—"

"What's the point of waiting? I'm sure about you, Tracey. I needed to figure that out but, with all that's gone on, if I hadn't been sure of you, we wouldn't be sitting here right now. But I'm here. I'm sure. I love you. And if I'm sure, why wait? I want—"

"It's so fast."

"What's time? We're not kids. You're old enough to know what you want. Do you want me?"

"Yes."

"And I want you. Your smile, your voice, they wipe away all the pain I thought I'd live with forever. With you I never feel like I have to be 'on.' I can just relax. Do you know how rare that is for me? I want you, Tracey. Everything that is you." He grasps a chunk of my hair. "This flowing hair. Those green eyes I lose myself in." He places a hand on my chest. "Your sweet, sweet heart and your fears too. Your struggles. I want it all."

My breath catches as I gaze into his green eyes that are almost like looking in a mirror. Rising against his hand, my chest feels so full it could burst.

He takes my hand. "I want a family again, and I want that family with you. I don't just mean kids, either. I want to know that you're my family. Forever this time. I'll do everything better. I'll make it work. I'll fight for us." He rubs his free hand against my arm. It sends shivers right through me. "And having kids, it could take years, right? So why not start now…or not now, but soon? I know you're who I want. Why not get the ball rolling?"

"The ball rolling?" I laugh, still overcome. He loves me. All of me. But—

"That's not the way to put it…I mean—"

Love isn't always enough. My joy fades. "Adrian," I hold the ring box away from me, "I don't want you to rush into this."

"I'm not."

"You are." My hand shakes. What am I doing? This is what I've wanted, what I've always wanted. What I want.

"I told you. I love you, Tracey. I—"

"What if it takes years? What if I have miscarriage after miscarriage after—"

"Stop."

"Do we even know each other? It's been just over a year."

"Tracey."

I close the box and stand, still clutching it in my hand. "What if you can't handle it?"

He rests his hand against my elbow. "We'll figure it out."

I shake my head and step away. Fear rushes through me

like a hurricane. "You'll change your mind. It's too soon."

"What does time—"

"No. You'll leave me. You could just leave me, and then what? You deserve someone better, without all this baggage." I hesitate. "Emotional and physical."

"I've got my share too."

"But—"

"Tracey, you're perfect."

"I'm not."

"Well, you're perfect for me."

"No, Adrian. I'm not. I'm—"

"Tracey." He steps toward me, but I hold my body away. He grabs my arms. "Where did you think this was going? You didn't see a chance I'd one day propose, decide it was time for us to start planning our lives? If not, what's the point of all of this?"

"Of course I did. But…I thought with more time, with living with me, really knowing me, you could make a more informed decision and…"

"And what?"

"And I'd know whether you could handle it, whether you'd—"

"I told you a long time ago, I'm not going to leave you over—"

"But just weeks ago you almost did, didn't you?"

"No…I—"

"You contemplated it." *Stop it.* The words scream through my mind. *Stop it. Stop it. Stop it. Just trust. Just—*

"Are you saying no?" He offers a crooked grin. "I haven't even actually asked yet."

"I…" My throat starts to close. The room pushes in, squeezing the life out of me. There are too many unknowns. My unknown fertility, especially, looming over us like a ticking time-bomb. If my body fails, if I fail, we may fail too. "I need to go."

"Go?"

"Yeah, just, is it hot in here? Or stuffy, it—" I rush to the window and crank it open.

"Tracey, it's freezing."

"I know. Sorry." I close the window, grab my purse and jacket, yank on my boots, and flee from the house. The snow falls in big flurry flakes, the sky is a deep grey, the playing kids and skating girl have all gone inside, and I have nowhere to go. My car keys are in the house. My phone is in my purse, but who would I call? It's five in the afternoon on Christmas day. I walk, hard and furious, until my hands and ears go numb. Why didn't I grab a hat and mitts? Eventually my pace slows. With the chill around me, my thoughts settle.

Adrian understands the fears he's dealing with, the unknowns of my situation in a way I can't, and yet he still wants me. The thought of putting him through the uncertainty and potential pain of having our hopes for a child raised and dashed, maybe time and time again, seems cruel. The thought of putting myself through losing him, while I also lose any hope of having my own child, seems impossible. And despite what he says, I could lose him. Life doesn't give guarantees. He could find he can't handle it, can't handle me: we could lose a child before we even really have it, and lose each other in the process.

The blowing snow creates a haze of white that blurs my path. It'd be easier to walk away now. It would have to be easier. People repeat their past all the time. If I walk away first, he can't. But if I walk away from him, what else will I continue to walk away from? When will the fleeing stop? My gaze turns toward the sky. Snow lands on my face and clings to my lashes.

I want him. He wants me. I ran from the man I love as he tried to propose. Ridiculous. The insanity of my actions swirls around me. I'm alone in a blizzard on the empty streets of Christmas day. Adrian could leave me, but he hasn't left me yet. I'm alone, but I don't have to be.

When I burst through the door Adrian is still sitting on the couch. He smiles in a way that tells me it's not too late. "That was dramatic."

I rush into his arms.

"Am I right to believe that was childhood? Or insecurity or—"

"Yes." I nod into his chest.

"Okay. So let's get this wet jacket off of you…and me. I really didn't need a taste of the storm."

I let out a small laugh and shed my coat.

"So that yes…"

"Yes. My answer is yes."

His eyes close. His smile is one of the most beautiful things I've ever seen. He opens his eyes and cups a hand under my chin. "I didn't actually ask you a question yet." His hand stretches out and closes around the box sitting on the couch beside him. "I've been thinking about this for a few weeks now, so if you need time I understand, I mean, I know I'm ready to work through whatever lies ahead, but if you're not sure…"

I'm sure enough. I'm sure as I can ever be. Sure that if I go through this with anyone, I want it to be him. He may not know one hundred percent what he's getting into, neither of us do, but he's here, he's seen me…like this, and he still wants me. The fear and pressure and uncertainty seep away; excitement and a willingness to trust fills its place. "Ask me."

"Tracey Sampson, will you be my wife?"

CHAPTER TWENTY-FIVE

A week after the proposal, Adrian walks into our kitchen. Scents of bacon and cream cheese and chocolate chip cookies waft through the air. "How much are you making?"

"Enough." I grin back at him. "It's a calculated plan. If our guests have full bellies, we won't have any sloppy drunks."

"You calling my friends sloppy?"

"Well," I turn my focus back on the jalapeno poppers I'm about to put in the oven, "Allison can put them back."

"Ah, so it's your friends who are sloppy."

"I'm trying to make sure no one is sloppy."

"I see." He reaches for my hand. The diamond glints in the light. "You ready for the big reveal?"

"Definitely."

"And you're sure you don't want to tell your family first? I mean if pictures get posted or…"

"We'll see them tomorrow, and neither of my parents has Facebook."

"It makes me nervous, you not telling them yet." He crosses his arms. "And you haven't even told your friends. You're in this one hundred percent, right? You're not ashamed or…"

"I didn't want to tell them over the phone. Just like you didn't want to tell your family that way, so we went to visit. But my family's farther away. To make another trip when we're seeing them tomorrow, it doesn't make sense."

"And you don't want to tell them the reason this is happening now and not a year from now?"

I take a breath, yank open the oven door, remove the first round of poppers and put in the second. "That's irrelevant." I turn toward him. "It's not really their business, right? Not anyone's business. We love each other. We're getting married. We want to start a family."

"They'll have to know sometime."

"If I have trouble. Only if…" I turn to the cookies on the cooling rack and start scooping them into a tin. "Maybe everything will be fine, we'll be pregnant a month after the wedding, and you'll be wishing you'd held back your proposal a couple of years."

Adrian gives my waist a squeeze. "Never."

"As for my friends, I'll tell them tonight. It's just been nice, our little secret. That's all."

Adrian pulls me against him. "It has been nice. And hey, if you want," he grins, "we could make something else our little secret, start baby-making now."

"And if I have a baby bump for the wedding?"

"It'll be cute." He rubs his arm along my shoulder. "I'm not entirely joking, you know. It's something we should talk about, consider. The doctor recommended you try before considering surgery, right? So maybe if we stopped preventing, then we could at least say—"

The doorbell rings and we turn our heads.

"Postpone this conversation until later?"

He nods and opens the door.

"Happy Housewarming!" Allison holds up two bottles of champagne. Eloise and Sheila stand behind her.

"You look fabulous." I motion for Allison to spin. Her hair falls in red waves around her face. Her dress, hugging every toned curve, looks like it was made for her. Vibrant green earrings dangle from her ears.

"Well, it is New Year's Eve." Allison grins and passes me

the bottles. "Plus," she glances into the apartment, "I was promised some eligible young men."

"Looks like we're the first." Sheila steps inside, looking lovely, but still like she could be going to a business meeting.

"You are indeed." Adrian waves the girls in.

"This is nice." Eloise passes me her coat. "And you moved in, what, two weeks ago?"

"About that."

She glances around the apartment then back at me. "It's interesting, the mix of your things and his. It works."

"I'd like to think so."

Before Adrian has a chance to close the door, several of his friends arrive. Within an hour, almost fifteen people filter through the rooms. I chat with some of Adrian's friends I haven't seen in a while, some I've never met, and then make my way to the teachers I invited. Charlise, her new baby bump proudly displayed, laughs at something one of Adrian's friends says then waves me into the circle. "This food is incredible." She pulls me into a hug. "I'm definitely eating more than our share." She rubs her belly. "And I love your new place, it's so—" She reaches for my hand then holds it up. "Is this what I think it is?"

Warmth floods my cheeks. I nod. "You're engaged?" She shouts the words and pulls me into another hug. She waves over some of the other teachers. A crowd forms around us; Eloise and Allison stand at the outskirts of it. Sheila's lips are pursed.

Adrian wraps his arm around my shoulder. "A week now. We've been keeping it on the down-low. We haven't had a chance to tell Tracey's parents yet. She wants to tell them in person."

"So save our congratulations?" asks Adrian's friend, Paul.

"Your public congratulations, at least."

"A toast!" says another.

"To Tracey and Adrian," one of his colleagues cheers.

"May they live long and prosper." A round of laughs and groans.

When the excitement settles, Eloise slips her arm around my waist. "Big news."

"Yeah."

"Congratulations."

"Thanks."

Sheila and Allison utter their agreement.

I step away from Eloise. "Why do I get the feeling you're not as excited as you should be?"

"We are. We are," says Eloise.

"If you are." Sheila glances from me to Eloise.

"What do you mean?"

"Never mind." Eloise waves her hand in front of her face. "Let's just enjoy the party. And celebrate. It's definitely a night for celebrating."

I look at each of my friends. "You're making me nervous. If you have something to say, say it."

"Don't freak. Enjoy. Another drink?" Allison raises her glass.

"Come here." I wave the girls into Adrian and my bedroom. "What is it?"

"Well," Eloise steps toward me, "you didn't tell us. You haven't told your parents yet…you let someone notice your ring instead of having a grand announcement. It doesn't seem like the Tracey who has been dreaming of this moment for years, who's had her perfect wedding planned since she was fourteen."

"When I was a kid."

"You still talked about it in University. And it's come up since then," says Eloise.

"You're not jumping for joy." Allison's expression is so uncharacteristically serious, it's unnerving. "Is this actually what you want? You're not rushing into it because here's your chance, or—"

"He asked me."

"Okay. But you've had a lot going on, the endometriosis, meeting your birth mother, learning your birth father is right here in town. It may not be the best time to make this kind of decision."

I close the door and turn to them. "Have you had a chance to talk about this or did you all spontaneously come to these same conclusions?"

Sheila crosses her arms. "I noticed the ring as soon as we got here. I was surprised I didn't know, so I asked these two. I was even more surprised to learn neither of them knew either."

"You think this is a bad idea?"

"No, no." Eloise waves her hands. "Adrian is great, and he seems great for you. We just don't want you to rush into something if it's for the wrong reasons."

"We've been together almost a year, and it's not like we're kids. It's not like we don't know what we're doing or what we want."

"I know." Eloise looks to the others. "It's like Allison was saying, all that's been going on, all that's still going on, these issues haven't been resolved."

"Well, my fertility won't be resolved, not without trying, probably not without surgery, which won't happen until we've tried for a while—"

"And your parents." Sheila cocks her head to the side and takes her court stance.

"What about my parents?"

"Have you contacted your mother again, your birth mother I mean, didn't things end kind of—"

"What does it matter how things ended? How does that have anything to do with this?"

"Just, if you're trying to distract yourself from these big life problems through a—"

"Adrian asked—" I lower my voice. "He asked me. I wasn't trying to distract myself from anything."

"And your father," Sheila uncrosses her arms and places

one hand on her hip, "have you—"

"What does he have to do with this?"

"Maybe you should meet Sebastien, meet—"

"What?" Flustered, I back away from my friends and bump against the foot of the bed. "I never told you his name. I never told any of you his name."

Sheila drops her arm. "You told me he was a lawyer who worked in the tower, that he had three kids, by the age he would be, he was the only one who fit."

"You researched—"

"I know him."

"You what?"

"Not well. He's in divorce law, but we've interacted at events and your brother—"

"My—"

"Patrick. Patrick Medina. I know him quite well. He's a prosecutor. We've shared a courtroom more than once."

My knees give out and I collapse to the bed. It feels as if a weight is pushing against my chest. "Did you…does he?"

"God, of course not." Sheila steps toward me. She presses her lips together before speaking. "I didn't tell him, any of them, about you, if that's what you're asking. I just—"

"What's he like?"

"Who? Patrick or—"

"Either. Both."

"Patrick is smart. Sharp. Driven. He can come across as a bit of a bastard sometimes, but he seems to have a good heart. It shows when he suspects he's defending someone who deserves to be in jail. He'll do his job, but sometimes it seems like a part of him wishes he hadn't."

I stare at the floor. Allison's feet shuffle back and forth. The bass of some song from the living room thumps in the background. A woman's voice squeals.

"He's a good guy overall. Doesn't seem to like his father a whole lot."

I look to Sheila.

"I don't know your father personally, as I said. He comes across as…presentable. Polished. Are you sure you want to hear this?"

"I asked, didn't I?"

"Apparently ten to fifteen years ago there was a scandal. A young woman. He was teaching at the University for a few semesters, a student or—"

"Sheila," Allison interjects, "she doesn't need to hear—"

A laugh escapes my throat. "So I could have even more siblings."

"I don't think…no." Sheila, who always looks composed, seems uncomfortable. "At least not from that situation."

"But it was apparently a habit for him. Cheating on his wife with young women. Is he still married?"

"I think so."

My voice comes out tense, just like the rest of me. "I wonder what she's like."

Eloise steps closer. "There's no need to wonder about any of this right now. It…it is what it is. We just want to know, want to make sure you're sure this is what you want, that you're not rushing into—"

"We're not eloping or anything. We're thinking a June wedding."

"So soon?" asks Sheila.

"We know what we want. Why wait? Especially with my situation. The sooner we start trying—"

"June." Allison cuts me off with a smile. "June's a good month."

I laugh at her sudden switch. "Shortly after school lets out. And far enough away that people can plan for it. Hopefully Autumn can come." I smile. "So you all can be my bridesmaids."

Allison sighs dramatically with a sweep of her hand. "Always a bridesmaid never a bride."

"Well, maybe you should get back out there," I nudge

her while trying to ignore the twisting stomach their words ignited. "Some of Adrian's friends seem pretty cool."

"Tasty." She adjusts her dress in the mirror, keeping a straight face while using our undergrad word to describe good-looking guys. "Definitely tasty. And I am looking fit to kill."

"You are," says Eloise. She turns to me. "So this is real, this isn't—"

"Yes." I keep my tone firm. "The fertility issue has something to do with it. It made us both consider how serious we were, how much we want each other and what we're willing to risk. It's sped the process, but that's all it's done, sped it. I'm not running away from the other issues. I'm not jumping into this because he's the first guy who's asked. I love Adrian."

Allison glances over from her primping in the mirror. "That's good enough for me."

"Me too." Eloise gives my elbow a squeeze.

Sheila lets out a little sigh. "Was it wrong of me to let that slip? Are you okay?"

I stand. "My life seems a minefield lately, what's one more bomb?"

"Do you really feel that way?"

"I don't know." I step away from the bed. "I don't have to figure out how I feel tonight."

"No, of course not."

"And we are missing a great party."

Sheila nods.

"So, congratulations," says Eloise. "And yes, we'll be thrilled to be your bridesmaids."

"Let us pick the dress." Allison gives a little clap. "Please, let us pick the dress."

"Sure."

We rejoin the party. Like a linebacker, Adrian weaves through the crowd toward me. "Everything good?"

I smile up at him, willing my body not to shake with the

new knowledge I hold. Someone I know knows Sebastien, knows my brother, Patrick. My brother has a name: Patrick. The knowledge makes my father, this other family, real. What do I do with that? "Great." I give Adrian a quick kiss. "Mostly just talking about the wedding. I asked them to be my bridesmaids."

"Mostly?"

I swallow, contemplating what to say. Cindy, one of Adrian's fellow journalists, pulls me toward the dance floor. "Later." I wave. "We'll talk later."

THE NEXT DAY, BEFORE we've even knocked on my parents' door, it swings open to reveal Jojo. She passes Neveah to Adrian then pulls on my arm with a smile. "Woman stuff," she says to Adrian as she drags me to her room. Once there, she practically pushes me inside then shuts the door.

"What the fuck?"

"What?"

"That." She points to my ring.

"How did—"

"Facebook, obviously."

"Someone—"

"No. I could see."

"Come on, Tracey. Come on."

"What? I'm sorry I didn't tell you. I thought in person—"

She throws her hands in the air. "It's not that you didn't tell me, it's just, now? Really? Now?"

"You're going to have to explain this better." I rub a hand to my cheek. Someone else not happy for me?

"It's...Arghh." She plops into the rocking chair in the corner. "Okay. I know I'm a rat and a baby, just, my life is shit right now. And the one thing I had over you was the kids and the consistent relationship, even though the rest of my life was basically an utter disappointment. And sure, the way I went about getting those kids Mom and Dad do not consider stellar, but still, having them, making it work with Damien, that was the one thing, you know? You couldn't make a relationship work, but I could. Then that all blows up and what do you do? Two seconds later you bring in this fabulous guy who Mom and Dad love, you announce you're moving in with him, and now you're marrying him. The timing could not be worse."

I almost laugh at her theatrics, but annoyance wins over. "You do sound like a child."

"Just…maybe take off the ring. Give it a few weeks or something, a few months. Wait until I'm perhaps out of the house, until I get my diploma or—"

"Jojo. Mom and Dad won't think like that."

"Oh, yes, they will. Mom at least. You don't hear the hints she leaves. The little mentions, 'oh, it'd be so nice if you were more like Tracey. Why can't you be a teacher and date a journalist and—'"

"She does not."

"Okay. Not in so many words but the sentiment is there." Her shoulders slump. "I'm horrible." She offers a strained smile. "So you love this guy? Like really love him, like even when life gets shit you'll still love him type of love?"

This time I laugh at the exaggeratedly pathetic look Jojo wears. "Yes."

"I still wish your timing was better but, congratulations." She sighs, looking more like my little sister than she has in years. "Never agree to polygamy."

"I don't plan to."

She hugs me. "Wait a few years before having kids, okay?"

"Don't say that."

"No, seriously. Not even for me and my rugrats being pushed to second tier, but for you and Adrian. Enjoy each other first. Kids change everything."

I consider telling Jojo why we can't wait, but the conversation could be a long one. "It'll happen when it happens." I walk toward the door.

"Two more minutes." She drags me back. "With all the Christmas cookies, the twins are bigger tyrants than usual. Just two more minutes of silence."

"Okay." I sit down beside her.

Before Jojo's required minutes of silence have elapsed, Mom's delicate rapping sounds on the door. "Dears, what are you doing in there?"

"Nothing, Mom." Jojo glances at me. "Sitting."

"Sitting?" Mom pushes open the door. "Is everything alright?"

"It's fine."

Mom glances from Jojo to me. "Then why are—"

"I wanted some quiet."

Mom clucks, then turns to me. "Tracey, where's my hug?"

"Sorry, Mom."

As I walk toward her, she gasps. "Oh, yes! Oh, yes, yes!" She reaches for my hand. "It's beautiful, darling. Just beautiful. When did he?"

"Christmas."

"And you never?"

"We wanted to tell you in person."

"Oh!" She squeals again. "More grandbabies. And he's such a nice young man. Henry! Come in here! Adrian, you too."

My father and Adrian make their way into the room, Neveah in Dad's arms and Adrian trailing a twin on each leg. "They're engaged!" Mom yells.

Dad grins and gives Adrian a friendly punch on the shoulder. "Good man."

"Have you thought about when the wedding will be?" Mom beams.

I glance to Adrian, then back at Mom. "We're thinking late June, once school's out."

"Perfect." Mom clasps her hands in front of her. "Just perfect."

Throughout dinner Mom asks questions about the wedding, makes suggestions, and brings up the possibility of more grandchildren again. Adrian and I smile and nod but make no commitments or concessions regarding anything. I enjoy the wedding talk, melding my ideas with hers, and especially enjoy my parents' offer of a significant donation to the wedding fund, though we assure them we want it to be inexpensive and low key (in case baby-making efforts get expensive, but we keep that detail to ourselves.) The talk of grandchildren makes me squirm. My non-committal answers feel like lies. I want them just as much as she does. More. When at last we leave, I lean into Adrian's side as we walk to the driveway.

"I think your mother's more excited about this wedding than we are." He squeezes me against him.

"I don't know about that." I laugh. "I'm pretty excited."

"She's excited about the wedding." He steps away from me to open the car door. "Me, I'm excited about the marriage."

"You charmer." I wink before sliding into the passenger seat.

Out on the main road, he glances at me. "Last night. The little huddle in our room. That was about more than our engagement, wasn't it?"

"I thought men were supposed to be oblivious."

"I'm no mere man." He puffs up his chest. "I'm a reporter."

"Ha ha."

"No, really." He grins that boy grin. "Observing people, not missing anything, knowing when people are concealing a story beneath the story. That's what makes me the best."

"The best?" I joke.

"Well," he laughs, "that's what makes me one of the few to still have steady work when departments are shrinking by the day."

"Too bad you couldn't leave that trait at the door when you leave work."

"I never leave work."

"Yeah." I hesitate. "There've been a lot of layoffs, though, haven't there? You said sections of the office look like a ghost town?"

"I'm not too worried. This Halifax/Toronto sex trafficking piece will be big. It's been on hold; I was scared they weren't interested, but it's because they wanted it bigger. It looks like the documentary may happen. If it does, I'll be around for a while."

"That's great."

"Yeah. Even if things fall through after that, I'm a scrapper, and people will always want stories."

"I'm proud of you."

"And," he reaches over to give my knee a squeeze, "I'm not distracted that easily. What was going on last night?"

I fill him in on the girls' fear that I was rushing into marriage because of my urgency to have children and create the life I've always imagined.

"Do you think there's any truth to that?"

"No." I rub a hand over my abdomen, the pain that's been brewing these last few days enters my consciousness. Right now it's not too bad but based on the last few cycles, in a day or two it will be all I can think of. I look to Adrian. "Not beyond what you said when you proposed—we know this is what we want, we know it could take a while, so why not start now?"

"Do you mean that? Actually start now, rather than in six months?"

Several breaths pass before I answer. The greatest harm would be getting married with a big belly, which would also mean our dreams had come true sooner, the road we'd lead together would not be as hard as we imagined. As to what others would think— "That's not what I meant." A smile forms. "But if you want, if you think—"

"I think. I want." He grins.

"Then why not?"

Adrian's expression turns serious. "Shit just got real."

After a few moments of laughter he glances over again. "What else?"

A half sigh, half groan escapes me. "Sheila knows my father."

"Your birth father?"

"Yeah. Or, she knows of him. She actually knows my brother. Like knows him, knows him."

"You don't mean…"

"No, no. I hope not. She's been opposite him in court, multiple times it seems."

"Shit did just get real."

"Seems like it."

"So…what does this change?"

"Nothing really." I tell Adrian about the student scandal. "This father of mine doesn't seem like someone I want to have anything to do with, and clearly he wants nothing to do with me."

"That was thirty years ago. People change, they realize the error of their ways."

"If he really did, he could have found Lydia. She found him, and from the sounds of it there's been no communication between them."

"What about your siblings? They're not to blame in all this."

"It's too much."

"Yeah, but—"

"Adrian." Irritation leaks from my voice. "Maybe one day. Not now. There's no rush."

"There could—"

"Adrian."

"Alright." He eases onto the highway, changes lanes, overtakes someone going several kilometres below the speed limit. "What about Lydia, did you reply to the Christmas card or—"

"Adrian."

"I think maybe all of this is happening for a reason. You know? Even that one of your best friends knows your birth father, that your birth mother is reaching out, all while you're facing the possibility of never starting your own blood family. It seems—"

"So about starting tonight." My voice is direct, even.

"How about this weather we've been having?" He grins as I roll my eyes at him. "Just trying to take a hint."

I can't help but smile.

CHAPTER TWENTY-SIX

The winter and spring fly by. Three weeks before the wedding, my life is full of exam marking, guest lists, and finalizations for the caterer. I sit at a table spread with envelopes, lists, and charts.

In the five and a half months since the engagement I've had less than four cycles, each one defined by raging pain and the visitor that tells me, yet again, my body has failed.

I try not to think of these un-pregnant months as failures. The wedding dress I didn't buy until two months ago, in hopeful anticipation of a size change, won't need to be taken out. But this is a good thing. Most definitely. One less stress.

It's not as if we've been actively trying, either. The only thing I'm charting is the length of my cycles. Those other measures I've read about—fluid tracking, temperature tracking, supplements—will wait until after the wedding.

According to the stats, for a healthy woman my age, five months is normal, right there around average. No need to worry yet. At eight months, the woman without a reason to think anything is wrong should perhaps get a little concerned. But I'm not a woman without a reason to think anything is wrong. One more month, or at least one more cycle, and I'll have a solid reason to be cut open.

But these are thoughts I don't have time for right now. I need to focus on the things in life I have some degree of control over: being an amazing teacher to my students, being the best fiancé I can be to Adrian, and making this wedding as dream-perfect as possible.

I need to believe that my life is just as it should be. I'm accepted by a man who wants me, despite the fact that I am, unequivocally, not perfect. Not only accepted, I'm desired, loved, worth fighting through life's challenges to be with. How can I not feel happy?

Names and addresses blur before my eyes. I blink, willing myself to focus. The pile of RSVPs in front of me seems daunting. If I could turn back time, I would definitely listen to Adrian's suggestion to do the e-response route, rather than the lovely little response cards I'm using, each one requiring manual inputs into my online wedding planner.

As I read the next card on the pile, my face lights up: the Andreys.

I call out to Adrian, who's in the kitchen. "Emily and Amalia are coming!"

He pops his head into the dining room, where I use the table as a massive desk. Pungent and amazing smells waft out. "Jakob's sisters?"

"Yeah."

"Sweet." He smiles then returns to his concoction.

I open several more envelopes, all Adrian's guests, then my hand freezes.

"Adrian."

"Yeah?"

"Adrian, get in here."

"What's up?" He wipes his hands on his apron and leans against the entry to the room.

"What is this?" I hold up the response card.

He steps close enough to read. "She said yes."

"*She* wasn't invited."

He pulls out a chair and sits. "I invited her."

"Who gave you the right to—"

"I have a right to invite people to my wedding."

"It's our wedding."

"Exactly, and it's important to me that my wife's mother is at our wedding."

My eyes close. I swallow, willing myself to control the anger swirling inside me. This is a betrayal. I glare at him. "My mother will be at my wedding."

He leans back in the chair, an unreadable expression on his face. "You have two mothers. And yes, both of them will be there."

"Should I be expecting a response card from Sebastien as well?"

"No."

My voice shakes. "What am I supposed to do about this?"

"Have her at your wedding." He takes the card from me. "Her and her plus one. Westin."

"Is this a joke to you?"

"No." He sets the card on the table. "I was trying to lighten the mood a bit. They're just guests, it's just…"

"No, Adrian. We've been through this before. They're not just guests. How will this work? Will she be invited to the rehearsal dinner? Will she be sitting in the row with my family?" I rub my hands across my face. "Should she be at the family table?"

Something bubbles over on the stove. Adrian stays seated. "I didn't think about all that." His face clouds, then clears as if all concern has vanished. "She could be part of all that, if you want. But either way is fine. Her as family or her simply as a guest."

"She'll have to meet my Mom and Dad," I say through gritted teeth.

"Who says that's a bad thing?"

"She doesn't deserve to be at my wedding."

"Deserve?"

"Just," I push away from the table and stand, "go get your food. No need to ruin one more thing tonight."

"Hey, hey." Adrian jumps up to block my escape out the

other entryway. "Don't run."

"I don't need this." I struggle in his arms. "You had no right."

"Okay. Maybe I had no right, but I thought it was best, and I honestly think it's not the traumatic disaster you seem to think it is."

"Let me go."

He holds me firm. "You can't run away whenever you're angry with me."

"Let me—"

"No. Listen. She'll come. They'll come. You don't have to do anything special. She'll just be here, and maybe one day if your relationship changes you'll be happy about that."

"She can't simply come. How do I introduce her to people? Where do I seat her? What do I say? Besides one email asking her to send the album, the last time I spoke to her I was yelling. I made a fool of—"

"And obviously she's okay with that. The card at Christmas. This." He picks up the response card and shakes it. "Obviously she wants you in her life."

"Well, that doesn't mean I want her. She abandoned me, Adrian. She threw me away."

"She didn't—"

"With the exams, the wedding, this—" I motion across my abdomen. "You just had to lay on one more thing."

"Isn't the wedding something you're supposed to be excited about? Something happy?"

"It is." I try to push out of his arms again as I fight back tears. "But it's also stressful."

"Okay." He pulls me tighter, sheltering me in his arms while I wiggle to get free. "We'll work it out. We can handle it however you want. She can be included as family or she can be treated as a casual guest, or something in between. At least she'll be there. She wants to be there." He releases me. "She's travelling all this way. That means something."

I step back and stare up at him. "I guess."

"It'll be fine."

"She'll have to meet my mother. My *mother*. You know how this will make her feel? She acts like this is her wedding half as much as mine. She'll see Lydia as an interloper, trying to steal her—"

"She'll be okay. She's not a child. She's probably tougher than you give her credit for." He rubs a hand along my arm. "Maybe she'll be thankful to Lydia, excited to meet her. After all the struggle she went through to have a baby, it's because of Lydia that she has you."

"The consolation prize."

"Stop it."

"Okay." I let out a long puff of air. "Invite Sebastien and I'm calling the wedding off."

"Noted." He grins. "I'm excited. I get to meet the woman who created someone as amazing as you."

"Nurture over Nature."

"You need to give her a break, Trace. She was young. She was trying to do the right thing. And from what it sounds like, she's punished herself plenty."

The memory of Lydia's tied tubes surfaces to my mind and something deep within me twinges. "Will you be the one to give my mother the heads up?"

"And have her hate me instead of you? No, no. I don't think so." I swat at him. He laughs. "If you wish."

Sizzles and pops travel from the kitchen. The scent of roasted garlic and tomatoes makes my stomach roar. "Get to the stove already." I push him out of the room.

THE NEXT WEEK I MEET my mother in the reception hall for the final walk through before the wedding. She trails her manicured fingers along the cream tablecloth on display. "Lydia, her name is?"

"Yes, Mom. Lydia. You know this."

"Yes. I know. Double checking." Her head is away from me and she nods at the table. "These are good. Lovely." Her words squeeze out.

"Mom."

"Mm-hmm?"

"Adrian invited her. It wasn't my—"

"It makes sense, sweetie." She turns and trails those manicured fingers along my jawline. "Why shouldn't your mother be at your wedding?"

"You're my mo—"

"Your birth mother." She walks over to the arch. "Semantics. Now, this would look nice at the entrance, don't you think? For your grand entrance." Her smile is broad.

"I was thinking behind the head table, actually."

She assesses. "You're having the wedding party sit with you, though?"

"Yes."

"It would look odd."

"Okay. The entrance it is."

"And your birth father, is he…"

"No. Just Lydia and her partner."

"Her partner?"

"Her boyfriend."

Mom lifts her chin. "This is very hurtful."

"Mom."

"You're my baby. I raised you. I took care of you. Night after night when you cried yourself to sleep, when you woke up sobbing, I soothed you. I calmed you."

"Mom."

Her voice raises. It's still low, but I know from experience this is her version of a full out yell. "What did that woman do?"

"Mom."

"She gave you away, that's what. She deserted you. She—"

"She took care of me for two years. She gave me life."

"She's not your mother."

I stare at the tablecloth, at my mother's hand still resting on it, surprised I've defended Lydia.

"And she just thinks she's going to come and—"

"Adrian invited her. What was I supposed to do?"

She turns her head. Several moments pass before she looks back, a fresh smile pasted on, a smile I've worn countless times. "Of course, darling. I'm sorry. Look at me. All the stress of the wedding." She stands straight, smooths her unruffled dress. "Just a silly little outburst. Forgive me. Of course it's great. It's just great, honey, that she'll be here." She scans the room, as if assessing it, then turns to me. "What will you tell people? I know the adoption makes you uncomfortable."

"If they ask, we'll tell them the truth. There are so many unknowns at weddings, though."

"Well, if she's at the family table…"

"I don't think she will be."

"You haven't done the seating plan yet? Tracey, it's getting—"

"She won't be." I snap, then reign in my tone. "She'll sit with Jakob and the Andrevs."

"Oh, she met them, didn't she? That will be nice." Her voice is too perky, too high. "Are you going for the chair slips?"

"They're too expensive."

"I suppose."

I step toward her. "Are you okay with this?"

"I don't see why it matters. You're a woman. You're getting married. You don't need your…me to be okay with it."

One of the venue managers strides into the room as she apologizes for the call she had to take. In fifteen minutes we've finalized everything that needs finalizing and are back in my mother's car, driving along the highway to Adrian's and my place. The setting sun casts a sharp orange glow against the glass of the office building next to our apartment. It looks aflame. I glance at my mother. She smiles, her jaw slightly clenched.

"I want you to be okay. I don't want to hurt—"

"I'm fine." She waves a hand.

"You'll be welcoming and—"

"Tracey Sampson. Am I ever not welcoming? And to this woman," she touches my cheek kindly, but the tone of 'this woman' is painful to hear, "I'll be thankful."

I put my hand on the door handle but don't push down. "Thank you for coming to see the venue with me."

"You're more than welcome. It'll be a perfect day. Just like you." She reaches over and smooths my arm. "My wonderful daughter."

Tension pulses through the air, masked, as it always is between us, with smiles and polite words. What right does she have to be angry about my mother, my real mother, coming to my wedding? I hesitate, hating her words—words I've heard so many times before—and the expectations they create. I let a small smile escape.

"I'm proud of you, you know. I love you."

I want so desperately to believe her, but love wouldn't make me feel guilty for this. Love would be happy the woman who gave me birth cares enough to book a flight. "I love you too. Again, thank you for all your help, for—"

She increases the pressure on my arm. It's not painful, just firm. She looks at it and not at me, but her poised smile melts into a genuine one. "That's what mothers are for."

※

I STEP INTO A DARK HOUSE. In the kitchen, a note is scrawled on our message board—*Chasing a lead, don't wait up! xoxo*. The couch looks inviting, so I settle into it then reach for my laptop. Toulouse slinks up to me, her motorboat purr the only sound as I scan through my emails. The mouse hovers over one from Lydia. Sighing, I click it. She wavers between excitement and hesitancy, expressing her thanks for the invite to the wedding and how much it means to her. She wants me to know that her identity at the event is completely up to me…an old family friend, someone I met while travelling, or, if I want, her birth mother. She has no expectations. She doesn't exactly ask me how I'm doing with my fertility issues but expresses her concern and hope that I'm doing well and have found some answers.

I stare at the screen so long it fades into an image from Autumn's wedding—all of us girls smiling and laughing. As that image fades into the next I shake the mouse to bring Lydia's email back. To say she's a family friend or a new acquaintance won't work. One look at her and no one would believe she's not family. But what's more important is her questions about my fertility. If she mentioned something about it in front of my mother, if my mother knew I'd told Lydia and not her…The tension of the past hour comes back. Phone in hand, I dial the numbers and wait.

"Hello?" The voice that answers is groggy.

"Lydia?"

"Yes," sounds of shuffling travel through the line: a thump, "who is this?"

"It's Tracey, I—"

"Tracey." The voice snaps awake. "Is everything okay? What—"

"Oh." It hits me. "I'm so sorry. I wasn't thinking. What is it? Midnight there?"

"Yes. Just past." Mumbling: Westin's voice, then Lydia's letting him know it's alright. "Are you okay?"

"Yes, I'm fine. I'm really sorry. I can call back tomorrow."

"No problem." She sounds fully awake now. "What's going on?"

"I got your email."

"Yes."

"I figured it would be easier to call."

"Okay."

"I just...I wanted to say it's fine, people knowing you're my mom. My birth mom. The truth is simplest, right?"

"Yes, of course." The sound of a chair sliding out. "I wanted you to know I didn't expect it."

"Right. That's nice. I mean I appreciate it."

"Okay. Umm. Good."

I'm botching this. "Also, the fertility stuff."

"Any change? Good news?"

"No. No change. No good news. It's just I haven't told my mom about it, any of it. So I wanted you to know not to mention it. Not that I think...just, it would hurt her."

Silence. The sound of a tap running. Lydia's voice. "I won't say a word. I'll tell Westin as well. Do you mind me asking," a pause, "why haven't you talked to her about it?"

Immediately my defences rise, like a wall that shoots up between us. "It's complicated. She had a lot of fertility issues herself, obviously. And...it's complicated."

Her voice softens. "So no good news? Does that mean bad news?"

I pause, debating how much to tell. "The pain is getting worse. It's pretty bad. Worse than I let on most of the time."

"I'm really sorry. I hate that you're going through this."

"Uh...thanks."

"Is Adrian—"

"He's great. Wonderful."

"I know I wrote it already but, again, congratulations. I'm really happy for you."

"Thanks."

"And so excited to be coming for it. To be included. We both are."

"Yeah."

"I used to wonder about this day when you were a baby in my arms. I'd see you there, so tiny, so perfect, and wonder what life held for you. I don't really pray, but I prayed you'd find a man to love and cherish you, who would treat you the way you deserve to be treated. And in recent years I've wondered…wondered so much." Her voice cracks. "He treats you right?"

"More than right."

I can almost hear her smile. "You have no idea how happy that makes me."

I laugh. "It makes me happy too." Several moments pass. "So, do you still have friends here? I know you changed your address three years ago, but when did you leave?"

"I left when I gave you up. I couldn't stay in the city. I didn't trust myself not to find you, to steal you back. There were many days when…" She takes a deep breath. "Well, you know the story…undergrad, here for graduate studies. I spent a few years back across the pond before securing this job at Oxford."

We talk until late into the night. When the call ends my body feels tingly: shocked and happy and hopeful. Eager. She is not only the woman who gave me life; in a way, an odd but real way, she's also my mother. And she's coming to my wedding. The knowledge is like a ball in the centre of my chest, heavy and burdensome these past weeks and now transformed into something different entirely: light and full of possibility. My mother, my birth mother, is coming to my wedding.

A shard of light cuts through the darkness. Adrian's form fills it. The silhouette eases off its shoes and closes the door. A shadow tiptoes down the hall. It stops. "Tracey?"

"Mm-hmm."

"I told you not to wait up." He flips a switch. A warm yellow glow illuminates us. "Is everything okay?"

Pushing myself off the couch, I loop my arm around his waist. "It is." I've found my mother. She cares. "Catch the lead?"

CHAPTER TWENTY-SEVEN

The day before the wedding our apartment overflows with activity and friends. Love seems to bounce off the walls. Jojo arrives looking better than she has in months and tells me all about her new job and the prospect of a small apartment about halfway between here and Mom and Dad's. Eloise, Sheila, Allison, Autumn and Emily work tirelessly to help make my DIY decorations and additions perfect. Amalia flits around like a little dryad full of excitement: helpful, and charmingly so. Charlise and Adrian's sisters have come too. Never have I felt so surrounded by affection. The bachelorette was incredible—all these friends and more celebrating, laughing, affirming to me that my years spent fearing I wasn't enough, thinking I had to tiptoe through my friendships, always hesitant one wrong move would sabotage people's acceptance of me, can be a thing of the past.

I have a whole host of people who support me and want to see me happy. They've comforted me and shown patience through the emotional meltdowns I've had the past few days, and they're all still here.

I stop a moment to take it in. Eloise and Autumn chat and laugh as they put together favours. Charlise and Jojo playfully bicker over how to best display the seating plan. Others labour at their tasks, clearly enjoying themselves. My mom walks in, back from an errand I sent her on. She's smiling and happy, as far as I can tell, free of the tension she held when she dropped me off last week.

I glance at the clock. We only have four hours before the rehearsal dinner, and I'd like to have all the prep finished beforehand. It's tight but possible. Despite this uncertainty, for the first time in a long time I feel at peace. Everything necessary is taken care of, and tonight at the dinner I will be surrounded by all the people here right now: my father, Adrian's family and friends, and Lydia and Westin. Lydia will be here. I look again at the clock. She and Westin should be arriving at their hotel now. I expect myself to be nervous, scared. But I'm not. No matter what happens today, no matter any tensions or pain, by tomorrow night Adrian will be my husband. I can't help but smile.

"Earth to Tracey."

"Hmm?"

Allison grins at me. "This vase. What do you think?"

"Perfect."

"That's what I was thinking!" She laughs.

A tap on my shoulder causes me to turn. Adrian's sister, Valerie, is holding a phone toward me. "This one's important."

"Who is it?" My stomach twists at the tone in her voice. We'd decided in order to lower my stress, my phone would remain off. All of the vendors were given Eloise's number, so the fact that Valerie is coming to me means whatever the problem is, it's personal.

"Adrian."

I take the phone and try to keep my voice light. "Hi."

"Hey." He lets out a heavy sigh and my chest clenches. "Not sure how you'll…"

"Adrian."

"Don't read more into this than it is. Okay?"

"What?"

"Plans had to be changed. It's Lydia. She's not coming."

The breath is pulled from my throat. "I had a message from her yesterday. She said everything was lined up, they—"

"I know. She says she's really sorry. She sounded really sorry, but Cooper took sick as they were about to head to the airport. They're not sure what's wrong. It could be appendicitis, but it could be something worse."

"Could be? His mother is there. He's supposed to be staying with his mother. How does that…"

He sighs again. "Would you leave your child if you thought he had appendicitis? Or something worse?"

"He's not her child."

"Yes, but—"

"You're defending her." My body feels foreign. Waves of pain course through me. All over again I'm standing in that room, clutching Buncey, watching my mother walk away.

"I'm not defending her. I just…I don't want you to turn this into something it isn't."

"Something it isn't? What would I turn it into that it isn't? It's my mother, my birth mother who claims she wants some role in my life, choosing to abandon me again, putting a child she has no real connection to ahead of her own blood daughter."

"That's not fair."

"What difference will it make, her being there? Cooper has his mother. And Westin could stay. Lydia could come alone."

"If you had a child and he was sick, wouldn't you want me to be with you?"

"This is ridiculous." My voice catches. "Why are you defending her? Defend me. She's just being the horrible, selfish woman she's always been. The woman who—"

"You're being selfish."

"What?"

His voice is angry. Frustrated. "Tracey, grow up. Be the person I fell in love with, the person who—"

"How can you say this? Today of all days."

"Tracey—"

"You know, sometimes you're a real imbecile." I click

the phone off then stare at it, shocked. I wait for it to ring. It doesn't. Do I call him back? A feeling of déjà vu settles over me. We've been here before. But this is worse, much worse. Eloise leaves Autumn and walks toward me. Her hand falls on my shoulder. "Trace?"

"Yes."

"What's going on?"

I turn from her and walk to the bedroom.

"You're scaring me, hun."

I laugh.

"Trace."

"I was a fool, you know." I plop down on the bed. "To think I'd been wrong. To think I was worth it. To think anyone—Adrian, my Mom—could really stay. Really want me."

"What?" Eloise closes the door. "What are you talking about? What happened?"

"Lydia's not coming. She's supposed to be sitting with us tonight at dinner. Her spot is reserved, tonight and tomorrow, and she's not coming."

"What?"

I tell Eloise all I know, including Adrian's defence of Lydia. By the end of it, my shoulders are shaking. No tears. Only shakes.

"Trace," Eloise rubs her hand along my back, "she's not deserting you. She's being a mom. The kind of mom she either didn't know how to be or couldn't be for you. You should be proud of her."

I glare. "Proud of her? Proud that she's a real mother to her step-children? Her step-children and not her own daughter. If it's appendicitis, he'll be fine in a few days, no big deal, but tomorrow is the most important day of my life and she's choosing not to be here."

"I'm sure it was a rough decision."

"So, you too?" Another harsh laugh escapes. "You're defending her too."

"Trace."

"Just like Adrian." My voice raises. "He was so quick to be on her side. He defended her like it was nothing, like her abandoning me—"

"She's not abandoning you. She made a choice." Exasperation leaks through Eloise's voice. "I thought you didn't even want her at the wedding."

I stare at Eloise. Shake my head. "And then I hung up on him. He was trying and…I wouldn't be surprised if he doesn't even want to marry me anymore." I shudder. "But why should I want to marry him? He'll leave one day. Most likely, anyway. What's the divorce rate? Why do people even try?" The tears start. "I don't think I could handle it, having him leave one day, having him…people are so damn unreliable."

"Stop it." Eloise hisses the words. "Just stop it. Of course Adrian could leave you one day. Of course he could stop loving you. So what? Anyone can leave anyone anytime. Anyone can reject you, disappoint you, decide they don't want anything to do with you. So what? Does that mean you stop living?"

"No, but—"

"Grow up." She leans back, showing a side of her I've never seen, at least not toward me. "I'm sick of it, the way you walk around on eggshells with people. So you got angry. You had cause to be angry, to have a reaction. And if he leaves you because of that, then yeah, you're better off. But he won't. One action won't erase how he feels about you. Love doesn't work like that. Just like I'm yelling at you right now and, honestly, I'm fed up with you and your insecurities, but I still love you. I'm still your friend." Her expression softens. "Could that change one day? Maybe. But I doubt it. Just," she scrunches her hands through her wild and wavy hair, her fingers increasing the beautiful mayhem, "think of all the people outside that door. They came because you matter to them, you with all your flaws, your crazy up-tightness, your barriers to intimacy, and your amazing heart. They're here because they love you and want to support you, not because you're perfect. Nobody's perfect. Nobody will ever be perfect. Would you leave Adrian just because he's not entirely the man you thought he was, or that you want him to be?"

"I'm thinking of leaving him right now."

"No, you're not, and whatever you are thinking, it's not because of who he is, it's because of who you are. Because you're scared." She gives a little smile. "Would you toss me off, reject me if I pissed you off, or was suddenly less perfect than we all know me to be?"

I almost laugh. "Of course not."

"You think you're better than everyone else?"

I take a deep breath. "I don't know if I can marry him, Eloise."

"Because of this?"

"Because of everything. Because he's already been through so much. Because I'm broken inside…and this dream I had of a family, of children who—"

"Sometimes people have to make new dreams. Adrian knows that's a possibility. If it were a deal-breaker—"

"He thinks he knows. He thinks he's okay with it. But what if he's not? What if the trying, the failure, it's too much for him?"

Eloise swallows. "You don't know you'll fail. And even if you do…it's not failure. It's just life. We can't predict life. You know that."

Her words die away, leaving silence in the room. She sits beside me. "Listen, you're going to do what you have to do. If you don't want to marry Adrian, if you don't love him, then walk away. Who cares about the wedding, the guests, any of it? Walk away."

"Of course I love Adrian."

"Then you have your answer. People fall out of love. They decide they don't want the choices or the people they thought they wanted. You're right, there's no guarantee. But you're a fool if you let that keep you from living." She pauses. "Don't be stupid, Trace. I've been there. Trust me. Don't let him get away."

I stare at Eloise. She knows what she's talking about. She's lived it. But the four-year-old inside of me is screaming, wanting to run into a room and hide. She's terrified that no one will ever really want her, that no one will stay. She doesn't know how to trust in love, at least not love that comes without a requirement of perfection: to be healthy, to be good, to smile always and never do anything to offend—these are the things that make sense to her. And so she wants to push love away, protect herself.

I shift my body toward Eloise. My voice is soft and hesitant. Childlike. "Why didn't she want me?"

Eloise sighs. "Trace."

"Enough. Why didn't she want me enough?"

"Maybe she did. Maybe she didn't. Maybe she truly thought giving you up was the best way to show her love, or maybe she was scared and young and confused and didn't know what to do. It sucks. It really sucks that she bailed on you. But think of it this way, right now she's trying to be the parent for this child that she never was for you.

"You're a grown-up now. You can handle yourself. Who knows, maybe she even thought you'd think poorly of her if she didn't stay, if she indulged her own desire to come to your wedding when at home a scared, hurting child sat wanting her. You don't know. And maybe you'll never know. But it doesn't really matter. You've got to let it go. You're not a little girl anymore, yearning for a home and someone to love her. You've got that."

I close my eyes. After several moments, I sense Eloise stand and make her way to the door. She pauses. "We have to leave for the rehearsal in an hour and a half."

I nod.

One part of me knows I'm being ridiculous. That, in a way, Lydia has made the right choice...or at least an acceptable choice. I should be past this by now. For a while there, I believed maybe I was, but I can't seem to shut up that child Eloise thinks no longer exists.

I hear Eloise's words, though, and I know they're true. I don't have to be perfect. Perfection doesn't translate to love. Eloise's friendship proves that. I've lied to her for years. I've lied to all of them. And still they're here, just like Adrian is still here, despite everything my imperfections may put us through.

A knock on the door draws me from my thoughts. "Yes?" Adrian steps in. I pop to my feet. "What are you doing here?"

He offers a small smile. "I thought my bride-to-be might need a hug."

"A..."

"Come here." His arms open and I cross the distance to step into them. He holds me tight, as if he's trying to absorb everything that roils around inside of me. After more than a minute, he releases his grasp and holds me at arms' length.

"I've been awful. I'm sorry."

"I know. You've been under a lot of stress. Not just today. But, Trace, this has to stop."

I step back. "What exactly?"

"This fear that people are going to leave you, not want you."

I take a breath.

"I'm on your side. I'm always going to be on your side. Sometimes that will mean disagreeing with you, supporting what I believe will matter to you most in the long run, not necessarily what matters to you in the moment."

I try not to see his words as condescending, although that's how I first hear them. I know better, though. They're said with love.

"I've given up before, but I'm not going to do that

again." He winks. "Help a fella out, though, come on."

"I don't mean to be this way."

"I know. Like I said, you've had a lot on your mind these past weeks. Go easy on yourself and go easy on the people around you. Alright?"

I nod.

"I'm not going anywhere. You're stuck with me," he smiles, "even if you sink to name-calling. Not saying I like it, but—"

"It's hard to believe."

"What?"

"That you won't leave. I'm a mess."

"We all are. I'm a mess too, but it's you and me, babe. Forever."

I grin. "Forever?"

He puts out his hand. "That's what tomorrow's all about. As long as you're still ready to do this?"

Am I? I expect my chest to constrict, expect fear to flow through me, telling me I'm not worthy of love, not enough. Instead, trust passes over me like a wave. It's not going to be easy, and I still have a lot to learn, a lot of ways in which I need to let go of my past, to heal. If my body keeps failing me, if we never have children, it's going to be rough, awful…I lift my gaze to Adrian's, this man who has seen me at my worst and is still here, who promises to be me with me no matter how hard life gets. I think of the people waiting outside that door. People who love me, just as I am. I take Adrian's hand.

"I'm ready."

A NOTE FROM THE AUTHOR

Dear Reader,

I hope you enjoyed reading *Forever In My Heart*. If it made you think, laugh, cry, or even took you out of your life for a few good hours, then I've done my job. If you like this book, it would mean so much if you took a moment to write a short, honest review on Amazon, Goodreads, or both! Reviews are incredibly important. They encourage readers to give a book a chance, which means your review may just help a fellow booklover find a new story to enjoy!

I'm excited to let you know that Tracey's story isn't yet done. In *Whispers of Hope* you can follow Tracey on her journey toward having the family she's always yearned for.

If you haven't read the first three books in the *A New Start Series* and you'd like to, you'll find information on each of them on the following pages.

To learn about future books, feel free to sign up for my newsletter at charlenecarr.com. You'll receive messages about my work, upcoming books, and giveaways. For a limited time, you'll also get a free novella, *Before I Knew You*.

Don't worry, I won't flood your inbox. I rarely send newsletters more than twice a month.

You can also learn about my new books and promotions by following me on BookBub. And if you've read *Forever In My Heart* as part of a book club, you'll find discussion questions on the following pages.

Read on, my friend,

Charlene Carr

OTHER BOOKS IN THE A NEW START SERIES

When Comes The Joy
Book 1

Jennifer's not perfect. Not even close. But she may just capture your heart.

At 27, Jennifer's out of work, her mom just died, and despite stellar qualifications, every job interview ends in rejection.
Haunted by the teasing, taunts, and fat jokes that defined her childhood, Jennifer blames her unhappiness on her ever-growing waistband.
And she's ready for change.
Messy and real.
Beautiful and harsh.
When Comes The Joy (previously titled Skinny Me) explores one woman's journey along the road of forgiveness, healing, and strength.

Where There Is Life
Book 2

What would you do if you woke up in a hospital bed, only to realize all your dreams were shattered?

Autumn's blissful newlywed life abruptly ends when she wakes after a life-threatening accident, unable to remember what happened or why her husband isn't by her side.

As the haze clears and Autumn's memory returns, will she be able to confront the truth?

Evocative and complex.

Honest and emotional.

The second book in the *A New Start* stand-alone Series, *Where There Is Life* is a riveting story about love, loss, and finding your way.

By What We Love
Book 3

Sometimes getting exactly what you want is the worst thing ever.

Dream job? Check. Man to make every woman you know stop and turn? Check. But when having one means giving up the other, what's a girl ...excuse me, *woman* to do?
Eloise Grant, a successful and driven Public Relations Consultant, has worked her whole life to make sure she never has to depend on anyone but herself.
But when she's offered a promotion she feels she can't refuse, depending on herself means leaving her friends, her family, and the man she loves behind.
Whatever choice she makes, it seems like Eloise's life is about to unravel.
Smart and engaging.
Heart wrenching and unpredictable.
By What We Love, book 3 in the *A New Start* stand-alone series, is the story of a woman desperate to have it all, while battling with memories of a past she'd rather forget.

Whispers of Hope
Book 5

The act every woman is supposed to be capable of, she's failing at, over and over again.

A year ago, Tracey Sampson met and married the man who helped her finally believe she is worthy of love, just as she is.
But she's yet to fulfill her greatest dream—to hold her own child in her arms.
As month by month that dream drifts further and further away, Tracey is forced to acknowledge that not everyone gets their happily every after.
Engrossing and inspiring.
Heart-wrenching and passionate.
As real as it gets.
Whisper of Hope, book 5 in the *A New Start* stand-alone series bares the heart and soul of a woman heartfelt and emotional story of a woman pursuing her life's dream despite heartache and disappointment. Witness the power of hope to transform a life.

ACKNOWLEDGMENTS

I would like to thank my wonderful beta readers who gave generously of their time and provided invaluable feedback. It amazes me, the little nuances you are able to see that help me make these stories so much more than what they were. I would also like to thank my editor and her keen eye.

BOOK CLUB DISCUSSION QUESTIONS

1. Do you know anyone who has been adopted or were you adopted yourself? If you've had the opportunity to discuss their experiences, how were they different or similar to Tracey's? Why do you think she felt the need to hide her adoption from those closest to her?

2. If you were in Tracey's position, would you want to search out your adoptive mother and other family members? For Tracey, her first inclination was to find her mother for medical information. With people you know, was medical information a prime factor for the search, or was it more the need to find blood relatives?

3. How did you react to the scene where Tracey shows up at Lydia's door? Was Lydia's response (dismissing her to her partner as some stranger looking for her cat) forgiveable? Understandable?

4. Were you surprised when you found out, contrary to Tracey's preconceived notions, her mother became an educated professional, teaching the same subjects as Tracey? Did this knowledge change any of your thoughts or feelings about her decision to give up Tracey for adoption and/or to not make an effort to find her as an adult?

5. Do you think Lydia's decision to give up Tracey for adoption was selfish, self-less, or something in between?

6. Jojo wasn't overjoyed to find out that Tracey was engaged, and yet Tracey was always a wonderful support to Jojo, even though she felt jealous over the fact that Jojo was her parents' miracle baby. Do you think Jojo was selfish for not wanting Tracey to tell her parents about the engagement until she could get her own act together again, or did make sense?

7. Adrian and Tracey have a lot on their plate—do you feel they're rushing into some pretty big decisions or, rather, are they embracing life? Do you think their marriage is likely to be a successful one? Why or why not?

If you have any questions about the discussion guide or would like a chance at having Charlene visit your bookclub through a webcall, email contact@charlenecarr.com

ABOUT THE AUTHOR

I'm a lover of words. Pursuing this life-long obsession, I studied literature in university, attaining both a BA and MA in English. Still craving more, I attained a degree in Journalism. After travelling the globe for several years and working as a freelance writer, editor, facilitator, and starting my own Communications business, I decided the time had come to focus exclusively on my true love - novel writing.

My goal is to write books that are almost impossible to put down, not because of some great mystery, or high-speed chase, or sexy scene, but because they're full of characters who enrage and delight you; Imperfect people in circumstances that could hit any one of us.

Characters full of human frailties who make awful, sometimes stupid choices …

But who don't give up when they're knocked down. Who struggle and fight and come out on the other side stronger, braver, ready to live a life of their own making.
Read more at www.charlenecarr.com/books

www.ingramcontent.com/pod-product-compliance
Lightning Source LLC
Chambersburg PA
CBHW030230100526
44583CB00013BA/655